Creative Writing
Education

NEW WRITING VIEWPOINTS

Series Editor: Graeme Harper, Oakland University, Rochester, USA

The overall aim of this series is to publish books which will ultimately inform teaching and research, but whose primary focus is on the analysis of creative writing practice and theory. There will also be books which deal directly with aspects of creative writing knowledge, with issues of genre, form and style, with the nature and experience of creativity, and with the learning of creative writing. They will all have in common a concern with excellence in application and in understanding, with creative writing practitioners and their work, and with informed analysis of creative writing as process as well as completed artefact.

Full details of all the books in this series and of all our other publications can be found on http://www.multilingual-matters.com, or by writing to Multilingual Matters, St Nicholas House, 31–34 High Street, Bristol BS1 2AW, UK.

NEW WRITING VIEWPOINTS: 11

Creative Writing and Education

Edited by
Graeme Harper

MULTILINGUAL MATTERS
Bristol • Buffalo • Toronto

Library of Congress Cataloging in Publication Data
Creative Writing and Education / Edited by Graeme Harper.
New Writing Viewpoints: 11
Includes bibliographical references and index.
1. Creative writing–Study and teaching. 2. English language–Rhetoric–Study and teaching. 3. Interdisciplinary approach in education. I. Harper, Graeme, editor.
PE1404.C724 2015
808'.0420711–dc23 2014044717

British Library Cataloguing in Publication Data
A catalogue entry for this book is available from the British Library.

ISBN-13: 978-1-78309-353-3 (hbk)
ISBN-13: 978-1-78309-352-6 (pbk)

Multilingual Matters
UK: St Nicholas House, 31–34 High Street, Bristol BS1 2AW, UK.
USA: UTP, 2250 Military Road, Tonawanda, NY 14150, USA.
Canada: UTP, 5201 Dufferin Street, North York, Ontario M3H 5T8, Canada.

Website: www.multilingual-matters.com
Twitter: Multi_Ling_Mat
Facebook: https://www.facebook.com/multilingualmatters
Blog: www.channelviewpublications.wordpress.com

The policy of Multilingual Matters/Channel View Publications is to use papers that are natural, renewable and recyclable products, made from wood grown in sustainable forests. In the manufacturing process of our books, and to further support our policy, preference is given to printers that have FSC and PEFC Chain of Custody certification. The FSC and/or PEFC logos will appear on those books where full certification has been granted to the printer concerned.

Typeset by R.J. Footring Ltd, Derby
Printed and bound in Great Britain by Short Run Press Ltd

Contents

Acknowledgments

Sincere thanks to the writers who contributed chapters and commentaries to this book. It has been a considerable pleasure working with each and all of you. Whatever this book provides, however it contributes, and in whatever way it advances discussions around the practice and understanding of creative writing is because of you. A big thank you to Philip Gross for his adventurous Foreword! I know Philip would have written an equally creative chapter or commentary, but to see what he did with the notion of writing a Foreword reminds us all why we choose to be creative writers. Thanks to Kim Eggleton, who guided the book along to its final stages of composition, and to Anna Roderick, who ensured the idea for it would be well supported in the first place. To the Multilingual Matters team, a heartfelt note of appreciation, for what you do and for who you are: simply great folks to work with. A word of thanks also to the two anonymous reviewers who provided lively and engaged responses to the manuscript from their locations in different parts of the world, and my thanks to Ralph Footring, whose copy-editing and production editing advice had both clarity and creativity in constant clear view. Finally, thanks and much love, always, to my wife Louise and to our sons Myles and Tyler.

About the Authors

Randall Albers, Professor/Chair Emeritus in the Department of Creative Writing at Columbia College Chicago, is Founding Producer of the Story Week Festival of Writers and recipient of Columbia's Teaching Excellence Award. His work is found in *Writing in Education, TriQuarterly, Writer's Digest, F, Brevity, Briefly Knocked Unconscious by a Low-Flying Duck* and elsewhere. Two chapters from his novel-in-progress, *All the World Before Them*, have been nominated for Pushcart prizes. For Story Week, he has interviewed Salman Rushdie, Jonathan Lethem, Henry Louis Gates Jr, Ray Bradbury, Jane Hamilton, Junot Diaz, Hubert Selby Jr, Richard Price, John Sayles, Irvine Welsh, Bharati Mukherjee and others. Featured in the Story Workshop® creative writing videotape, *The Living Voice Moves*, he has presented at AWP, NAWE, NonfictioNow, AAWP and many other conferences on writing and the teaching of writing.

Craig Batty is Associate Professor of Screenwriting at RMIT University, Australia. A screenwriter, script editor and script consultant, he has worked on various short film, feature film, television and online drama projects. He is the co-author of three books – *Writing for the Screen: Creative and Critical Approaches* (Palgrave Macmillan, 2008), *Media Writing: A Practical Introduction* (Palgrave Macmillan, 2010) and *The Creative Screenwriter: Exercises to Expand Your Craft* (Methuen, 2012) – and the author of two books – *Movies that Move Us: Screenwriting and the Power of the Protagonist's Journey* (Palgrave Macmillan, 2011) and *Screenplays: How to Write and Sell Them* (Kamera Books, 2012).

Brooke Biaz has published a number of creative works, including short stories, novels and some creative non-fiction. Currently residing above Zap, a coffeehouse and bakery in the small coastal town of Lightening Cove, future works include a new novel and a cultural history of invisibility.

Bob Broad is Professor of English at Illinois State University in Normal and directs Just Words Consulting Group. His interests include empirical qualitative research, writing assessment, rhetorical theories, and pedagogies that promote democratic culture. He is author of *What We Really Value: Beyond Rubrics in Teaching and Assessing Writing* (Utah State University Press, 2003) and co-author of *Organic Writing Assessment: Dynamic Criteria Mapping in Action* (Utah State University Press, 2009). His articles and book reviews have appeared in *College English, Journal of Writing Assessment, Assessing Writing, Research in the Teaching of English, Teaching English in the Two-Year College, African American Review*, and *Works and Days*.

Kevin Brophy is the author of 13 books of poetry, fiction and essays. He teaches Creative Writing in the School of Culture and Communication at the University of Melbourne.

Maggie Butt is an ex-journalist and television documentary producer whose fifth poetry collection, *Degrees of Twilight*, is due out from the London Magazine in 2015. Previous books *Sancti Clandestini – Undercover Saints* (Ward-Wood Publishing, 2012) and *Ally Pally Prison Camp* (Oversteps Books, 2011), the story of 3000 civilians imprisoned in London during the First World War, are both illustrated. They follow her first collection, *Lipstick* (Greenwich Exchange, 2007), and a collection of short poems, *petite* (Hearing Eye, 2010). Her edited collection of essays, *Story: The Heart of the Matter*, was published in 2007 by Greenwich Exchange. She is an Associate Director at Middlesex University, with more than 20 years' experience of teaching Creative Writing; she was Chair of the National Association of Writers in Education (NAWE) and has recently co-written the new Creative Writing A-level. She has a PhD in Creative Writing from Cardiff University. Website http://www.maggiebutt.co.uk.

Liz Cashdan is a tutor and assessor for the Open College of the Arts. She also tutors for the WEA and does workshops in schools. Her latest publications are: *Iceland Stories*, in collaboration with digital artist Pat Hodson and sound artist Jessica Rowland (2012); and *Things of Substance: New and Selected Poems* (Five Leaves Publications, 2013). She is Chair of the National Association of Writers in Education and a peer reviewer for their higher education journal, *Writing in Practice*. She is also poetry editor for Jewish Renaissance and reviews for *The North*.

Katharine Coles is a professor at the University of Utah. Her fifth poetry collection, *The Earth Is Not Flat* (Red Hen, 2013), was written under the auspices of the National Science Foundation's Antarctic Artists and Writers Program; 10 poems from the book, translated into German by Klaus Martens, appeared in the summer 2014 issue of the journal *Matrix*. Her sixth collection, *Flight*, is due out in 2016. She has also published two novels. Recent poems and prose have appeared in *Poetry Northwest, Seneca Review, Virginia Quarterly Review, Image, Crazyhorse, Ascent* and *Poetry*. In 2009–10 she served as the inaugural Director of the Poetry Foundation's Harriet Monroe Poetry Institute. She has received grants and awards from the National Endowment for the Arts, the National Endowment for the Humanities and, in 2012–13, the Guggenheim Foundation.

Fan Dai holds a PhD in linguistics, an MA in human geography and an MFA in creative writing. She has taught one of the few creative writing courses in English as a second language at Sun Yat-sen University in China since 2009. She is currently teaching the first bilingual creative writing course. She writes in both Chinese and English, with four collections of essays in Chinese and, in English, the novel *Butterfly Lovers: A Tale of the Chinese Romeo and Juliet* (Homa and Sekey Books, 2000). Her work in English has appeared in *Drunken Boat* and *Asia Literary Review*. She is Professor of English and Director of the Sun Yat-sen University Center for English-Language Creative Writing.

Sieneke de Rooij is a Creative Writing Consultant, Writer, Editor and Creative Writing Teacher in the Netherlands. She was an editor for various Dutch publishing houses; her own books, articles and apps have been published since 2000. She organizes workshops and courses for students of all ages and coaches writers working on their manuscripts, and has been an advisor for new writing initiatives in the Netherlands. In 2014, she started a new initiative for Creative Writing teachers, with poet and CW teacher Margriet van Bebber, Dactylus (the Academy for Creative Writing Teachers), which is now training 12 students a year to be creative writing professionals and is providing courses and master classes.

Dianne Donnelly is the Associate Director of the CCCC-Award winning composition program at the University of South Florida and the Chair of the Local Arrangement Committee for the 2015 CCCC Conference. In addition to her interests in rhetoric and composition and writing program administration, she is a creative writer and craft critic who addresses the theory and pedagogy of creative writing. Her pedagogical works include *Does the Writing Workshop Still Work?* (Multilingual Matters, 2010), *Establishing Creative Writing Studies as an Academic Discipline* (Multilingual Matters, 2011) and *Key Issues in Creative Writing* (with Graeme Harper, Multilingual Matters, 2012). She is a frequent presenter at the creative writing pedagogy forums at CCCC and AWP; reviewer for *Pedagogy*, *TEXT*, and multiple presses; senior creative writing editor for Writing Commons; and associate editor of the 'New Writing Viewpoints' book series.

Toby Emert is Associate Professor of Education and Chair of the Department of Education at Agnes Scott College in Decatur, Georgia. His interests include English education, 21st-century literacies, arts and education, and technology in language arts classrooms. He teaches writing instruction, creative writing and children's and young adult literature. Additional research interests are teaching as an art form and authentic and alternative assessments.

Philip Gross is Professor of Creative Writing at the University of South Wales, in the UK. His poetry publications include *Later* (2013), *Deep Field* (2011) and *The Water Table* (2009), winner of the British T.S. Eliot Prize. *I Spy Pinhole Eye*, with photographer Simon Denison, won the Wales Book of the Year Award in 2010. He is the author of 10 novels for young people, from *The Song of Gail and Fludd* (1991) to *The Storm Garden* (2006), and his poetry for children includes *Off Road To Everywhere* (winner of the CLPE Award 2011). His academic writing includes chapters like 'Then Again What Do I Know: Reflections on Reflection in Creative Writing' (in R. Marggraf Turley, ed., *The Writer in the Academy: Creative Interfrictions*, 2011).

Maureen Hall is currently researching cognitive-affective approaches in teaching and learning, the integration of contemplative practices for deepening learning, and how reading and writing can change lives. She spent a year in India over 2010–11 as a Fulbright–Nehru Research Scholar researching the Super Accelerated Learning Theory (SALT). Part of her sustained interest in India involves learning more about the origins and ideas underpinning various contemplative practices, as she finds that these practices hold great possibilities for deepening student learning.

Simon Holloway is the Programme Leader for Creative Writing at the University of Bolton. His research interests focus on the pedagogy of creative writing, and the processes of textual composition, specifically the actions of authors as they work: he has published on this in the *Blackwell Companion to Creative Writing*, *TEXT*, *Writers in Education* and *Creative Writing: Teaching Theory and Pedagogy*. His short fiction and poetry have appeared in places such as *Stand*, *New Writing: The International Journal for the Practice and Theory* *of Creative Writing, The North American Review, New Contrast, Litro, The Rialto* and *The North*. For the last six years he has also coordinated 'Great Writing: The International Creative Writing Conference'. His latest novel, *The Words We Use Are Black and White,* was published in 2014.

Gill James completed a PhD in Creative and Critical Writing in 2007, shortly before she came to the University of Salford. Previously she taught creative writing at the University of Portsmouth and the University of Wales, Bangor. She is a published author who writes fiction for young adults and children and also writes shorter fiction for adults. She frequently visits schools in order to give readings and workshops about her work and to introduce school children to the idea of studying creative writing in higher education.

Nigel Krauth is Professor and Head of the writing program at Griffith University, Gold Coast, Australia. He has published four novels for adults (two of them national award winners) and three novels for teenagers, along with stories, essays, articles and reviews. His research investigates creative writing processes and the teaching of creative writing. He is co-founder and General Editor of *TEXT: Journal of Writing and Writing Courses* (http://www.textjournal.com.au).

Jeri Kroll is Dean of Graduate Research at Flinders University and Professor of English and Creative Writing. She has published on Samuel Beckett, contemporary poetry and fiction, children's literature and creative writing research and pedagogy. Past President of the Australasian Association of Writing Programs, she is on the boards of *New Writing: The International Journal for the Practice and Theory of Creative Writing* and *TEXT: Journal of Writing and Writing Courses*. Recent books include *Swamp Soup* (Picaro Press, 2012), *Workshopping the Heart: New and Selected Poems* (Wakefield Press, 2013) and a crossover verse novel, *Vanishing Point* (Puncher and Wattman, 2015). Her most recent scholarly book is the co-edited *Research Methods in Creative Writing* (Palgrave Macmillan, 2013). A staged reading of *Vanishing Point* took place at the Kennedy Center for the Performing Arts 'Page to Stage' Festival in 2011 and a MainStage production at George Washington University in October 2014. Subsequently, the play was selected for a full production at the 47th Kennedy Center American College Theater Festival held in Cleveland, Ohio, in January 2015.

Elizabeth MacFarlane is the author of *Reading Coetzee: A Critical-Creative Nexus* (Rodopi, 2013). She teaches Creative Writing in the School of Culture and Communication at the University of Melbourne.

Asma Mansoor has been serving as a Lecturer in the Department of English at the International Islamic University, Islamabad, Pakistan since 2006. Currently pursuing a PhD degree in English Literature, she found teaching to be a field in which she could satisfy her penchant for literature. During this tenure, she has taught a wide range of subjects ranging from 'Classical Poetry' to 'South Asian Literature in English'. Being a writer herself, she has also taught 'Writing Skills' and 'Creative Writing' to under-grad students of English Literature. In addition, her work, both creative and research-oriented, has been published in international journals including the New Writing: The *International Journal for the Theory and Practice of Creative Writing*, the *South Asian Review* and *Pakistaniaat*. A few of her papers have also been presented in international conferences including in the USA and the UK.

Steve May is Professor of Radio Drama and Dean of the School of Humanities at Bath Spa University in the UK. He has won awards for drama, poetry and fiction. He has been judge for the Sony and Imison Radio Awards and the Ravenglass Poetry Competition. His book for undergraduates (*Doing Creative Writing*) was published by Routledge in 2007. In 2011 he became Chair of the Higher Education Committee of the National Association of Writers in Education. He is an active member of the School Contemporary Writing Research Centre. A specially commissioned and translated version of his play *Chess Wars* was broadcast in Germany in 2006. His prophetic play *Horizon* was broadcast in 2008 and eight plays in the *Higher* series (written as Joyce Bryant) were broadcast between 2008 and 2012.

Moy McCrory is Senior Lecturer in Creative Writing at Derby University. She has published a novel and several collections of short stories and been widely anthologized. Areas of research are Irish women's writing, the Irish diaspora, post–memory and narratology.

Nigel McLoughlin is Professor of Creativity and Poetics at the University of Gloucestershire, UK. He is a published poet with five collections in print, the latest of which is *Chora: New & Selected Poems* (Templar Poetry, 2009). Since 2008 he has been Editor of *Iota* poetry journal and he has served as a guest editor for *TEXT: The Journal of Writing and Writing Courses* and for the journal *American, British and Canadian Studies*. In 2011 he was awarded a UK National Teaching Fellowship. A recording of his poetry can be found on the Poetry Archive at http://www.poetryarchive.org/poet/nigel-mcloughlin.

Paul Munden is Director of the National Association of Writers in Education (NAWE) and currently Postdoctoral Research Fellow (Poetry and

Creative Practice) at the University of Canberra. His poetry has received an Eric Gregory Award and a new collection, *Analogue/Digital*, is scheduled for 2015. For the British Council, he has been writer-in-residence at several Anglo-Swiss conferences, most recently on the Role of Cultural Relations in Addressing Conflict, and edited the anthology *Feeling the Pressure: Poetry and Science of Climate Change* (British Council, 2008). He worked closely with AQA in developing the specification for the new Creative Writing 'A'-level and was recently awarded the Ken Goulding Prize from Middlesex University for his Professional Doctorate by Public Works. He is author of *Beyond the Benchmark: Creative Writing in Higher Education*, commissioned by the Higher Education Academy (2013).

Gail Pittaway is a Senior Lecturer in the School of Media Arts, the Waikato Institute of Technology, in Hamilton, New Zealand. A member of the New Zealand Communication Association, the Tertiary Writing Network, the New Zealand Society of Authors, Gail has also been an executive member of the Australian Association of Writing Programmes since 2004 and has published poetry and papers in *TEXT* journal, as well as having stories produced for radio.

Marcela Sulak is the author of the poetry collections *Decency* (2015), *Immigrant* (2010) and *Of all the things that don't exist, I love you best* (2008); four book-length poetry translations from the Hebrew (Orit Gidali, 2016), the Czech (Karel Hynek Macha, 2005; K.J. Erben, 2012) and the French (Mutombo Nkulu-N'Sengha, 2011), and several essays, which appear in the *Iowa Review*, the *Los Angeles Review of Books*, and elsewhere. She is the co-editor of *Family Resemblance: An Anthology and Exploration of Eight Hybrid Literary Forms*, forthcoming from Rose Metal Press. She directs the Shaindy Rudoff Graduate Program in Creative Writing at Bar-Ilan University in Israel, where she is Senior Lecturer in American Literature.

Michael Theune is Associate Professor of English at Illinois Wesleyan University in Bloomington, Illinois. He is the editor of *Structure and Surprise: Engaging Poetic Turns* (Teachers and Writers Collaborative, 2007) and the host of the Structure & Surprise blog (https://structureandsurprise.wordpress.com). With Kim Addonizio, he co-edits Voltage Poetry (http://voltagepoetry.com), an online anthology of poems with great turns in them. His poems, essays and reviews have appeared in numerous publications, including *College English, The New Republic, Pleiades*, and *Spoon River Poetry Review*.

Accounting for the Unaccountable: A Foreword in 42 Tweets

Philip Gross

Don't expect us to make you a writer, I found myself saying at a recent Open Day. *Do not expect a proper job, maybe ever. I promise nothing.*

#

Some writers I know accuse us who work in universities of beguiling students with dreams of success. Nothing could be further from my mind.

#

Nothing, said King Lear, *will come of nothing*. Everything that followed showed how wrong he was. Five acts, a world of story, drama, poetry.

#

Never have we writer-teachers been so put on the spot to say *So what's it for, Creative Writing? What are the Outcomes? What can come of it?*

#

Who in their right mind would say *Nothing*, leave that box unfilled by so-available jargon that says *Just say me; that's all you have to do*?

#

I'm not negative, by habit, no naysayer. But I can feel the bite, the clarifying sting, the astringent dab on the hurt, of the *via negativa*.

#

It does hurt sometimes, the required language we find ourselves using. Hurts because just under the surface of it we know *something* is true.

#

I say this with respect for those of us who work at the borders with official language (some in this book) – guides, translators to and fro.

#

In the world of faith the *via negativa* isn't doubt. It's the wiping of smeared thoughts from a window between us and what we trust is there.

#

Or for Lear, who could not abide the *nothing*, a tragic long tale of being stripped bare until he acknowledged (OK, too late) something true.

#

And what if the true thing is too simple and too subtle to express in the language in which we are required to justify what we teach and do?

#

The truest thing for anybody who is in some sense a *maker* is that *Yes!* when you the feel the work quicken with something you did not intend.

#

Or not... The language of control calls on us to say what will be *delivered*. If we are serious about 'creative', maybe nothing will be born.

#

Maybe nothing. Or worse, repetition. We could guarantee that, no problem. Or something uncalled-for. All that 'creative' guarantees is risk.

#

How's this for a writing game: fill out the Risk Assessment form – yes, in earnest, being honest with yourself – when you sit down to write?

#

Writing could change your life! Your earnings (no joke this, for mature students leaving paid jobs for lives as writers) are likely to fall.

#

Do I dare to *promise nothing* ... that is, except disciplined space, with demands, the first of which are: be alert to language, and each other?

#

In other words, creative process. But let's handle the term gingerly. Somewhere between the fey and the industrial lives the work of making.

#

And of unmaking too. No, this isn't magic. Nor so twitchily shy we can't find terms for it. But one of the terms we need may be a ? Or Zero.

#

The Uncertainty Principle. Keats' Negative Capability. No lack, but a tool of our trade. Without it, you can cross out that word 'creative'.

#

Another word to write in: 'serendipity' – i.e. not just chance, but the chance that happens more when you're alert and ready, primed for it.

#

Like many CW educators of my age in the UK I was a working writer doing odd jobs, school visits, evening classes, anything so I could write.

#

(This is circumstantial: my time, my age, my place. Unashamedly. I do not speak for other writers in this book. Our strength is our variety.

#

This is writing knowledge too – let the specific speak to the specific. Generalities approximate. Be true, be specific. Then we can relate.)

#

So, 1989, Bath, serendipity... Me standing there by chance with chance-acquired skills, when in the universities a need, an appetite, arose.

#

Sitting on an interviewing panel today would I feel able – would I *be* able – to offer a job to a candidate as unaccounted-for as I was then?

#

And the workshop – its uncertain outcomes? Unknown quantities inside every head. Isn't that what is wrong with it? Or could it be the point?

#

Not to be smug or sentimental about these things... Let's say it out loud: the unaccountable is serious. Even, that it can be accounted for.

#

Someone is paying us to do this. Ultimately, our students. Can we level with them, trust them to recognise the real thing, if we speak true?

#

Let's talk transferable skills. Who could teach this life-mathematics, handling these unknown quantities, better than we could, if we chose?

#

Of course most of our students won't become great writers. But they learn how to handle themselves, each other, their materials, creatively.

#

Few students now in any discipline will end up doing what they're planning for, any more than I did. What we teach, they need: adaptability.

#

Imagine a discipline not as a hoard of knowledge but a disciplined space out of which we can look in all directions, 360°, the compass rose.

#

There *is* knowledge, of course... the knowledge that goes into creating that space, into holding it open, including the unknown quantities...

#

And the arbitrary tasks, the games, the wild cards... This tweet form for example: 140-characters-including-spaces. How to account for that?

#

There's nothing in it but this clear small lens to magnify the grain of language, and of ourselves in the process. Just like our discipline.

#

Or like the workshop: shape made not just of characters, but of them and spaces. Grasping the spaces between us, words and us, is the point.

#

Or take these tweets as birdsong (yes, even a cheap pun serves us now and then). Most days I walk to the train through a wood. Stop. Listen.

#

Those tweets, the real ones, say nothing to me except *Notice*. Create a space around me in several dimensions... myself in it, listening out.

#

Then on to work. Do I twitter like this to the Quality subcommittee? No, I probably fill the forms in as required. But something is changed.

#

A poem: not just the words but the space in which they resonate. Its architecture, built of said and unsaid, thing and no-thing, yes and no.

#

Like a quick cold splash, first thing, to get the blood flowing. I feel it in my skin all day. The real thing. What it says is *Don't forget*.

Creative Writing and Education: An Introduction

Graeme Harper

1.

Creative writing is the action of writing creatively, informed by the human imagination and the creative and critical understanding of the creative writer, influenced by personal history and by culture, guided by forms and types of individual knowledge that so often do not stay within the disciplinary boundaries of colleges or universities or schools as they have been defined in the late modern period. Creative writing is not always assisted by these contemporary institutional structures and functions, wherever these might be in the world, because these structures and functions relate to relatively fixed time frames (at the macro level for such things as completion of college degrees and at the micro level for such things as completion of work to be assessed) and the actions of creative writing most often do not, and because creative writing practice and understanding are highly individualized and our contemporary educational institutions are not.

So our universities and colleges, for example, dealing in modern mass education, produce programs and courses that refer to holistic entities and relational characteristics of the individuals within them. That is, a creative writing student is either part of a 'class' group or is an individual (say, a graduate student) as part of a cohort of other individuals (in this way defined in relation to other individuals in that cohort). What this means is that an exploration of creative writing and education begins with the realization that those looking to truly teach it are often attempting to find some way to reconfigure the environments, time frames or contexts in which they are working in order to more successfully teach the reality of the practices with which they, and their students, are engaging.

This is what I refer to as the 'myths' about creative writing and education. Others might call some of the contributions made by these myths 'tensions'. In this vein, for some years we have heard expressed both formally in documents concerned with creating post-secondary education courses and informally in the statements of some creative writers asked to teach creative writing in institutions versions of the statement that 'creative writing cannot be taught'. This, too, is a figurative reflection of the myths or tensions encountered. We see some reference to these in the thoughts expressed in Philip Gross's Foreword to this book and you will read more of this also in chapters throughout *Creative Writing and Education*.

These myths include the idea that there is a single conversation that can be had concerning creative writing and education, a single conversation with varying perspectives. Such a view is more a reflection of the centralizing impact of mass educational practices than it is an expression of a reality of creative writing. A discussion of creative writing and education is not one conversation with various viewpoints but many conversations – much as creative writing is not one action but many and creative writers are not defined solely by a culture or society but also by the nature of their individual self and their personal experiences.

Equally, we find in today's creative writing discussions examples of conclusions about creative writing and education drawn from national histories rather than more widely, from the practice of creative writing and its many appearances and histories and contexts around the globe. This is natural, and it is often also useful, as long as those conclusions are placed in juxtaposition to others or shown in comparison or contrast to those occurring elsewhere in order to identify characteristics defined by their origins. In this way, different meanings will be expressed, based on differing individual and cultural experiences, and some of the knowledge gained in this is the result of our puzzlement about how terms and ideas are being employed. To do anything other than allow this to happen would be to suggest that creative writing and education relate to each other in a jejune way defined by expressions such as 'becoming a writer'. While this idea of 'becoming' certainly has a utilitarian purpose in what in modern times has often been an education consumer culture, it fails to recognize that with creative writing the becoming never ends, and that the expression 'a writer' is a modern occupational invention borne on the back of the defining technical or mercantile roles in an industrial world. Neither 'to become' nor being defined as 'a writer' is a definition of actual learning for those who wish to learn or teach something about creative writing.

2.

The authors in this book explore creative writing and its various relationships to education based on their experiences of both creative writing and education. As you will see, their experiences are strong and many. This is meant to be a book of many conversations – and the attentive will quickly notice that this fact is further indicated by the number of the chapters that are jointly written. The conversations in this book are meant to be open, personal and empowered.

It also should be said that this is not a book necessarily to gladden those who teach English Literature or Language, Composition, Rhetoric or Writing (more generally defined) or anything else but Creative Writing. It might not even make those teaching Creative Writing all that relaxed, because the authors in the book were encouraged to focus on what they believe to be important, to write about what they felt needed to be said. Because of the variety of responses, readers will almost certainly find something in the book that aligns most with their own responses – and that might be the route for an initial foray into some of less aligned chapters, where I am confident a reader will at least form a sense of, if not a passion for, other possibilities.

Similarly, by a way of a direct apology: this is not a book of something called 'Creative Writing Studies'. I have indeed co-edited a book with that title (Harper & Kroll, 2007). I'm fairly sure my co-editor and I did not intend to create a box into which we could put all creative writing investigations. What we meant was that it was possible to *study* creative writing, but that all those who engaged in it did not necessarily have to, or might not want to, *study* it. Thus we called the book *Creative Writing Studies* to suggest it was for those who were interested in studying it or teaching those who were studying it. Dianne Donnelly later published an excellent book entitled *Establishing Creative Writing Studies as an Academic Discipline* (2012), which did not suggest creating a box for a discipline either; rather, her book explored ideas about specialized knowledge concerned with the study of creative writing. She makes a good case. This current book I personally do not consider to be a book in a field called 'Creative Writing Studies'. I consider it to be a book about creative writing and education.

I have long believed in the statement made by the writer Irwin Shaw that 'a good editor ... understands what you're talking and writing about and doesn't meddle too much' (see Mathieson *et al.*, 1979). I have not meddled too much in the opinions of the writers in this book. While I have my own opinions, and I do express some of these later in this Introduction, this is not a book written by me and it is not a book in which I define my editor's role as being the intellectual, creative or spiritual core for all the authors who present work in the book. However, it was indeed I who selected these authors, knowing each of them well enough that I felt they would have something to say. I replied to any queries from them about the focus or intention of their chapters. I responded to some drafts along the way and I gave some instructions about what the chapter might consider. Those instructions for the chapter writers went exactly like this:

> Your chapter [is] likely to be trekking along one or more of the following trails:
>
> - the chapter focuses on methods related to the teaching or learning of creative writing and/or
> - the chapter focuses on a notable issue that impacts on good practice in the teaching of creative writing and/or
> - the chapter investigates critical ideas that relate to creative writing and to education and/or
> - the chapter draws on empirical research from a period of teaching creative writing to suggest how creative writing relates to education and/or
> - the chapter makes recommendations for progressing the teaching of creative writing.
>
> Open to 'A.Nother' approach, if you wish. So these are, to quote pirate philosopher Geoffrey Rush, 'more what you'd call "guidelines" than actual rules'.

For those who are not familiar with Jerry Bruckheimer's *Pirates of the Caribbean* film series, the last comment refers to a speech in *Pirates of the Caribbean: The Curse of the Black Pearl* (2003) by a Captain Barbossa (played by Rush):

> First, your return to shore was not part of our negotiations nor our agreement so I must do nothing. And secondly, you must be a pirate for the pirate's code to apply and you're not. And thirdly, the code is more what you'd call 'guidelines' than actual rules.

The intention was to give the authors something to ponder, and to encourage them to pursue their own ideas and directions. Although they were all welcome to 'return to [the] shore' of my suggestions they were not at all obliged to do so and could simply treat my coded message as guidelines.

The chapter writers were also asked for the following, based on the same 'guideline' philosophy:

> each chapter to conclude with a (up to) 10-point exploratory guide to Issues, Ideas, Actions in the area of Creative Writing and Education. Heading: 'Exploration'.

The idea of this 10-point concluding statement is that it allows a grounding for the (globally diverse) chapters and experiences, while leaving the content (and writers) of the chapters room to explore according to experiences and knowledge based in practice, theory and response.

Because the results of creative writing come in a wide variety of forms, I felt a good method for not creating a book about creative writing and education that largely avoided that simple fact was to ask some of the writers to comment more freely, without any of the structural or formal requirements of academic chapter writing. Thus the inclusion in the book of a number of 'Commentaries'. Commentary writers were asked to contribute in exactly these words:

The plan: a short exploratory piece of your making, and of your interest, and in the style you choose.

These commentary writers were given a guideline length for their contributions of 1000 words. Many exceeded this, but no restrictions were placed on them doing so. Further, originally all the commentaries were to be placed at the end of *Creative Writing and Education*. The idea was that they would act as a kind of coda to the book, completing the exploration by showing that creative writing produces works in many forms and that while formally constructed academic discussion was one way of exploring creative writing there could most certainly be other ways, and those other ways might reveal other things. A reviewer of an earlier version of the book thought this approach didn't work and suggested instead interspersing the commentaries and the chapters, and using the juxtapositions to create interesting connections, contrasts and comparisons. I liked this suggestion and I have therefore used it. I thank that reviewer for their contribution to the book.

3.

In an article entitled 'Persistent myths in the history of education', education historian Edward J. Power, once suggested:

Throughout education's long history legends and myths that have been generated in misinformation and cultivated by indifference or incorrigible obstinacy have attached themselves to a core of historical knowledge to distort the dimensions of its accuracy. (Power, 1962: 140)

Power's general observations are not out of place when exploring creative writing and education. If there have been misinformation, indifference and obstinacy in the contextualizing of education generally, then there have been more in relation to education in and about creative writing. This has occurred not because those contributing to it have actively sought to limit our understanding. This has occurred because, as Power noted in the wider context, 'validity goes unchallenged' (Power, 1962: 140).

To that end, it is the aim of *Creative Writing and Education* to present views without the distortion of indifference or obstinacy, and to present them directly from those who, by their enthusiastic engagement in creative writing in educational settings (most specifically in post-secondary education), have a desire to share individual experiences and to contribute to group expertise. Individual and group expertise founded on an obliqueness of vision, and remaining unchallenged, likely has prevented more concerted attention to creative writing generally in institutions concerned with education. We are reminded of some of this by Mark McGurl when he writes in the concluding pages of his *The Program Era: Postwar Fiction and the Rise of Creative Writing* (2009) that:

> Outwardly, the task of the academic creative writer is to produce, in her writings, unconscious allegories of institutional quality, aesthetically pure because luxuriously useless. More simply, these writers contribute a certain form of prestige to the university's overall portfolio of cultural capital, adding their bit to the market value of the degrees it confers. In this role they are somewhat like varsity athletes, but whereas varsity athletics typically symbolizes the excellence of competitive teamwork, creative writing and the other arts testify to the institution's systematic hospitality to the excellence of individual self-expression. (McGurl, 2009: 408)

McGurl's book added to a relatively small number of books concerned with the history of creative writing in universities. About some of these I have admittedly been critical, not because they are poor pieces of scholarship in themselves, but because they have largely not addressed questions of mythologizing and distortion. Historiography can of course perpetuate untruths as much as it can seek to expose truths. What McGurl's statement does neatly is remind us that the political economy of education and the cultural politics associated with such things as literature, with the artifacts of the creative industries more broadly, and even with the ascent into prominence of certain creative writers, are not in fact the practice of creative writing, even if they do have a relationship with it. We're reminded in this, once again, of how national characteristics of the history of education can potentially distort a view of the human practice creative writing and potentially make us impatient for a view that fits our history. While readers will not get a singular view in this book, it is hoped they will see far more truth in what follows, and something more of what McGurl rightly calls 'individual self-expression'.

4.

To offer then one moment in which the editor of this book explicitly expresses some thoughts, those thoughts are these:

We need to consider why the human practice of creative writing – which can indeed be nothing other than human – remains so often depicted as primarily related to a singular material artifact emerging at the end of these human actions. This association is today as much in the popular imagination as it is in formal educational thinking because of the persistence of myths that have made the final artifacts of the practice of creative writing the predominant focus of educational and other attention. 'Other attention' meaning, not least, the kind of attention during the industrial age directed toward tradable manufactured commodities.

Create an artifactual culture – one that defines much human exchange on the basis of the production and consumption of material goods – and it makes sense that formal education will follow and itself emphasize material end points. This is part of the reason why it remains difficult to begin discussions of creative writing and education by questioning the primacy of material outcomes. Such outcomes seem so fundamental to our understanding and engagement with creative writing, as well as to our shared knowledge about creative writing, that to suggest they are not primary to education concerned with creative writing appears to challenge human meaning as much as it appears to challenge cultural beliefs. This is largely what is behind the creation and maintenance of myths or 'tensions' when it comes to the teaching and learning of creative writing.

With this in mind, we might return to the point that, although the end result of creative writing is important, creative writers spend the majority of their time engaged in the practice not engaged with the material end result. Add to this that creative writing uniquely uses words as its principal creative tools and therefore has a strong relationship with the application and exploration of human language in all its many dynamic forms. Consider also that creative writers produce evidence of their actions during their creative writing, but also before and after it, and that, while there might be an end goal, the many pieces of evidence (whether drafts of work, correspondence, complementary or supplementary texts, or other evidence of their creating) are significant also in the human practice that creative writing happens to be. Focus for a moment on one or more of these points and the idea that when creative writing is in formal educational situations we should privilege singular end results makes very little sense. Certainly, recognize, examine and put into individual and cultural context those end results of creative writing; but privileging them misses so very much that is pedagogically significant.

In this, a thought comes momentarily to mind that the title of this book, *Creative Writing and Education*, is too ill-defined and too generic to be widely useful. Based on that thought, the temptation is to break creative writing and education relationships down into graspable chunks, or differing routes of educational engagement, or contrasting groupings of thematic chapters, so that something of the complexity of the relationship might be simplified for readers, and the variations in it might be explored. Candidly, I tried and I failed in an earlier draft of this Introduction to make any sense of creating such divisions. An anonymous reviewer energetically pointed this out to me. My suggestion had been that there were three possible ways of looking at how the book's title might encapsulate our conversations. These three perspectives I labelled brightly:

(1) education in creative writing
(2) creative writing in education, and
(3) education about creative writing.

This dividing up was my partial attempt to undertake a thought experiment concerning how relationships between creative writing and education were formed, what systemic elements they might contain, what functional characteristics they might employ and whether there were any evolution-ary characteristics identifiable in any of these subgroups (so, for example, whether 'education about creative writing' was attempting to evolve knowledge of a teaching field, or whether 'education in creative writing' was clearly aimed at progressing a student's ability to do creative writing). I therefore suggested the following things:

Education in creative writing could be considered education associated principally (though not solely) with the undertaking of creative writing. Whatever was discussed critically in this version of creative writing and education would be related directly to the practice of creative writing and critical undertakings would bear the strongest link to situational knowledge (Harper, 2013: 284) applicable to creative writing projects being undertaken.

Creative writing in education could be imagined to be somewhat different to this, in that its principal interest would be creative writing applications more generally in educational settings. The act of using creative writing as an investigative tool would underscore *creative writing in education*, and thus its role in our creation and dissemination of human understanding more generally.

Education about creative writing contrasted somewhat with the earlier versions of creative writing and education by being discussions about the practice and results of the practice, but not necessarily accomplished through the undertaking of creative writing. So education about creative writing could perhaps incorporate some things seen in researching and teaching rhetoric and composition (as found, for example, in universities and colleges in the USA); though, more so, it could incorporate that seen in the study of literature, media and drama. It might no doubt also include elements of the study of music and computer games.

This dividing up looked convincing at my initial glance. So, ultimately, what was wrong with this bright and deliberate tripartite structure? Firstly, at least one reviewer had little idea of why I had suggested it, and even less about what it really meant. That's no criticism whatsoever of that reviewer: I simply hadn't convinced them of the structure's validity. If I hadn't convinced a reviewer of the manuscript, who was obliged to give attention to the book's shape, then how would other readers react who might not feel so obliged? Not well, I suspected. Secondly, it was exactly for people like that reviewer that I was suggesting these divisions in the first place. I was attempting both to bridge distinctively national characteristics of historical understanding concerned with creative writing and education (especially the teaching and learning of creative writing in post-secondary education) and to counter any future criticism that this book was too loosely structured, too open-ended. Obviously, based on the initial reaction, I hadn't even convinced myself that such divisions made sense! Consequently, in this mistake lay the solution to how to introduce, and explain, the structure and intention of *Creative Writing and Education*, more genuinely.

5.

Thus, this is what you will find here:

You will encounter a variety of thoughts concerned with creative writing and education. These two terms – 'creative writing' and 'education' – define the book, for me and for the writers in it. How these terms (and, indeed, these two sets of human practices) relate is not going to be limited by me now or in what you encounter in the rest of the book. So you will not find in what follows a deterministic exploration. Where you reach in reading this book, or how you read this book, will be decided by you.

In that vein, I'm thankful that the book is not structured to deal with perceivable gaps, constraints, difficulties or identified key themes – at least it is not structured *by me* to deal with those things. If you find discussion of any of such things emerging in the book, this will indicate the ideas and concerns of the authors in the book, and their comments will be presented to you largely unfiltered by me. I believe the authors have enough expertise and experience to make excellent decisions about what they believe is significant.

Clearly, the thought that there are different ways to engage with creative writing and education has some validity. As an individual and cultural human practice, this will always be so. But what the thought brings to mind above all else is that these ways are not easily separated from each other, that creative writing does not by nature stay contained in one mode of engagement, that the word 'creative' represents a fluidity of actions and results. If formal late modern education has dealt in slicing up knowledge in order to package it for sale, for consumption, or for presentation to the political or economic forces of our time, and in this way generated and supported misinformation when it comes to creative writing and education, resulting in myths and distortions, then the principal question becomes, what can we do now to move forward more productively? That was the question that brought about this book.

Creative Writing and Education aims to give you a sense of contemporary thinking, to provide some alternative points of view, and to offer examples of how those involved in creative writing and education feel about how these activities relate. As one of our most widely undertaken and greatly valued human practices, creative writing makes much of the critical and creative understanding that all human language entails. It is not produced without our actions, in whatever form or forms those actions take. The results of our actions are as many and as varied as there are thoughts and ideals that inform creative writing in the first place. While the sheer extent of possible points of entry and exit to the practice of creative writing make it an individual and, certainly, a many-sided practice, its diverse nature, combined with its human origins, should tell us that it relates to something fundamental about our individual selves, whoever and wherever we are.

In my view, therefore, if the teaching of creative writing is to be genuinely about creative writing, it must begin with those things that draw each of us to the practice, and from there consider our actions while undertaking it and the results we produce across the length of time we undertake it. A demythologized creative writing teaching would surely be one that horizontally positions our actions and our results, action and result similarly valued. An undistorted creative writing teaching would look beneath the surface of this human practice and its results and explore what it is that occurs in our creative and critical thoughts *during* the practice of creative writing. If we are not indifferent to this goal – and the fact that you are reading this book suggests you are not indifferent to it – then misinformation won't be acceptable and obstinacy about what has been valued in the past in one educational situation or another will not dissuade any of us from further exploration.

The possibility of improving our understanding and our individual pursuits in creative writing by approaching it in this way is likewise considerable. What we discover in pursuing the further development of creative writing in educational settings will repay our interest and commitment not because we are developing creative writing as a subject of study or as an academic discipline, but because we are seeking human knowledge that we have long felt important but not always pursued with clarity.

How the Editor Reads the Book

As you'll have gathered already, I very much envisage this book as a series of conversations. Those conversations are between each writer and each reader, between all the writers and every reader of the book. Individual readers can and will make their own choices as to how they read the book. The advantages of reading an edited collection should be that you can dip into it at various points, without feeling you have undermined the overall experience. If, for example, you weren't reading this Introduction I'd certainly never know about it, and there's a good chance you wouldn't be disadvantaged by not doing so. But if you are reading this and thinking 'but he must have made some decisions about how to place each piece of work in the book, even though he wants the book to directly reflect the responses of the chapter writers', you are correct. Beyond my previous note that an earlier version of the book had the commentaries gathered at the end, and that this was changed due to the astute observation of a reviewer of the manuscript, here is my reading:

I have placed the contribution by **Randall Albers and Steve May** as Chapter 1 because I feel it usefully bridges individual experiences in American and British post-secondary education. The two writers, one from the USA and one from UK, have worked together for quite a while, across the Atlantic, and presented a number of conference papers together at creative writing conferences. They've built exchanges between their institutions, and taken leadership roles in creative writing programs within their individual institutions. Their chapter mentions a number of well voiced topics and terms in creative writing teaching and learning, from 'process' and writer 'development' to 'competence and confidence', 'imagination' and the idea of 'truth', which frames their chapter.

Liz Cashdan and Moy McCrory have also often worked together. I've placed this chapter at this point in the book partly because I read it as a contrast with the first chapter, but also because its focus on identity highlights the question, for me, of how we support individuality when we consider creative writing and education. Liz and Moy offer an exploration also of the question of cultural influence in creative writing and creative writing learning.

Following their chapter, I've placed the first of the book's commentaries. **Marcela Sulak**'s piece usefully demonstrates one of the reasons why I wanted to combine formal chapters with less formal commentaries. In the more open commentary format, she remarks poignantly on her work in the Middle East, directing an international creative writing program. While the Middle East is a geographic area in which creative writing is clearly taught and learnt, how many readers of *Creative Writing and Education* know anything about this? My own knowledge was scant. I read Marcela Sulak's contribution as not only an exploration of cultural difference but also as a personal comment on the challenge of teaching in a multilingual situation when dealing with an art that is so dependent on written language.

'Creative writing assessment in higher education institutions should be transparent and accessible to all stakeholders', writes **Dianne Donnelly** in 'Embracing the learning paradigm: How assessment drives creative writing pedagogy'. The challenge Donnelly discusses is identifiably within the formal mechanisms of contemporary post-secondary education. How do we negotiate a practice, such as assessment, which is fraught with student as well as teacher concern, and produce a viable model reflecting the nature and intent of engaging in creative writing? **Toby Emert and Maureen Hall** also focus on the classroom, but this time in relation to teacher education. They introduce the term 'service learning' (which might be unfamiliar to some readers outside the USA – it refers to projects undertaken in the community as part of a course of study). Emert and Hall explore reading and its text-making contributions, and in that regard their chapter could have been placed elsewhere – beside Nigel McLoughlin's chapter, for example, which also discusses reading. I like encountering it here, in relation to what Dianne Donnelly calls the 'learning paradigm', but I would point the reader at very least in the direction of McLoughlin's chapter, for further connections.

In 'Poetry by heart', the second of the book's commentaries, this time by **Paul Munden**, Director of the UK's National Association of Writers in Education (NAWE), we continue in the community, with Paul describing an exciting initiative of the Poetry Archive, involving a national recitation competition for students aged 14–18. Paul comments: 'Creative Writing is all about the new, and yet sometimes, dare I say it, our approaches to the subject seem anything but.' Food for thought!

Given that I have included other pieces earlier in the sequence that are not American, British and Australian contributions, the placing of **Fan Dai**'s chapter here is not so much about offering it as a contrast as it is about it offering some greater historical and contextual understanding. For example, she notes: 'In 2009, Shanghai University set up its Center for Creative Writing (in Chinese), followed by the International Writing Center in 2010 at Renmin University of China'. I suspect few readers outside China were aware of this, and given the global context of creative writing teaching and learning it is significant knowledge. This seems a good reason to include the chapter here, at what approaches the middle of the book. That is a personal preference. I'm assuming some readers did start at the beginning of the book and, when reading from the beginning of a book, I like to find somewhere around the middle a sense that there'll be enough new to keep me interested until the end. That might be a sign that I'm an impatient reader.

Perhaps due to that impatience, or perhaps because I see an opportunity for putting heads together, I've included something of a mid-book gathering of interconnected topics. To start, there is an investigation of language and heritage, with **Asma Mansoor** recounting in her commentary aspects of her work in Pakistan. Marcela Sulak's earlier commentary and Fan Dai's chapter are comparatively relevant here, while Asma adds to these with her thoughts on what she refers to as the 'palimpsest of memory'. Her commentary is followed by an interview I conducted with three of my former creative writing PhD students, who now all work as teachers and researchers in post-secondary education, **Craig Batty** in Australia and **Gill James and Simon Holloway** in Britain. The questions and answers in this chapter largely relate to the definition of the relationship between creative writing and education, and to what the interviewees believe is (or can be) learnt. The mid-book section concludes with a commentary from **Katharine Coles** on, among other things, care and risk in creative writing teaching, a topic I felt was well suited to provide the book's fulcrum. She writes: 'A possible way to think generally about the tension between the need to master technique while at the same time taking risks is to distinguish *care* from *carefulness*, aiming for the former while trying not to tip over into the latter'.

Nigel McLoughlin's chapter is entitled 'Interpretation, affordance and realised intention: The transaction(s) between reader and writer'. Nigel, a poet, is Professor of Creativity and Poetics at the University of Gloucestershire, UK, and he frequently researches between and amid creative practice and the theoretical understanding of creative writing and creative writing pedagogies. His chapter is a good example of his methods, in this case responding to the work of literary theorist Stanley Fish, which elicits a wider scrutiny of notions of cooperation in textual construction and interpretation.

In **Gail Pittaway**'s contribution, movement and visuality come to the fore but, more so, she questions the notion of what best stimulates the creative writer's imagination and mind. Play, sound and intertextuality all appear in this chapter and it works as a lively discussion of sensory experiences in the teaching of creative writing. Gail is writing from her home in New Zealand. **Sieneke de Rooij** presents her commentary from her home in the Netherlands. She seemingly offers not only a perspective from another hemisphere but a hemispheric challenge to Pittaway's preceding discussion. Sieneke de Rooij notes: 'To help my students find more variation in their writing, I created some lessons and assignments in which I forbid any visual input from entering a text'. In fact, de Rooij's explorations with students in workshops in the Netherlands, using sensory connections of scent and sound, identify a remarkable trans-global exchange between two creative writing teachers. I'm sure Gail Pittaway and Sieneke de Rooij did not speak when composing their contributions to this book. I'm fairly sure they have not yet even met.

Kevin Brophy and Elizabeth MacFarlane take us into the realm of technology, not least the 21st-century rise of massive open online courses (MOOCs) and blended physical–electronic environments for teaching and learning. Can such a phenomenon as MOOCs work for creative writing courses? I admit to being a critic of a certain kind of MOOC (the largely asynchronous kind that seems to be to miss the point about direct human interaction and productive learning processes). The writers comment that they 'aim to recognize and exploit the versatility of the lecture by bringing it into contact with new media and new digital platforms – as far as our present skills allow'. Their suggestions seem to offer some potential, not necessarily for the preservation of the 'traditional lecture' format, but for the investigation of new electronically enhanced formats of many kinds.

So it is to **Jeri Kroll**'s chapter, focusing on the doctoral degree in creative writing. When she suggested focusing on this topic I was pleased to hear it. It would be disingenuous of me to suggest that this is a chapter emerging solely from Australian and British practices. Firstly, the writer of the chapter was born in the USA and she knows its educational practices well. Secondly, the USA has long included 'creative dissertations' as possible routes in its PhD programmes in subjects such as English, so the idea that doctoral work in creative writing is mostly located outside the USA would be false. But this is a chapter about 'creative writing research' and that is an interesting term when considered as a component of teaching, given that the idea of research through creative writing, research about creative writing or research in creative writing does not appear in a similar guise across the world.

Maggie Butt's commentary is placed directly after Jeri Kroll's chapter because its focus is at the other end of what some research sponsors (or funders, as they are often called in the UK, for example) call a 'pipeline'. A pipeline in research funding terms, and indeed in terms of levels of education, refers to the creation of connected educational practices and results. So, for example, a pipeline program focusing on the development of stronger medical research might begin with the championing of medicine with students entering their first year of high school, involve differing types of support and intervention, include postdoctoral researchers in dedicated laboratories, and end with the appointment of more medical researchers to full-time positions in post-secondary education. Maggie discusses the development of a British Creative Writing A-level. As she points out, 'the "A-level" is the exit qualification from secondary school (age 11–18) or further education college (age 16–18) and operates as preparation and entry qualification for degree courses'. In this sense, therefore, by developing a 'Creative Writing A-level' the educational pipeline in creative writing is being strengthened.

Value and self-understanding are examined in **Michael Theune and Bob Broad**'s chapter 'The poetry of evaluation: Helping students explore how they value verse'. With a discussion of research, pipelines and indeed care and carefulness, and the interrelation of writers and readers, a chapter on value I read as being well placed here. The chapter might also be related to the contributions made by Dianne Donnelly and Nigel McLoughlin, but I leave it to the reader to determine how much Bob Broad's phrase 'dynamic criteria mapping (DCM)' compares or contrasts with points made about evaluation elsewhere in the book.

The final chapter in *Creative Writing and Education* seemed to me to have to be **Nigel Krauth**'s investigation of the 'radical future', not least because it is forward looking. But also because it is about the multidisciplinary; it is about addressing the contemporary; and it is about speaking plainly about where we might need to re-examine current teaching practices. This might not be the easiest chapter to read for anyone concerned about losing the qualities of much we have known in relation to books and literature. Equally, it seems to me an essential conversation to have.

That final chapter is followed by the final commentary, by **Brooke Biaz,** as a coda to the book (another useful suggestion of a reviewer). Perhaps, for me, it is this part of the commentary that bests sums up its intention:

Because the human activity of creative writing has existed for so long, and in so many cultures, and in so many forms, we can be confident that human beings value it, and value it for many reasons. That sense of human value must make us ask what it is in creative writing that we value and how any education connected with creative writing can best support that valuing.

Needless to say, that is my own reading of *Creative Writing and Education*, the placement of the chapters and commentaries, and the perspectives, considerations and contributions of the many authors. Another reader might see the whole thing differently. I offer my thoughts only as guidelines, not actual rules.

References

Donnelly, D. (2012) *Establishing Creative Writing Studies as an Academic Discipline*. Bristol: Multilingual Matters.

Harper, G. (2013) Creative writing research. In G. Harper (ed.) *A Companion to Creative Writing* (pp. 278–290). Oxford: Wiley-Blackwell.

Harper, G. and Kroll, J. (eds) (2007) *Creative Writing Studies: Practice, Research and Pedagogy*. Clevedon: Multilingual Matters.

Matthiessen, L., Morris, W. and Marquand, J. (1979) Irwin Shaw, the art of fiction no. 4 (continued). *Paris Review* no. 75. Available at http://www.theparisreview.org/interviews/3395/the-art-of-fiction-no-4-continued-irwin-shaw (accessed 13 July 2014).

McGurl, M. (2009) *The Program Era: Postwar Fiction and the Rise of Creative Writing*. Cambridge, MA: Harvard University Press.

Power, E.J. (1962) Persistent myths in the history of education. *History of Education Quarterly* 2 (3), 140–151.

Chapter 1

Revelation, Transgression, Disclosure and the Tyranny of Truth

Randall Albers and Steve May

This chapter is written in the form of a dialectic, with some fortunate moments of agreement.

Randall Albers: One of the oldest saws in the teaching of creative writing is 'Write what you know'. This canard ranks right up there with 'Show; don't tell' in popularity and half-truth. (Do Flaubert, Faulkner, Woolf and others limit themselves to showing? No, they do both.) The dictum seems to imply: Writing must draw on the writer's own experience, what the person has lived and seen, in order to have any claim to the attention of an audience. If writing what you know were limited to writing only what you had experienced or seen first-hand, fiction would be a pretty paltry thing indeed.

Steve May: Only if one's experience were paltry – isn't the key issue the implication that only those blessed with magnificent experience can be magnificent writers? So the question is, how do those of us with paltry lives (like Baudelaire, 1861: 250) turn 'miserable sludge' (*boue*) into gold?

RA: Hemingway, in *A Moveable Feast*, tells of times when he would not be able to get a story going. Standing in front of his fire, squeezing the peel of an orange into the flames to watch it sputter, he would look out over the Paris rooftops and tell himself, 'Do not worry. You have always written before and you will write now. All you have to do is write one true sentence.' And invariably, he would write that one true sentence and then go on: 'It was easy then because there was always one true sentence that I knew or had seen or had heard someone say.... Up in that room I decided that I would write one story about each thing that I knew about' (Hemingway, 1964: 13).

SM: But what is this 'truth' that Hemingway – and, we might venture, writing teachers and students – hope to claim?

RA: Writing what he 'knew' seems coincident with what he felt was 'true' and was necessary to story. Hemingway's notion of felt truth departs from what some philosophers have tried to prove about objective truth, but it recalls Keats's linking of the two in asserting that 'axioms in philosophy are not axioms until they are proved upon our pulses' (Keats, 1818). The key point here is that truth is discovered in the mind – and heart – of the beholder.

SM: So, while the external world, sludge or no, may be the source of our writing, ultimately truth is found in what we make of our experience, not simply in scientific examination and fidelity to external fact.

RA: It doesn't take Hemingway to remind us that truth is an internal, felt response more than an external, objective reality. And it doesn't take Coleridge to remind us that what we know is as much a product of imagination and dreams as of experience – Hobbes, Locke and the empiricists notwithstanding (Coleridge, 1817: 167). In fact, conflating knowing and truth can be a trap. While Hemingway may use his feeling of the truth of something he has known or seen or heard as a means of engendering his sense of possibility and of pushing past the paralysis of writer's block, for others hyperawareness of the need for maintaining fidelity to the way things 'really' happened may actually prompt that paralysis. Writers may not be aware of the cause. They may simply find themselves sitting at their computer, trying to write a scene and not able to get it out. They can't see it clearly enough, can't find the right language, can't hear their voice on the page. And suddenly, they feel the weighty presence of the monkey censor on their shoulder, whispering 'You can't write that! What will the critics think? What will your friends think? What will your *mother* think? My lord, you'll never hear the end of it!' And that's followed by 'You know, you'll just never be good enough. If you wanted to tell fictions, why didn't you just listen to your mother and become a lawyer? It would've paid better.'

SM: Blake (1793) put the same point rather differently:

How do you know but ev'ry Bird that cuts the airy way,
Is an immense world of delight, clos'd by your senses five?

So, we want the bird, we want the truth about the bird, that is the goal. And in order to locate that truth, some grasp of the airy way through which it travels would be useful, if it is air or ether and whether it permits a vacuum. Trouble is, there is no 'available objective reality'. To expand: 'available' means available to us as creatures, 'objective' means untinged or untainted by perception and 'reality' means 'in quotes reality' because we can't have it without the modifying inverts. So, there might be a reality, an objective reality, an unambiguous and fully consistent reality, but it is not available to us, either as poets, novelists, playwrights or physicists. The flat fish with two eyes on the same side of its head will see a moon other than the moon of the toad. Indeed, the toad may be a two- or three-moon creature, depending on its state of amphibiousness at any particular time:

> In short, it seems as if language is like a great balloon, anchored to the ground of nonlinguistic fact only by a number of widely scattered and very thin (but all-important) ropes. (Putnam, 1975: 4)

For our purposes here, the main out-thrust of this proposition is that 'truth' is not an invariable objective, but a subjective variable, a product of our closed senses. This is hardly a heartening place to start for the new writer, nor indeed any writer. For one thing, Creative Writing traditionally celebrates the senses, and has a rich history of prompt exercises that depend on sight, smell, taste, sound and touch. If we apply some or all of these to the bird, it seems we are not finding its true essence, but constructing a distorted wraith. Further, our distorted wraiths are all different (if they were all the same, we might begin to have evidence of an available objective reality).

RA: Without getting any more deeply (and unreferenced) into the epistemological debate carried on by Bertrand Russell, Gilbert Ryle and others, we might ask 'How do teachers and students of creative writing understand "truth" and how do they respond to its call within themselves?' With Emerson's self-reliance: 'To believe your own thought, to believe that what is true for you in your private heart is true for all men, – that is genius' (Emerson, 1841: 147)? Or perhaps with Wilde's less sure view: 'The truth is rarely pure and never simple' (Wilde, 1895: 35)? More practically speaking, how do teachers help students break free of truth's tyranny in order to silence the monkey censor, realize their own unfolding vision and write fiction, non-fiction, poems or plays not bound by notions of 'correctness' (political, moral or other). And how, correspondingly, do we help students learn to be open to suggestion, avoid unalterable, solipsistic belief in their own world-view and respond to the wider social matrix in which they live and write?

SM: Try this simple experiment:

> Show an object to one group of people. Get them to describe it without naming it. Let them read their descriptions one by one to another group, who have not seen the object, and who then try to draw the images evoked in their minds by the descriptions. (May, 2007: 46)

RA: It doesn't sound simple.

SM: Trust me. The drawings will usually vary widely, as will interpretations of the 'meaning' or 'reality' of the evoked objects. Why? Not just because some people are 'better' at describing things, or because some are 'better' at understanding or drawing, but because the differing preconceptions, knowledge and experience of the writer and reader make it impossible that the two versions of the 'thing' are the same. Nor, of course, can the perceptions of two different readers be identical. Or even six.

RA: Reminds me of the tale passed down from ancient India of the six blind men touching different parts of an elephant and finding that it is like six different things – a pillar, a rope, a tree branch and so on. None of them is 'right' in the sense of knowing the full picture; each has his own picture, his own experience of the object, his own version of elephant reality. And while, it must be said, each has the potential for telling a perfectly fine and true story about that reality, putting all six stories together as readers will not ultimately get us any closer to the objective 'truth' of the beast than any one of them. Just as for Blake's bird.

SM: Let's hop down a different path in the rose garden. Let's deconstruct a somewhat jaundiced version of what we are asking of our students in the classroom:

> Dear class, I'd like you to write something that fulfills the expectations first of your peer group within this classroom, and then, possibly in the future, that fulfills the expectations of a larger group of public persons and makes you a modest but respectable income. Now, don't get me wrong, this is not a simple business, nor can it be entirely conscious. Setting out to write a 'bestseller' (or a cult book, or even a TV repair instruction manual, if they still had them) is not generally considered a good plan. Why? There will be a large number of expectations and assumptions of which neither you nor your audience are aware, and so hitting these will be a process of trial, error or luck (we call this workshopping). Because there is no available objective reality, it is up to you to create a 'reality' that floats the boat, tickles the boxes and hits the spot for the majority of your audience.
>
> Please don't take this for the heartless process it might appear; indeed, arousing the emotions of your audience is probably going to be one of the boxes to tick, enlisting their sympathy, making them believe, making them want something good to happen to someone, or bad to someone else – you may often find yourself in tears, or in fears, or in a transported state – all the better. It may also be of benefit if you appear not to be conforming to the assumptions and values of the culture you

are courting. Witness how the chattering classes of the UK respond with shuddering pleasure to a bit of rough in the form of (say) the novels of Irvine Welsh. Vicarious transgression (so long as everyone can get home safe for tea) is probably a plus. Gender, social and racial stereotypes are good ground for the manipulation of expectation and response: the skilled artist can go beyond mere reversal (woman as strong instigator – very *passé*) to the double or triple inversion – woman appears strong, is weak, finds strength later on. Finally, don't tell me you are writing what you are writing because it's 'true'. The so-called truth almost invariably spoils a good story and, as we all know by now, there is no available objective reality, so throw that stuffed bird out the window. And we will not be expecting you to write with precision – how can you be precise when the thing you're describing is imprecise?

Let's leave that classroom and see what we've got.

If there is no available objective reality, then our best efforts will leave us with a metaphorical room full of drawings, containing a variety of shapes and textures, triangles that could be beaks, pronged things, feathery protuberances, beady, bulging circles. Have we got anywhere as writers – any further than if we simply called it a bird and shut the bird book?

RA: Students faced with the blank page and forced to decide between naively asserting the truth of their own experience and wholeheartedly accepting the truth of a table-thumping audience of peers and teacher find themselves in a precarious position, even an utter quandary. Do they simply put forth their own vision of the bird and insist upon its validity, any objections notwithstanding, or do they give themselves over to the will of the group – and, more often than not, the teacher – in order to please that audience and hope for the aforementioned modest but respectable reward?

Writing is a complex activity, bringing many areas of the brain into play at once.[1] It demands free play of the individual's mental faculties. As Lad Tobin has ably shown, the writing classroom is fraught with power relationships – student to student, student to teacher, student to group – any of which have the potential to inhibit this free play by directing the student writer's attention to what cannot or should not be expressed rather than to what can be – *must be* – if imagination is to do its work (Tobin, 1993).

Teachers need not be *Paper Chase* tyrants in order to convey subtly, even unconsciously, that certain kinds of student will be set above others or that certain kinds of behavior will be rewarded.[2] We have all seen classrooms, and may have been students in them ourselves, where grandstanding is the name of the game, where those in the front row vying for the teacher's attention manage to get it, where students from a certain class, carrying a certain brand of educational preparedness, of a certain gender or race or ethnicity, displaying a certain facility of expression, are allowed to run the show – all regardless of talent, motivation, creativity and so on.

SM: Attending a script-writing course where the tutor had developed a singular style of character self-narration (e.g. BILL: And Bill rises in a fury to strike Ben), it was somewhat disturbing to find that all but one student attending the course were writing their scripts in the same way by the end of the week. Lord knows what had happened to our morals.

RA: The problem for developing writers is compounded when the will of the external negative audience has been internalized, when the desire to please that audience has been so inculcated through years of straight-line, follow-the-rules schooling, when the voices of parents, relatives, friends or the frowning wider audience result in a self-censorship so pervasive and so profound that any notion of personal power has been negated by the power of the group. Not to say that all audiences are bad in this regard. The desire to please an audience that is not judgmental except in the sense of wanting the best that the person can do can be enabling and helpful in producing excellent writing. And helping students experiment with different kinds of audience in order to find the most enabling and helpful should be part of the teacher's effort in the classroom. Meanwhile, students who lack this experience and who carry around the internalized version of a negative, judgmental audience may feel exposed, that they are revealing too much as they set pen to page or fingers to keyboard. A student writing a novel in which one of the main characters is a cutter will often get the question from one or more classmates: 'Is that *you*?' The question presents a dilemma for her. Should she avoid answering? Should she show her own scars and say yes? Should she lie and say 'No, I just happen to have known some cutters in my life' or 'No, I just did research and made a character out of it'?

SM: Or the mature student who is writing the 'true' story of her horrifying childhood (which her family strenuously denies). Her father, mother, uncles, aunts and friends were satanic abusers. She has a frightening power of imagining herself into that child, and to see and hear and smell and touch with that child, and convey those sensations to the reader. We are with the horror of the child being passed round a circle of leering men, beside a crackling coal fire, the whiff of their spittle, the cackles, the murmurs, the sensation on our surprised and vulnerable bodies. How might her workshop tutor and fellow students respond to her work in progress?

RA: It's the writing, not the writer?

SM: So, for example, suggesting that in the scene involving the father, the two uncles, and two other unidentified men, might it be more effective to reduce the number of abusers to three? This would focus the scene, reduce repetition and, by the principle of less is more, actually increase the anguish and pain.

RA: And she replies – 'But there were five'.

SM: And never sells the book, I think.

RA: But wrote it to her own satisfaction?

SM: Her father, who denied it all, died while she was writing it.

RA: Students in creative writing classes must find ways of confronting the tyranny of truth and mediating between internal and external claims to knowing. Between Bishop Berkeley's assertion that nothing exists without a perceiving mind (Berkeley, 1710: 62) and Dr Johnson's gruff, foot-stomping response 'I refute it *thus!*' (Boswell, 1791) there would seem to be precious little space to move.

In the end, of course, all except legal prohibitions are internal. Since the immediate audience of the writing classroom acts as a stand-in for the wider audience, it posits a social context that appears to be external but which students internalize. Our goal as teachers must be to help developing writers retain ultimate ownership and agency for their own work while also creating an environment enabling them to take in suggestions of others in the workshop openly, to reflect upon them without giving those voices undue power, and to sort out what might be 'true' for their own story and what is not.

Areas of vulnerability are many, for example:

Voice. The message is given, consciously or unconsciously, that some voices, dialects, language and so forth are not permitted, including non-standard English or anything but the high literary style.

SM: *Subjects.* Material from some cultures, economic classes, genders or gender orientations, educational backgrounds or genres are not permitted – or at least that they are, overtly or covertly, unvalued.

RA: 'Sorry, no more stories about the streets, immigrants, the working class, dysfunctional families, abuse, sex, rape, food, coming out, extramarital affairs, sci-fi fantasies or post-apocalyptic survival will be allowed. They've all been done, so find something else.' You might well ask 'What's left?'

SM: *Perfectionism.* Students perceive that products are privileged over process and that their manuscripts have to be perfect before shared with the world, even (or especially) the world of the workshop.

RA: *Research.* The writer becomes straightjacketed by 'fact', maintaining less focus on effective storytelling than upon whether events really happened in just this way or places are described accurately or characters are judged true to the reader's experience. The result may well be that these writers stop writing because they feel that they don't 'know' everything or that their version won't be acceptable to the audience.

SM: *Revelation.* The material is too raw, hits too close to home for parents, siblings, friends or (very often though they won't admit it) the writer him- or herself.

RA: The writing is ultimately too revealing, and the writer can locate no clear path to transgression, can't figure out a way to disguise it enough if fiction or can't figure out a way to honestly reveal what may have happened if non-fiction.

SM: Clear cases of the 'truth' getting in the way of a good story.

RA: This list is not exhaustive, and any writing teacher will no doubt have elements to add. But it does begin to indicate something of the pervasiveness of the problem faced by creative writing students and their teachers. A great deal of the teacher's focus – more than many teachers are willing to countenance – must be upon helping students find ways of silencing the censoring voices they carry within them. This focus on ensuring the widest possible permission for voices and subject matter represents the beginning of the process, the first step on the transgressive path.

How do teachers set about fostering permission for voice and subject matter for all students in a writing workshop?

SM: It isn't enough simply to tell them to feel free to write about anything, to take risks, to break whatever rules they might feel compelled to break. In fact, with some students, saying these things will only make their struggles worse by calling attention to their *lack* of permission and by encouraging their already well entrenched focus upon pleasing the teacher rather than listening to the wisdom of their own stories.

RA: We are, then, teaching a process, not simply creating products. We are, moreover, conveying that the process, the experience itself, as Graeme Harper has eloquently argued, possesses an intrinsic value at least as important as the objects produced (Harper, 2010: xviii). If students have a good process, they will be more likely to take the risks and incorporate the techniques enabling them to create good products. As teachers, we help them by focusing initially on giving tools to move past their barriers, internal and external, to find their own voices and learn how to write their own stories, not the ones that we or the workshoppers necessarily want or demand. It calls for awareness on our part of the dynamics at work at every moment in a class, as well as deftness in handling each student's individual process, recognizing that our students may move through many stages – just as we ourselves may have done in our own writing careers – and need different things at different times.

In order to find their own, authentic voice, the thing that makes their writing unique, students must be encouraged to locate authentic subject matter – that is, subject matter authentic to their own knowing, speaking to their experience without being strictly bound by fact, possessing the potential to evoke their own curiosity and desire and sense of emotional connection. Lacking strong material, material that means something to them, students will find their voices flattening, their language turning lifeless or arch, their syntax twisting to some approximation of what they think the teacher wants. In other words, those elements most essential to a creative writing student's development – discovery of their own, authentic voice and strongly cathected content – work together. If the connection breaks, the writing – and perhaps the writer – falters. If the connection is maintained and explored, anything – everything – becomes possible.

SM: As teachers of creative writing, then, we need to ask two questions crucial to our students' development as writers: (1) how do we help them gain permission to tell what they know; and (2) how do we help them gain credibility for their 'truth' by reflecting productively on its relationship to the truths of others?

RA: The most important elements for establishing this framework have to do with: (1) creating a safe classroom, one conducive to experimentation and risk-taking, for all students; (2) helping students actually hear and use the power of their own voice; (3) teaching voice as a means to making distinctions about stronger and weaker material, more effective and less effective ways of telling; (4) focusing on process rather than exclusively on product; (5) giving students assignments that encourage reflection upon their own writing process, including those that help identify, acknowledge and then deal with obstacles to permission that they encounter within themselves; and (6) exposing them to techniques enabling them to render their material effectively, however close or distant that material might be to their own experience and their own lives.

Each of these elements could easily generate its own chapter in order to explicate successful approaches fully. But we can offer a few basic suggestions that creative writing teachers might find helpful to establishing an environment conducive to exploration, risk-taking, effective decision-making and wide-ranging permission in a writing workshop:

SM: Openly explore the cultural specificity of exemplary works: choose assigned and in-class readings, older and contemporary, that reflect the widest possible range of subjects, voices, cultures, forms, styles and registers of English and that dramatically exhibit the way in which permission will be encouraged for people of many different backgrounds, skills levels and so on.

RA: Give manifold opportunities for reading aloud from published work as well as from the students' own writing, thus enabling students to hear the author's voice behind the words on the page and learn to practice the power of their own individual voice addressing the immediate audience of the class.

SM: Encourage the extensive use of journals, where students can explore widely and freely, and take risks at their own level of confidence.

RA: Emphasize positive rather than negative critiquing in order to sift out what is especially effective and help students learn to build from strengths.

SM: Treat writing as a process of seeing and re-seeing through successive drafts, not the mere manipulation of words on the page.

RA: Focus at all times on the writing itself, not the writer, on what makes the writing effective, what possibilities might be opened up for consideration, what else might be tried as an experiment – at all times protecting the right of students to their own voice and choice of material, thus ensuring that final ownership rests with the writer.

SM: Banish all reference to readers' 'liking' or 'not liking', but concentrate on understanding, and trying to find out why pieces work or don't work.

RA: These various elements represent crucial concerns for enabling students to build competence and confidence in their own creative problem-solving strategies and learn their application to a wide range of writing modes and tasks, in and out of the university. Students become more able to write free from the introjected, often censorious forces that may have inhibited them from finding their own strongest material and hearing their own, authentic telling voice. Moreover, they are able to mediate more effectively the tension between blind allegiance to their own narrow vision of the truth and equally blind adherence to the tyrannical vision of truth put forth by others. The world of the classroom thus becomes not simply a testing-ground but rather a productive proving-ground, an incubator for trying out skills and realizing agency useful in the wider world.

SM: In the description–drawing exercise, what are we *really* asking students to do? To look at something ordinary, and see it with new eyes, their own eyes, asking them to fire the bird within their own oven of context. When you conduct the experiment with objects and drawing, you will almost invariably discover that the objects themselves are paltry and uninteresting compared with the descriptions, and indeed the images wrought in the imaginations of the audience/drawers. As writers, we do have a sacred power, to transform the dullness around us into the exciting, the inspiring, the thrilling, the moving. Cast your mind to that stuffed extinct avian specimen bottled in 1903 in the museum and 'The windhover'. As teachers, we have a duty: to help students discover the transformative power of their imagination through language.

Exploration

(1) What is Truth?

(2) How does a writer deal with the spurious authenticity of 'fact'?

(3) How does a writer explore and establish his or her own 'reality' in the face of open and hidden tendencies to 'normalisation'?

(4) How does a writing workshop tutor avoid turning every student into an issue or style clone?

(5) How do we exploit our cultural specificity without being slave to it?

(6) Are our senses liberating, imprisoning or deceiving?

(7) Does the Truth spoil a good story?

(8) Why are you telling me this?

(9) Did you shut the window?

Notes

(1) The UK Arts and Humanities Research Council has recently started supporting research in this area, see http://www.ahrc.ac.uk/News-and-Events/Events/Pages/Will-Self-Memory-Network.aspx (accessed 2 July 2014).

(2) *The Paper Chase* is a 1973 movie directed by James Bridges, in which a Professor Kingsfield teaches contract law in tyrannical fashion.

References

Baudelaire, C. (1861) *Les fleurs du mal*. In F. Scarfe (ed. and trans.) *Baudelaire: The Complete Verse*. London: Anvil Press (1986).

Berkeley, G. (1710) *The Principles of Human Knowledge*. In D.M. Armstrong (ed.) *Berkeley's Philosophical Writings*. New York: Collier Books (1965).

Blake, W. (1793) *The Marriage of Heaven and Hell*. Luce: Boston (1906). Online at https://archive.org/details/marriageofheaven00blak (accessed 4 January 2014).

Boswell, J. (1791) *The Life of Samuel Johnson*. London: Penguin Classics (2008).

Coleridge, S.T. (1817) *Biographia Literaria*. London: J.M. Dent & Sons (1971).

Emerson, R.W. (1841) On self-reliance. In S.E. Whicher (ed.) *Selections from Ralph Waldo Emerson*. Cambridge, MA: Riverside Editions/Houghton Mifflin (1957).

Harper, G. (2010) Foreword: On experience. In D. Donnelly (ed.) *Does the Writing Workshop Still Work?* Bristol: Multilingual Matters.

Hemingway, E. (1964) *A Moveable Feast*. New York: Charles Scribner's Sons.

Keats, J. (1818) Letter to J.H. Reynolds, 3 May 1818. In R. Gittings (ed.) *Letters of John Keats*. London: Oxford University Press (1970).

May, S. (2007) *Doing Creative Writing*. Oxford: Routledge.

Putnam, H. (1975) *Mind, Language and Reality.* Cambridge: Cambridge University Press.

Tobin, L. (1993) *Writing Relationships: What Really Happens in the Composition Class.* Portsmouth: Heinemann Educational Books.

Wilde, O. (1895) *The Importance of Being Ernest.* New York: Avon (1965).

Chapter 2

Dragging the Corpse: Landscape and Memory. Two Writers Consider How the Role of Identity in Their Own Writing Leads into Educational Practice

Liz Cashdan and Moy McCrory

The Landscape of Memory and Home

This chapter was developed from a paper, 'Whose landscape is it anyway?', which the authors gave jointly at the Great Writing Conference, 2012. This was one of a series of annual conferences organized by Graeme Harper at Imperial College London. Originally, we were interested in this topic from a writer's point of view, but gradually realized how important the idea of belonging was not only to published writers but also in the field of education, where writers act as tutors and teachers of writing.

In our own writing we recognized a similar difficulty we shared in expressing the idea of 'home' – a word which takes up plural and different meanings, but is not easy for either of us to name instantly and which difficulty we had both, at various times, written about.

> She was crawling on all fours through turf, it clung to her, sucked her down. She was dragging a corpse behind her when it began to sing … there was wind screaming for the dead in every corner of her room. (McCrory, 1989: 126)

In this image of the corpse, the weight of both history and the lived past reveals itself as something dragged, something that cannot be shaken off or lost, which many experience as the fate of those of us in the Irish diaspora, while for Cashdan, a Jewish person of Russian descent, this image, while immediately recognized, provoked an uncertainty: was that corpse being dragged Russia, Israel or on some occasions England itself?

The sense of identity is something which challenges the way writers use the language they have acquired and has provoked us to consider a joint response to our respective senses of identity, both formed from expatriate histories. We may be looking at the same place or landscape, but we both wonder where we might belong in it, and how this informs what we choose to write about, and how this impacts on how we educate others.

Moy McCrory

Coming from an Irish background, born in England, my perspective on the descriptors of nationality in relation to place, home and country have placed both question mark and emphasis on those words. How do I describe my nationality, or my sense of it, when it is located elsewhere and where a return to a past, which was not mine, is equally impossible?

As a writer, I have always felt as someone who does not own such easy words. In their place is the disruption of comfortable terms, for at every turn they will thwart me. The ground I occupy is broken up. Instead, up-bringing, background and family are the formative influences in my sense of nationality. Just as the self cannot exist in isolation and is created by the sum of external forces, my genetic code bequeathed me burn-in-the-sun Celtic skin and light eye color, while my inherited culture bequeathed me an image bank full of an ancient sensibility, with phrases and songs rising like incense. My family's daily life was governed by invisible laws, older realities which seemed to coexist with the present. The house was full with memories, as the ever-watchful dead lived side by side among us. I grew up in a life that was imagined differently, where the inanimate took on its own reality, and life was writ large among ordinary people who experienced extraordinary meaning in the slightest of things.

An idiom-rich speech, where chairs 'sat' and tables 'waited', suggested that there was life in everything. And in speech, my family's background and its historic severance were rooted. They spoke accented English, not Gaelic, but their phrases and constructions had originated in an earlier language, still spoken by a minority, even as the Irish language societies and leagues would not accept loan words, but kept that language in its virgin state, untrammeled since the 16th century. Our learnt Gaelic, then, was an archaic form, impossible to take God out of the equation, placing man as the recipient of God's will, a victim to the natural world. Even emotions fell upon us, like a calamity. Witoszek and Sheeran (1991) consider that a fatalism which they feel is part of Irish Catholic experience is governed by the earlier language structure, with its verbs expressed as happening to – rather than performed by – the subject.

But, with the displacement of my childhood, I was growing into the local vernacular, the voice of the historic oppressor. This displacement is central to my writing.

Liz Cashdan

Some years ago I heard David Dabydeen talking about a sense of belonging and the writing of poetry. He was giving a talk and reading at a poetry festival in Galway. So there I was, an English poet in Ireland listening to Dabydeen, who was wondering whether he belonged to Guyana or England, whether he should continue in the vein of *Coolie Odyssey*, using Guyanan English, or turn to the English he had been using more recently while studying in Cambridge. At the same time, we were treated to some poetry readings in Irish, which, of course, I could not understand but both Dabydeen as speaker on that occasion and myself as ardent listener felt that at least the Irish signified a sense of belonging to those poets who wrote in Irish. Not, of course, that Irish poets have to apologize for using English – our literature would be so much the poorer without them.

But all of that made me ask myself where I belonged and whether I ought to ask my students to work out where they belonged before they started writing. Coincidentally, it was perhaps an even earlier time spent in Northern Ireland, before I had started teaching Creative Writing, that made me have to come to some sort of decision about my own belonging. As a teacher in a secondary school I had to take an oath before a JP to say I would not upset the Queen's government in Northern Ireland.

> First time living north of London, you're invited out
> To supper, but they've had their tea at six o'clock so
> All you get is a sandwich and a cuppa well past nine.
> It would have been ignorant to ask. They're Protestants
> 'And are you a Protestant Jew or a Catholic Jew?' they ask.
> Simple answer to that one: orthodox Jews are Protestant.
> But when it comes to the Intifada, you know you'll be Catholic.
> (Cashdan, 1995: 36–7)

Not long after that I paid my first visit to Israel and it was after several visits there meeting new Russian immigrants who had not yet learnt Hebrew, and recognizing the plight of Palestinians who had lost their land, that I came to recognize that the end of diaspora for one person could well signify another person's loss of homeland.

How do you say?

Galina has come to clean my sister's house.
In Russia she was a school teacher.
...

On TV four hundred Palestinians turn to Mecca,
their faces touch the snow of no-man's-land.
How do you say that in Hebrew?
Jews know the word for exile in every language.
...

'I am afraid of Arabs,' Galina says.
Yesterday the Arab who had come to empty
her dustbin stopped to greet her.
'He would kill me,' Galina says.
She uses the conditional particle in Russian.
'He would kill to save his children.'
...

I know the Russian for children, and the Hebrew
but how do you say children in Arabic?
(Cashdan, 1995: 49)

The Viewer Forever on the Borders

> Liminality is a condition in which one's sense of identity is diffused, leading to states of dislocation and disorientation but also to the possibility of new perspectives. (Institute of Contemporary Arts, 2013)

Liminality, from the Latin *limen*, meaning a threshold, also suggests a viewer forever on the borders, situated forever between stepping out of their home and remaining inside it. Such a position is familiar to those with diasporic and disrupted backgrounds. The author John Walsh (2000) uses the image of the angels cast from heaven, not arriving on earth, but always being between the two states. The assimilation of the Irish into Britain is not a done deal. Despite whiteness, language and a shared Christianity, the second-generation Irish feel as if they are 'placed at the intersection of two nations' (Hickman & Walter, 2002). Jewish and immigrant families are removed by belief and language, and lean in from such a threshold, understanding that in order to cross it, accommodations must be made.

Stephen Wilson claims that 'Jews brought up in the UK are enriched by two cultures yet tend to feel divided by their dualistic heritage' (Wilson, 2012: 273). He examines the way in which their poetry represents their experiences of anti-Semitism and, by a curious coincidence in view of our experiences, how he himself as a poet and other poets use the metaphor of magpies looking like nuns to represent anti-Semitism.

As practitioners, we realized that we had in fact exchanged experiences at one point. Moy McCrory had worked in Israel and Liz Cashdan had lived in Belfast; both experiences had produced creative work, writing about a dislocation which was not necessarily our own.

Moy McCrory

Displacement can be both external and personal, and can provide the writer with new ways of considering relationships to place and land. For a time I had worked as a foreign volunteer on a kibbutz near the Golan Heights, with the machine gun towers and curfews, which were not dissimilar to my experience of Belfast during the Troubles. Among the many survivors I met and talked to, an elderly man who obsessively collected detritus and created a museum in which to display it struck a chord with me because of an odd autobiographical detail. I had grown up with a father who was a hoarder. However, the kibbutznik stood out for reasons other than hoarding; he went his own way and he did not 'belong', even though his history was backbone to the early kibbutz movement. When I began work on the story I started to see how a fictive collecting stood in for irrevocable loss. A man who has lost everything slowly begins to reclaim the past from everyday life. The story is recounted by an observer, to whom things are told, about a character, who remains an enigma, a stranger to everyone.

> It was Avram in the post room who told me that his father, whose job it had been to check the documents, on first seeing Yehudabach's photograph threw up his hands. 'A shwartzer? Nu, look what they send us.'...
> I began to hear stories about Yehudabach's museum. Now after work he spent his time in the old corrugated hut, refurbishing, sorting, always working.... He was a zealot, indexing, cataloguing every exhibit, a life's work and not to be put off. (McCrory, 1994: 43)

I also considered a detail of his refusal to speak his native German, that he acquired his Hebrew with difficulty, yet continued this next stage of his life through this disrupted spoken form. Here he speaks English to the narrator and she hears something else inside the phrases:

He swept an enormous veined hand, directing me to look towards his hut.

Museum?

He started to explain. 'Bo-ones and sto-ones,' he said. He stretched the words, pulled them out of shape so the hollow ow rattled like the inside of an empty tin. Wind blew through his words; they were like something that had long vanished. His voice repeated them slowly, as if he was doing this for my benefit, and would continue until I could feel their meaning, the real heart of a word. Empty. At the centre of everything, Yehudabach knew, there was nothing, just a gaping hole. (McCrory, 1994: 46)

And in his collection were remains found in the ruined Arab village just outside the perimeter fence, a place the narrator talks about visiting on her afternoons off, when she sits in the broken buildings and imagines them as homes which have been lost to their owners:

Of the people, all that remained were the bits of broken pots and the marks left by fires burnt into white stone in the corners of rooms. (McCrory, 1994: 46)

The narrator finally understands the importance of memory and Yehudabach's determination that nothing further should ever be lost from history, with all the contradictions this implies. The question of whose history it is to tell causes me to create narrators who are outside the main actions. Equally, in a story about Belfast I have used in places an indirect chorus of observers: students who huddle together in a freezing house, 'like hens, one winter', while the main narrator, who tells the story years after the events, admits to having problems in her personal life. Does she relate this story to a therapist, a confessor?

Both stories are about not belonging, but in the latter there is a feeling of exclusion which is both personal and societal; of being in the wrong situation – drinking in a loyalist pub while she is a Catholic – and being excluded from her house, while a party takes place that she and the rest of her housemates have not been invited to. The narrator's memory of her student days is of being with 'outcasts'. Later, even this sense of belonging appears to desert her.

The night the bomb went off in the phone box down our street I'd been up the road, drinking Guinness with Loyalists. Everyone thought it was the IRA. It was only a frightener, not meant to kill anyone, but a girl we knew had been making a call. Some man she'd never seen before turned up banging on the phone box windows and she got out fast in case he was a lunatic. Whether he was or not, that madman saved her life. It's the details you remember. She'd been ringing the speaking clock....

On wintry days if the sun shone it was warmer out on the street because the house stood in shadow. Nothing thawed. Coats left hanging in the hall grew stiff with frost overnight....

Over that dark, disconsolate winter ... Bernie decided she wanted nothing to do with us and carved out a new social life.... We felt like outcasts while she was having this whale of a time, or if not a whale exactly, something large like a shark maybe, circling in dark waters. (McCrory, 2013: 38–39)

Finally, the narrator is an outsider even to herself, and the outsideness/strangeness is both of a personal state and of those social divides which amplify her condition of non-belonging, now extended to her own family:

Relatives can make you feel awkward just for living. It's not as if you have to do anything. (McCrory, 2013: 39)

Liz Cashdan

I visited Bialystok, where my parents came from. It was Czarist Russia when they lived there but it's in Poland now. There was no way I belonged there, although there was something emotional about standing in places where they had stood. I decided to write about my visit in a sequence of poems, not in my voice but in the voices of local people I met, trying to judge how they would have seen me as the tourist/traveler/nostalgia-seeker. One day I went to my mother's townland, as the Irish would call it, just outside Bialystok. In this case, both the disappearance of population and buildings and a language I didn't know shut me out from a past I could only imagine.

Bus Driver: Bialystok to Zabludowa

You don't get many tourists on this route,
mostly locals shopping in town or going
to register, going for work.
She pays, doesn't understand our money
as far as I can tell. Then looks
in her phrase book, tells me
her mother was born in Zabludowa before
the First World War. Doesn't look old
enough – dyes her hair, I shouldn't wonder.

There's a nice new town hall and co-op
I tell her but she doesn't seem to care.
Seems more interested in the old folk
with their horses and boat-shaped carts.
She's taking a lot of photos of them.
Of course she won't find the old wooden
synagogue with its upturned eaves like
something from China. Not that I ever
saw it. But my grandfather can remember
when Zabludowa was full of Jews. Like
they were all Jews in the street where
he lives now. Well, times change.
(Cashdan, 1995: 61)

Perhaps more disturbing was the brief glimpse into a past I hadn't expected, the past owned by an American Catholic Pole who had come back, like me to find where his wife's family had lived. In my own family's defense, I have to say that my father did support striking workers, Catholic or Jewish.

American Tourist: Bialystok

…

The wife's people came from here,
that's why we've come back –
when this English woman rushes up
to us, all excited, flapping
the guide book: 'Translate this please.'

…

'Towards the end of the nineteenth century
the big Jewish textile firms included –'
The woman grabs Maria's arm, points
to the names. 'That's my grandfather.'

Something stiffens inside me but I don't
say how Maria's grandfather emigrated
because he couldn't keep his family
on the wages paid by the Jewish
factory owners…. I think
of our farm back in Wyoming.
(Cashdan, 1995: 59)

Considering Identity and Belonging as Tools for Our Educational Practice

We are aware that students who haven't themselves been displaced or whose families haven't moved are less likely to be concerned with the idea of belonging. In a recent Travel Writing class of mature students, Liz found that most wrote from the perspective of being at home in England, and so their travel was no more than travel, and home they came.

The exceptions were two students, Leila B, who was born in England but whose parents came from Pakistan, and Batseba Tesfaye, who was born in Eritrea, brought up in the USA and who now lives in England.

Leila had been to Pakistan with her parents when she was 13 but found that it was a strange land that she couldn't fit into. Batseba had been back to Eritrea, where she had experienced both the horrors of being conscripted into the army as a teenage soldier but also a spiritual feeling of being at home after her years in America.

Here is a bit of Leila's writing on her visit to Pakistan:

I am ambushed as dozens of beggars hanging around on the dangerous Islamabad roads seize the chance to fill their pockets for the day by begging during the wild traffic rush hour. 'It's like as if we are in the zoo!' My brother declares. 'It's worse than being in a zoo.' I reply. My ears are immersed with chaos and impatient drivers beeping their horns. Shadows are cursed through my side of the window as if the twelve o'clock sun is foreshadowing the poor beggars' fate because their fate rests solely on my shoulders. The pressure builds up in mountains as the soaring heat troubles us as sweat patches form through my shalwar-kameez (A type of clothing worn by Muslim men and women). The merciless beggars are hungry for money....

I grapple for a spare ten rupees in my Debenham's purse and plunge my face out of the window before handing the convincing boy the ten rupees that he believes he deserves to have. The strange scent from his murky Kameez immediately hits me because of this, it hypnotises me almost casting a spell on me, tiring out my muscles from usual as the scent channels through my airways. Luckily, the scent isn't strong enough to bribe my eyes to shut. (Leila B, 2012)

Her writing, apart from the fact it's not quite idiomatic English (and yet she went to school in Rotherham, with only a couple of months' break in a school in Pakistan), is striking because of the way, as a Yorkshire lass, she finds the sights and smells of Pakistan strange – she does not belong there: she actually titled her piece 'Adapting to a culture that is not mine'.

Here is how Batseba Tesfaye described her visit to a shrine near Asmara shortly after leaving the USA. Batseba goes to her old homeland to 'replenish my spirit'.

> Our bus then headed out of Asmara towards the east. The weather as always was beautiful, the morning sun warm on my face as I looked dreamily out the window. The scenes and images of rural living passed along like a large painting; Shepherds coming home with their flock; farmers with their oxen ploughing their fields, young children with donkeys on their way to fetch water, cowherds taking their cattle to the pastures and in the distance the villages with the silhouettes of pointed huts rising against the morning sun.
>
> We were on our way to Debre Sina, where every year in June, thousands of pilgrims would flock to the sacred site to celebrate the festival of Saint Mary.... Me and my cousin had both decided to go. Salem was going to recover from a personal tragedy and I was going to replenish my spirit. (Tesfaye, 2012)

The Home as Site of Background

Our experience of student writing is not identical, since Moy teaches mostly at university, both undergraduate and postgraduate courses, while Liz teaches at university and schools with an age range 5–18, but also in adult education, where the accent is on personal development and leisure pursuits rather than the gaining of qualifications. Liz's experience has been that younger students are less concerned with place and belonging, than with their own belongings, unless they come from ethnic minorities. Moy's experience has been that all students are concerned with their sense of identity and how they might express this. We realized the image of the house, the home, the street figured prominently. Such a trope was something we could all relate to and a sense of ownership of one's history could be expressed in that private region, where our laws were our own and we made our days.

Asking students of writing to consider how they see themselves in relation to where they live – country, nation, gender, self – allows all possibilities to exist, allows those from fractured backgrounds to consider cultural disruption, allows those with continuous experience of a place to reflect on its history. In this guise, the home/house becomes something both personal and universal; as an image bank it is vast.

In reconsidering their sense of self, Creative Writing students can write about what they know, rather than what has been imposed, and in this way create their own terms of belonging which are authentic and relevant and do more than merely avoid the stereotypical, as they offer genuine experience, often rendered for the first time into writing.

Exploration

Issues
(1) Belonging, not belonging.
(2) Whose history is it to tell?
(3) Whose language is it?
(4) Whose culture is it?
(5) Whose landscape or place is it to claim?

Ideas
(6) The teaching or learning of creative writing is enhanced by looking at ways of inspiring responses which enable a consideration of self in relation to family and place.
(7) Such work allows an investigation of critical ideas of acculturation that relate to creative writing and to education. It allows students to explore the idea of inclusiveness.

Actions
(8) For developing writing, imagine a house with many rooms. Each room represents something about you. The past, the present, the future. Walk in and out of those rooms. Sometimes a room may be shut, or viewed through a half-open door. Listen in, and note what you find.
(9) Imagine you are leaving the place where you live now. What would you take with you? Not just personal belongings, but also landscape, culture, language, environment. What would you be pleased to leave behind?
(10) Imagine a walk through a house (an actual or imaginary place), where each characteristic of the narrator can be represented by a different room. Consider, for example, Jeni Couzyn's poem 'House of changes' (Couzyns, 1990).

References

Cashdan, L. (1995) *Laughing All the Way.* Nottingham: Five Leaves Publications.

Cashdan, L. and McCrory, M. (2012) Whose landscape is it anyway? Unpublished paper given at the Great Writing Conference, Imperial College London.

Couzyns, J. (1990) House of changes. In P. Abbs and J. Richardson (eds) *The Forms of Poetry* (p. 84). Cambridge: Cambridge University Press.

Dabydeen, D. (1988) *Coolie Odysssey.* London: Hansib/Dangeroo.

Hickman, M. and Walter, B. (2002) *The Second-Generation Irish: A Hidden Population in Multi-ethnic Britain.* London: Economic and Social Research Council.

Institute of Contemporary Art (2013) Exhibition notes to 'Points of Departure', as collaboration between the Delfina Foundation, ArtSchool Palestine, the British Council and the Institute of Contemporary Art, 26 June 2013–21 July 2013.

Leila, B. (2012) Travel writing class, Sheffield Institute of Life Long Learning, October 2012. Permission granted July 2013.

McCrory, M. (1989) The Water's Edge. In *The Water's Edge and Other Stories.* London: Sheba Press.

McCrory, M. (1994) Yehudabach's Museum. *Metropolitan*, issue 2 (summer), 43–47.

McCrory, M. (2013) Combustible world. *The Warwick Review* 7 (4), 38–49.

Tesfaye, B. (2012) Travel writing class, Sheffield Institute of Life Long Learning, October 2012. Permission granted July 2013.

Walsh, J. (2000) *The Falling Angels: An Irish Romance.* London: Flamingo.

Wilson, S. (2012) *Poetics of the Diaspora.* Oxford: Ben Yehuda Press.

Witoszek, N. and Sheeran, P.F. (1991) The tradition of vernacular hatred. In G. Lernout (ed.) *The Crows Behind the Plough: History and Violence in Anglo-Irish Poetry and Drama* (pp. 11–27) Amsterdam: Rodopi.

The Breath and the Bomb, or, In Praise of the Uneducable

Marcela Sulak

When I first began directing an international creative writing program, I was somewhat stymied to hear the word 'educable' employed by colleagues evaluating potential candidates: 'I'm not sure we should admit him. He doesn't sound educable.' Since the person whose educability was in question, likely as not, already possessed a couple of graduate degrees – perhaps in engineering or medicine or journalism – it was clearly not aptitude nor intelligence nor the ability to take instruction that was at issue. After looking into the matter, it seemed the term in this context meant 'someone who values, or will learn to value, what I value'. One could also turn the question and ask: is my skill set as an instructor adequate to the goals this potential student has articulated?

When one teaches students who are linguistically, culturally and socially similar, the word 'educable' is not so problematic. But education is incredibly dependent on context. A seemingly neutral skill, such as the ability to express an idea or concept clearly, will be valued differently depending on one's age, gender, social status, and the cultural context in which one writes. This is why the same sentence may be deemed aggressive if a woman writes it, powerful if a man writes it, clear if an American writes it, rude if a Japanese student writes it. So what does 'educable' mean when teaching in an international creative writing classroom in which the students' native languages are not the language of instruction, and whose literary and cultural backgrounds are distinct from one another and from that of the instructor? What if, for example, the English-language graduate creative writing poetry class is composed of native speakers of Arabic, German, Dutch, Hebrew, Portuguese (Brazilian) and English (British and American), and only two (the Arabic and Hebrew speakers) were born in the country in which the seminar is being taught? This describes my writing seminar last fall.

I cannot teach my students to value particular styles of writing above others. English-language poetry values originality – don't ever write something if you have heard it before, I say – and the startling, true image. The Arabic-language writers have taught me that good poems in Arabic must acknowledge certain conventions and traditions that English-language students might find flowery or, well, conventional. The Brazilian writer's poetry sometimes feels too emotional for the American writers. The German-language writers can be rather heady; the American poems might be deemed soulless, if witty. I can tell students what is generally unacceptable today in poetry written in the English language, though not all of the writers may intend to keep writing in English after the program is over. Some of them are enrolled in this English-language program because it is the only degree-granting creative writing graduate program in any language in Israel. There are skills the enrolled writers want to learn, that they feel they can learn, studying in English, skills that are transferrable into Hebrew or Arabic or Portuguese.

Thus, my task is to teach tools that I hope transcend a particular language. And most of all, the students and I can practice learning to *listen to* and to *hear* one another through and across language and culture. To that end, I teach a course called 'Prosody and genre', in which meters, rhythms and poetic genres are tools we can learn to manipulate in order to create certain effects. Here is the course description:

> Poetic forms and genres emerge in response to the way people over time have expressed their most intense joy, grief, thanksgiving, nostalgia, exaltation, despair, love and fear. Forms and genres shape readers' expectations and perceptions; they shape poets' arguments, and most importantly, they allow poets to glean from the past the ideals, values, and stories that shape our present moment. In this class, we will practice using various formal tools to shape ideas and perceptions into music by writing poetry in specific forms, modes, and meters. We will also become familiar and confident with the interpretative tools that enhance our understanding of poetry and allow us to communicate about this multi-faceted art form in a thoughtful manner.

This approach, placing technique in the foreground, allows a lively exchange on aesthetic tradition and cultural values to arise and permeate the discussion in a non-confrontational, if challenging, manner. Just as, in a good sonnet, the form is as meaning-making as the content, so it was in the class. I could teach tools and traditions; students could learn them now and decide later how they valued these tools as writers situated in particular communities. Focusing on form, rather than content, was also helpful in workshop, as we discussed what the poem was trying to accomplish, rather than what we, as individuals, valued or liked.

We began with prosody, examining meter and rhythm, how to make the reader's heart pound and skip in such a way that would have inspired Plato to evict poets from the Republic all over again on charges of getting the populace too worked up to think. We discussed how rhyme, when carelessly deployed, is a mental soporific, but that the expectation created by rhyme was a great tool for creating points of resistance. Yoking two discordant or unexpected ideas together in rhyme jolts a reader into a new realm. The Hebrew and Arabic speakers explained rhyme as opened and closed syllables. Opening ourselves to the experience of new sound sensations and to new ways of hearing (and listening) proved vital, as well as cool.

Because we lived in the Middle East, extracurricular events soon found their way into our classroom, and for a miraculous few weeks we were sometimes able to use the framework of prosody and poetic genre to articulate and frame our experience of these events. Our seminar took place during an exchange of missile fire between Gaza and Israel. Some of my students in the south of the country had been living in bomb shelters for a month before the first missiles hit Tel Aviv or Gaza. The rest of us in the center of the country lived about 10 days totally attuned to the stresses of air-raid sirens, the boom of a striking bomb and the tense silence just after. We began to feel in our bodies as if we had all slipped into an enormous line of poetic scansion. We read Auden's *Age of Anxiety*, written in accentual verse during the Second World War, and the prosody felt in harmony with our own pounding pulses – the two strong stresses on either side of a caesura; the harsh exactitude of each line. We realized how much tension an unstressed syllable can hold, walking around Tel Aviv on the single day that a missile siren failed to sound, scanning buildings and streets looking for where we would go when we heard it.

I worried what the conflict would do to our class both physically and emotionally, for we were Muslim, Jewish and Christian, of the broadest range of political ideology. During the fighting, everyone came to our weekly meeting except the new immigrant whose three children (aged five and under) were not in pre-school, since the schools were shut down in her town due to the frequency of the falling missiles. I brought chocolate and cookies and worry. But the students were warm and thoughtful. One or two brought in poems about bombs and shelters. But most of them wanted to claim the deeper humanity that was at stake when the cliché of the bomb replaced the nuance of conversation.

There may be no poetic form better equipped to handle the wide range of volatile emotions that emerge from a group of students with six different native languages, seven different native cultures and obscene challenges to their basic humanity than ottava rima. Odd as it may seem, Wayne Koestenbaum's *Model Homes*, which I'd assigned rather nervously at the beginning of the semester, when I had no idea what the class would be like, broke down the last defense of students for whom the missile exchange was the least of their worries.

My students this fall had unusually heavy life challenges. We had just lost a student to leukemia a few months earlier and we felt her absence in our class. Other students were writing about the dissolution of a 30-year marriage (as it was happening), very recent suicide attempts after dealing with the PTSD from gang rape; witnessing the deaths of women laboring to give birth in refugee camps in Darfur when the lone attendant in the hospital (one of our students) could not save everyone at once; the inability to become pregnant in a society that values women by the number of male offspring they produce; the death of a child. Some of the younger students expressed the concern that they did not even know how to talk to the classmates as victims struggling to survive. In the end, they spoke to one another through the language of poetry criticism and workshop feedback. One of the students who had suffered the most comforted me in my own fumbling attempts: 'there is no right response to a situation that never should have happened', she said.

Wayne Koestenbaum's outrageous *Model Homes* seemed at first an unlikely salve. Its 13 ottava rima cantos coyly hint at something unseemly that happened in the young Wayne's childhood home while it self-consciously and flamboyantly invokes the clichés of urban gay life. Too witty and skittish for any expression of sincerity other than the sweet realization in the end that Wayne's partner is not perfect, but he's close enough for Wayne, the book nevertheless demonstrates amazing strategies for writing and speaking about real-life trauma. Centuries ago, ottava rima originally carried long poems and heroic themes but, like everything else, the form quickly became used for mock-epic or mock-heroic work. Today, the form permits the main character to be the hero in a world in which events have cosmic and earthly impact, and the hero's actions have great consequence in the world of the poem, while ruefully acknowledging that the world of the poem is at an ironic distance from the real world in which the poem is crafted. The speaker (and writer) can both mean it and not mean it at once. Thus, the form allows for the catharsis of a good joke, but with the extended nuances of a good story.

Ottava rima's six iambic lines of alternating rhyme enable writers to gain quite a bit of depth and poignancy, for the couplet at the end of each stanza rescues everyone with a punch of comic relief. Using this form felt similar to how one of the Hebrew-language poets described writing in English: 'Since it's not my native tongue, what I write in it doesn't quite feel real. That's why I can write the unwriteable.'

The form is also a metaphor for how I try to teach the unteachable, which is all that those of us who are 'uneducable' can do: question every value by contextualizing it. Understand that every genre is born in a particular culture or society and in a particular period (or season) for a particular activity, and each form is transformed according to the culture and the time of the writer. Every rhythm comes from the cultural and social registry, as well as from the individual human blood-beat; a breath and a bomb.

Chapter 3

Embracing the Learning Paradigm: How Assessment Drives Creative Writing Pedagogy

Dianne Donnelly

I'm almost always aware that grades are present; they are the elephants I am trying unsuccessfully not to think about. (Tobin, 1993: 60)

Few important or long lasting changes can occur in the way we assess student writing ... unless we attempt to change the theory which drives our practices and attitudes toward assessment. (Huot, 1996: 551)

The Assessment Divide

It's not surprising that many creative writing teachers find assessment practices problematic. They view the assessment of creative writing through two distinct lenses: one suspect of evaluative practices that do not value or characterize the distinguishing ways in which creative writers learn, think, write, read and respond; the other keenly aware that creative writing 'lives in the borderland between art and academic' (Kerridge in Harper & Kerridge 2004: 4) and, in that frame, the assessment of student work, courses and programs are accountable academic practices. Such duality in perspectives also manifests in the variable teacher definitions of creative writing (*art, craft, literary, commercial*) and in the way teachers construe students' intentions as writers. Complicating these tensions are *conflicts* between (1) teacher authority associated with grading/marking student work *and* collaborative authority offered by workshop participants; (2) formative assessment facilitated in workshop settings and individual conferences *and* summative assessment associated with the assignment of grades/ marks;[1] (3) student-centered learning environments conducive to exploration, risk and playfulness *and* grading practices that threaten to depress students' efforts, confine experimentation, and instill in students and in the classroom writing community elements of fear, anxiety, competition, defeat, resistance and/or apathy; (4) incongruences associated with teachers reading work that may reflect students' personal experiences followed by the evaluation of those pieces; and (5) grading as consequence *versus* the value of constructive feedback and the promotion of good writerly habits.

Some teachers minimize negotiating these polarities by assigning 'A's as a course completion grade for all students. Ostensibly, the advantage of this recourse is that students are not bound by summative evaluation and are likely more receptive to constructive feedback and revision efforts. Case in point: as soon as Jack Ridl (2008), poet and teacher of 27 years, suggested to students that 'they could do something else with an ending or a line break or change the tone, all they heard was a grade plummeting. Defenses rose. They refused to see any alternative to the way they had composed the work, and stood firmly for the A grade they deserved.' Many educational theorists support Ridl's position, having long suggested that grading actually *reduces* students' interest in learning (Kohn, 1999), *reduces* deeper and/or more challenging discoveries, as students connect the grade with the effort and do not wish to risk penalty (Milton *et al.*, 1986), and *reduces* critical thinking, as students' prioritize grades rather than learning (Butler, 1988). Ridl (2008) reflects that his students 'wanted to create an effective work ... but understandably because of school and its achievement evaluation based on measurement, they had to make their grade not their first priority but their first concern'. His answer was to eliminate grading of their work, to better 'connect their priority with their concern'.

Putting aside the precarious impact on faculty tenure or promotion review, eliminating grading either by delivering a 'pass/fail' option or by universally assigning all 'A's regardless of effort or performance is not a realistic alternative for most of us. Implementing pass/fail options typically do not work for a number of reasons: (1) getting administration to agree is difficult, (2) the course may be devalued and viewed as substandard by those critics who still marginalize creative writing as an academic discipline, and (3) despite student motivations that may include taking the creative writing course for self-fulfillment of one's potential, grades still seem to matter to students, in that they impact the quality of their degrees. Assigning all 'A's may also complicate our commitment as teachers to maintain the integrity of our courses, programs, universities and accreditation processes by submitting meaningful grades. After all, charting the progress of students' work and encouraging further development are important for creative writers in the academy. Assessment is a significant part of our literate activities when we consider how often we evaluate reading and writing, and how often creative works are read and ranked by readers, editors, agents, reviewers, judges and committees. Moreover, most writers appreciate the value of assessment as a means for writing growth and improvement.

How do we remain 'accountable to our institutions to report grades that accurately and usefully describe students' performances in a course' while also being 'responsible to our students to establish conditions that enable real learning'? (Huot, 2002: 168). Reconciling this double-bind situation *is* possible if we stay grounded in the theory (the *why*) and the practice (the *how*) of assessment.

The Learning Paradigm: Theory and Practice

Interrogating the theory that undergirds our course assessment practices leads to a better epistemological understanding of why and how assessment drives our pedagogy. Brian Huot contends,

> all of our practices are theoretically driven, since they are based upon beliefs and assumptions. It's important, then, that we become more conscious of our theories concerning assessment and how they affect not only our assessment practices but the entire act of teaching writing. (Huot, 2002: 62)

When our course outcomes are student-centered, not only do students gain perspective on their performance in a particular course or in a writing project or assignment, but they also discover what they are doing well; and through formative feedback, they learn in what areas they might improve. In addition, students' self-reflective practices increase motivation, enhance creativity, critical thinking and self-confidence, and improve learning. Reflective practices are also a means by which writers can lead readers through their process of discovery, and by which they can offer critical spaces for knowledge processing, meaning-making and critical analyses in a safe environment, as well as provide valuable connections between knowledge acquisition and knowledge gained. Such practices position students to assume increased responsibility for their own learning.

Consider the instructor of an introductory class who discloses to her student-writers in a posted online syllabus: 'I do not believe in assigning a letter grade to creative work because it limits your ability to follow your instincts and curiosity as a writer by forcing you to write work you think I will like'. In line with the double-bind that many teachers feel, she clarifies: 'That said, we are in an institution that wants me to give a grade for this class.

Therefore, completing the following objectives with gusto will determine your grade.'[2] This teacher assigns 50% of the students' grades to community participation and the remaining 50% to a portfolio of student work, the criteria for assessment to be negotiated by the class. The definition and any possible measurement of 'gusto' are vague in this context, but this teacher's classroom practice de-emphasizes grades and promotes a student-centered learning environment in which there is some shared governance.

In contrast, the syllabus of another introductory creative writing class references participation as 'a competitive activity' in which the 'seriousness of [students'] comments are very important'. There is an expectation that every student will 'speak in the class, both when the instructor calls upon the student and in a voluntary fashion'. There follows a statement that not attending a 'conference' will result in a grade reduction or possible course failure, a description of procedures and then a warning that students who 'are not prepared to participate in all of these procedures, [should] drop the course immediately', and on the occasion that 'a student leave the classroom for any reason, he or she should not return to the classroom'. The landscape of this course is clearly communicated when the instructor says 'the notion that creative writing is without rules is nonsensical, and the student should dispel him/herself of it immediately. Any notion that one writes only for him- or herself must be left outside the classroom'. Finally, there is a caveat that 'simply showing up for class and responding when called upon will not earn [students] more than a C grade at best in this critical area'. He empha-sizes: '**DO NOT BE AFRAID OF TALKING**'[3] (original caps and bolding). This instructor's classroom practice, which promotes grades, compliance and line governance, positions learning as teacher-centered and controlled.

What cannot be ruled out, with these two instructor approaches, is the influence that teachers have on students' perspectives of grades.

Assessment is most effective when it is located in practice, when *what* we want our students to learn is reflected in *what* we teach them and in the learning environments that we value and create. In this 'learning paradigm' (a term coined by Robert B. Barr and John Tagg) our teaching aligns with student outcomes so that 'student learning and success set the boundary' (Barr & Tagg, 1995: 13) for what is possible in our programs and in our colleges and universities. Kathleen Yancey reiterates this position that writing assessment creates knowledge about our practices. She claims,

> When writing assessment is located within practice, its validity is enhanced, to be sure. But equally important, it reflects back to us that practice, the assumptions undergirding it, the discrepancy between what it is that we say we value and what we enact. It helps us understand,

critique, and enhance our own practice, in other words, because of its location – in practice – and because it makes that practice visible and thus accessible to change. (Yancey, 2009: 140–141)

In the courses we teach, assessment of our students' creative writing activities (broadly defined as the acts/actions, practice/performance of creative writing) better represents the value of student work when it centers on outcomes-based teaching and learning. Best practices associated with writing assessment include some of the following:

- Define which specific components are gradable and which not gradable.
- Link coursework to student learning outcomes.
- Highlight student learning outcomes in the course syllabus.
- Make connections between direct methods of assessment (portfolio, homework assignments, learning journals, reflections, workshop critiques, reading responses, critical essays, writing exercises) and the learning outcomes each method will satisfy.
- Consider Carl Vandermeulen's suggestions to structure coursework 'in two distinct movements – a long one focused on learning, then a short one for finishing and evaluating the best products of that learning' (Vandermeulen, 2011: 186). In this particular design, the grading of *creative* work is delayed and could occupy a small place in the overall grading scheme. However, rather than delay grading, students' reader responses, critical essays, workshop critiques and such might be graded throughout the course of the semester.
- Offer students improvement opportunities. For example, Vandermeulen and others require a mid-term portfolio, which is graded and on which ample feedback is provided. Students then have opportunities to revise and grow as writers. Final portfolios are collected at the end of the semester. Vandermeulen feels no compulsion to fold the mid-term portfolio grade into the final grade.
- Provide criteria for the measurement of levels of performance.
- Construct rubrics that define objective criteria and share these rubrics with students prior to assignment deliveries.
- Be cognizant of the ideologically based methods of assessment (reader-response, objective, mimetic, expressivist) that will be applied.
- Assess what is most important for optimal student learning.

Teachers should also define for students the other qualities that will affect their final grade. In considering the limitations of 'emphasizing qualities over quality' and how 'in the drawing of attention to craft, we might slight other ways of valuing literary art' (Vandermeulen, 2011: 188), I am reminded of the parallels made between M.H. Abrams' (1953) four theories of art and the taxonomy of pedagogies discussed in *Establishing Creative Writing Studies as an Academic Discipline* (Donnelly, 2011). Abrams is careful to observe that the four theories (objective, expressive, mimetic and pragmatic theories), which he defines as the 'total situation of a work of art', vary 'according to the theory in which they occur' (Abrams, 1953: 6).

As ideologically based methods, values and emphases influence current approaches to the evaluation of student writing, it becomes more critical to define our practices and be cognizant of where we place meaning in the artistic communication transaction (artist, work, audience, universe) and how our privileging affects our pedagogy, assessment practices and students. The teacher who places authority on the 'text' (objective theory), for example, regards the work in isolation from any external reference. Expressivist pedagogy places the artist in the critical element in the composing process, with the belief that it is she who not only creates the work but who establishes the criteria by which it is to be judged. The pedagogical design of mimetic or imitable theory privileges the concept that '[a]rt imitates the world of appearance' (Abrams, 1953: 8). Pragmatic theory, as reader-response, is aimed at audience; as Terry Eagleton concludes, 'for literature to happen, the reader is quite as vital as the author' (Eagleton, 1983: 74).

While no single pedagogy dominates in a creative writing class, this taxonomy of pedagogies has some bearing on what teachers assess and where they place emphasis. The objective and mimetic pedagogical approaches are often associated with what is taught in creative writing classes, particularly at the undergraduate level. As such, teachers often assess how well students demonstrate their understanding of craft in their own creative works, in the work of their peers and in their critical analyses of selected models. But in assessing 'the total situation of a work of art', it is hard to ignore the social constructs associated with the pragmatic theory and the originality and imagination reflected in the expressivist theory.

Some considerations for measuring these less tangible and more indirect methods of course assessment include the following:

(1) Assessing effort. Particularly in introductory creative writing courses, teachers do not expect perfect poems, short stories or plays, but evidence of effort and participation is something that is reflected in a student's final grade. How, then, does a teacher sum up effort? Vandermeulen suggests that *effort* might be those *extras* we think about if we were to write a letter of recommendation for students (Vandermeulen, 2011: 193) – in this case, teachers would reflect on student effort invested, those qualities that perhaps set this student's earnest attempts apart from others.

(2) Assessing participation. What evidence can be measured in *participation* grades? The answers to this question and those related to *effort* depend on individual teaching practices, but the critical assessment of student participation depends on how clearly teachers define criteria that measure this participation and student learning outcome. It is not unusual, then, to find student *participation* as sometimes representing 30% or more of a student's final grade in creative writing. We hope to see our students committed to growing as writers, readers and critical thinkers, and we need some way to measure their energy in this regard.

Moreover, the writing communities that we develop in our courses are critical to the functioning and success of our course. As such, we value the level of engagement, commitment, attendance, attentiveness, citizenship, attitude and what one respondent in Vandermeulen's recent survey of creative writing teachers refers to as 'all the fuzzy stuff that makes a class work' (Vandermeulen, 2011: 193). Defining assessment criteria that go beyond counting student attendance as 'participation' or counting thoughtful in-class interplay/discussions will help to make the grading of student participation less vague for both teachers and students. Depending on our aim, we might describe the language that best represents our assessment of 'A' levels and 'C' levels and let students infer the 'B' level or just provide the 'B' level, 'since competence is easier to define than excellence', or only define the 'A' level, as Vandermeulen does, 'because mere competence is not something to aim for' (Vandermeulen, 2011: 190).

It is also good practice to ask our students to evaluate their own contributions to the writing community. Vandermeulen proposes this practice so students can 'observe how their own contributions connect with and relate to those of others' (Vandermeulen, 2011: 192). His students evaluate their participation at mid-term, which offers them an opportunity to change their participation performance subsequently, so that, at the end of the course, they can make comparisons and reflect on the nature and extent of their participation.

(3) Assessing context. In more advanced coursework, do we assess for 'the way the "context" of the piece participates in cultural, social, political, philosophical, religious debates? And if so, what criteria do we use?' (Boulter, 2004: 137). Even if we ask students to address their intended context in an accompanying critical piece, Amanda Boulter wonders how 'we balance the creative wisdom that self-reflection and self-awareness are essential for all writers, against a theoretical acknowledgement that a writer may not fully understand their own work?' (Boulter, 2004: 138). Similarly, if we privilege an awareness of the reader, we are challenged to show students how to avoid solipsism and self-expression.

(4) Assessing originality and imagination. Boulter legitimately asks if we, as teachers, 'are so well read that we can spot genuine originality' (Boulter, 2004: 137). If our grading criteria, for example, emphasize qualities representing the empirical elements of craft, how might we reward originality, and how might we measure originality and help students to understand the criteria that influence their grade in this component and that then justify originality in a student piece? How should we teach or demonstrate this quality? Is it, as Fay Weldon wonders, 'one of the supposedly unteachable qualities, something you can encourage, but not control?' (Weldon, 2009: 170).

Closing the Loop: Program Assessment

Assessment, as the systemic process by which universities identify their mission, purposes and objectives, (1) measures the value that institutions, programs and courses have as it relates to increased student learning; (2) evaluates student learning outcomes; and (3) closes the assessment loop with the making of needed curriculum changes after review of the assessment findings. The first step in creative writing program assessment is to develop program goals and objectives that creative writing faculty will see as reflective of their undergraduate and/or graduate programs.

Michael Carter (2009: 276) provides some general considerations for brainstorming program objectives and outcomes, not all of which are included here: (1) Imagine an ideal graduate from your program. What kinds of skills, knowledge or other attributes characterize that graduate? (2) What is it that attracts students to this program? (3) What value does this program offer a student? (4) How do you know whether your students possess the kinds of abilities, knowledge, skills and attributes you expect of them? (5) What kinds of assignments or other activities do people in this program use to encourage the kinds of abilities, knowledge and skills you have identified? (6) What kinds of jobs do students in this field generally take? (7) What kinds of skills are appropriate to jobs in this field? I would add another: (8) In addition to learning outcomes, how might you measure success in your academic program? Responses to these questions can lead to more specific student learning outcomes. While these outcomes may vary depending on program levels (introductory, intermediate, advanced, undergraduate studies, graduate studies), criteria should be student-centered, faculty-driven, transparent, identifiable and understood by all participants.

Learning outcomes should assess (1) the content and methods associated with knowledge assessment and (2) the techniques and approaches related to skills outcomes. Assessment of these areas should be collected/measured in direct and indirect methods. Direct evidence should include work that represents variable writing performances written for multiple purposes over an extended period of time. Indirect evidence should yield further insight into our students' learning experience; it may come from student surveys, focus groups, exit interviews and reflective essays, as well as student assessment of programs. In addition to assessing what is most important in terms of student learning, creative writing programs should also assess whether their goals align with their ability to produce measurable results.

Assessment data are analyzed and results are connected to external benchmarks or indicators of success. The findings are then used to make improvements that enhance student learning and practices, to close the assessment loop.

Conclusions

If we are to regard creative writing assessment as an integral to program enhancement, we should create opportunities to map the efficacy of our student-centered writing programs and to develop evidence-based curriculum decisions. Embracing these paradigms boldly positions creative writing as a proactive, knowledge-based discipline, one which situates student learning at its center and one in which assessment is the impetus that drives our pedagogy.

Moreover, if writing assessment challenges our disciplinary identities behind classroom walls, as Gerald Graff (2009: 160) suggests, then why not also challenge the isolation of our university identities as well? Creative writing assessment in higher education should be transparent and accessible to all stakeholders and, as such, there exists a corpus of creative writing accounts that informs our pedagogy. How might our conversations at institutions and national conferences, as well as our dialogue through global connections and in journals, explore the ways such a rich body of data further develops theories of creative writing assessment particular to the unique skill sets that situate creative writing apart from other subjects?

Exploration

(1) Creative writing assessment and the benchmarks that measure particular subject areas and skills should value and characterize the distinguishing ways in which creative writers learn, think, write, read and respond. As epistemological markers, these unique skill sets situate creative writing apart from other subjects.

(2) Reconciling the double-bind of (i) creating environments that enable learning and (ii) remaining accountable to institutions by reporting grades/marks *is* possible if teachers stay grounded in the theory (the *why*) and the practice (the *how*) of assessment.

(3) While outcomes may vary depending on course and program levels (introductory, intermediate, advanced, undergraduate studies, graduate studies), assessment criteria should be student-centered, faculty-driven, transparent, meaningful, identifiable and understood by participants.

(4) Learning assessments should assess content and methods associated with knowledge assessment and techniques and approaches related to skills outcomes.

(5) Assessment results, connected to external benchmarks or indicators of success, should close the assessment loop and lead to program improvements that enhance student learning and practices.

Acknowledgment

My gratitude to James Livingood (University of Virginia), Rita Ciresi (University of South Florida), Gary Hawkins (Warren Wilson College), Tom Hunley (Western Kentucky University) and Anna Leahy (Chapman University) for their feedback on creative writing assessment at their universities.

Notes

(1) In the context of this chapter, the term 'grade' as used in the USA is synonymous with 'mark' as used by practitioners in the UK and Australia.

(2) English 227, Section 4: Introduction to Creative Writing Syllabus, Illinois State University. At http://eng227sec4fall09.wordpress.com/about (accessed 22 October 2013).

(3) English 50: Introduction to Creative Writing Syllabus, Penn State University. At http://www2.hn.psu.edu/faculty/jmanis/eng50syl.htm (accessed 22 October 2013).

References

Abrams, M.H. (1953) *The Mirror and the Lamp.* London: Oxford University Press.

Barr, R. and Tagg, J. (1995) From teaching to learning – A new paradigm for undergraduate education change. *Change: The Magazine of Higher Learning* 27 (6), 13–25.

Beck, H.P., Rorrer-Woody, S. and Pierce, L.G. (1991) The relations of learning and grade orientations to academic performance. *Teaching of Psychology* 18 (1), 35–37.

Boulter, A. (2004) Assessing the criteria: An argument for creative writing theory. *New Writing: The International Journal for the Practice and Theory of Creative Writing* 1 (2), 134–140.

Butler, R. (1988) Enhancing and undermining intrinsic motivation: The effects of task-involving and ego-involving evaluation on interest and performance. *British Journal of Educational Psychology* 58 (1), 1–14.

Carter, M. (2009) A process for establishing outcomes-based assessment plans for writing and speaking in the disciplines. In B. Holt and P. O'Neill (eds) *Assessing Writing: A Critical Sourcebook,* (pp. 268–286). Boston, MA: NCTE/Bedford St Martins.

Donnelly, D. (2011) *Establishing Creative Writing Studies as an Academic Discipline.* Bristol: Multilingual Matters.

Eagleton, T. (1983) *Literary Theory: An Introduction.* Minneapolis: University of Minnesota Press.

Graff, G. (2009) Why assessment? *Pedagogy: Critical Approaches to Teaching Literature, Language, Composition, and Culture* 10 (1), 153–165.

Harper, G. and Kerridge, R. (2004) Editorial. *New Writing: The International Journal for the Practice and Theory of Creative Writing* 1 (1), 1–5.

Huot, B. (1996) Toward a new theory of writing assessment. *College Composition and Communication* 47 (4), 549–566.

Huot, B. (2002) *(Re)Articulating Writing Assessment.* Logan, UT: Utah State University Press.

Kohn, A. (1999) From degrading to de-grading. *High School Magazine.* Available at http://www.alfiekohn.org/teaching/fdtd-g.htm (accessed 11 September 2013).

Milton, O., Pollio, H.R. and Eison, J.A. (1986) *Making Sense of College Grades.* San Francisco, CA: Jossey-Bass.

Polio, H. and Beck, H. (2000) When the tail wags the dog: Perceptions of learning and grade orientation in, and by, contemporary college students and faculty. *Journal of Higher Education* 71 (1), 84–102.

Ridl, J. (2008) Degrading the grade. Available at http://ridl.wordpress.com/2008/02/19/degrading-the-grade (accessed 10 October 2013).

Steins, L. and Solomon, A. (2006) Effective faculty feedback: The road less traveled. *Assessing Writing* 11, 22–41.

Tobin, L. (1993) *Writing Relationships: What Really Happens in the Composition Class.* Portsmouth, NH: Boyton/Cook Heinemann.

Vandermeulen, C. (2011) *Negotiating the Personal in Creative Writing.* Bristol: Multilingual Matters.

Weldon, F. (2009) On assessing creative writing. *New Writing: The International Journal for the Practice and Theory of Creative Writing* 6 (3), 168–174.

Yancey, K. (2009) Looking back as we look forward: Historicizing writing assessment. In B. Holt and P. O'Neill (eds) *Assessing Writing: A Critical Sourcebook* (pp. 131–149). Boston, MA: NCTE/Bedford St Martins.

Chapter 4

Greater Satisfaction from the Labor: Creative Writing as a Text Response Strategy in the Teacher Education Classroom

Toby Emert and Maureen Hall

> *Artists work harder, but they also derive greater satisfaction from their labor.*
> Louis Rubin (1983)

Reading and writing are acts that connect us to the world of experience: '[t]hrough engagement with language, human beings enter into a conversation which allows them to transcend their own egos, to transcend the boundaries of their own skin' (Waxler & Hall, 2011: 184). In her seminal article 'Toward a transactional theory of reading', Louise Rosenblatt defines a distinct method of transaction between a reader and what she or he reads, which she labels 'aesthetic' reading. In this type of interaction with a text, 'the reader is concerned with the quality of the experience that he [or she] is living through under the stimulus and guidance of the text' (Rosenblatt, 1969: 39); the reader is engaged in meaning-making, not simply information-gathering. In other words, reading in the aesthetic mode invites readers to develop a 'relationship with the text' (Rosenblatt, 1969: 35) and to be actively aware of the history of experiences and cultural expectations that color the interpretation of the ideas they encounter in any reading. The emphasis in what has been come to be known as 'reader-response theory' is on attending to the meaning each reader makes of a text and an acknowledgment of 'the exuberant multiplicity among individual readings' (Harkin, 2005: 412).

It is sensible to admit, of course, that reading for different purposes calls for different reading strategies. In this chapter, we describe our efforts to broaden this concept. In our instruction, we build on Rosenblatt's theory about readers' interaction with texts to develop learning strategies that incorporate creative writing as a mode of response, privileging the efficacy of what Keene and Zimmerman (1997) categorize as text-to-self connections. We have found that asking students to write imaginatively about their interactions with scholarly readings strengthens their understanding of the important philosophical questions embedded in content.

The aim of such an effort is to encourage a distinctly critical interaction with the themes of any given course and to invite students to focus more circumspectly on what they perceive to be the significant ideas in the texts they encounter. This stance toward response recognizes that the background, the culture any of us brings to the classroom, 'creates the frame of reference through which we perceive the world' (Jackson, 2011: 80). When teachers utilize creative writing to help students 'enter' a text from an unexpected angle, they activate possibilities for more thoughtful responses to the text and promote the ethos of a more liberal learning environment. William Cronon suggests that education should aspire 'to nurture the growth of human talent in the service of human freedom' (Cronon, 1998: 74). Introducing imaginative writing assignments in classrooms in which they are not typically included unlocks the potential for this kind of educational experience, nurturing the students' creativity and focusing their thinking about the uses of language as a tool of expression.

Though we work in distinctly different educational settings (Toby chairs the Department of Education at a small, select women's college and Maureen is Associate Professor in the STEM Education and Teacher Development Department at a medium-size state university), we both teach courses that (1) prepare literacy teachers to enter middle-school and high-school classrooms and (2) offer professional development for teachers already employed by cities and districts. In this chapter, we outline specific strategies we have developed in our work as teachers of teachers, each of which incorporates artistic and creative expression. Our objective in writing this chapter is twofold: to offer a rationale for the pedagogical choice to require creative writing in courses that typically privilege more traditional forms of academic writing; and to illustrate how these instructional choices are operationalized.

Rationale for the Inclusion of Aesthetic Responses to Texts

It is important to note that we are not suggesting that the kinds of teaching activities highlighted in this chapter are wholly sufficient as indicators of students' comprehension of ideas and texts. In fact, we believe that learners need to employ a variety of modes of expression in order to demonstrate their mastery of complex ideas. However, many teachers tend to privilege certain modes of thinking and writing, often premised on empirical methods of gathering and reporting data, and ignore imaginative expression. Providing opportunities for students to develop aesthetic responses to texts has a dynamic effect on their connection to what they read, and asking students to write creatively about course content and readings offers an alternative approach to knowledge-building. Moreover, the responses students develop when they work in creative modes deepen their connections to texts and inform other types of writing (Emert, 2010). In some cases, preparing for discussions of provocative readings by engaging with texts imaginatively alters the tone and content of the ensuing conversation and elicits a more considered response and a more nuanced dialogue. Artists hone, and it is the act of struggling to render something 'beautiful' that challenges the creator to reshape, rediscover and revise. We recognize the potential of creative writing, when used as a teaching strategy, to amplify the act of learning. In the descriptions of the assignments that follow, we demonstrate how we have asked our students to interact with ideas with an eye toward creative meaning-making.

Example Assignments that Feature Creative Writing as a Response to Texts

Example I: Found poems as responses to 'difficult' texts

I (Toby) teach a foundation course for the Master of Arts in Teaching (MAT) degree, EDU 630: Understanding Learners. It serves as an introduction to philosophical and social contexts for teaching and learning. Among other topics, the course explores 'culturally responsive instruction', which precipitates discussions of prejudice, bias, inequality, stereotyping and intolerance. We tackle the thorny issues of race, class, ability, sexual orientation and gender. Even for advanced students accustomed to weighty discussions, the conversations around these issues are routinely charged. One of the course texts is Lisa Delpit's well known collection of essays titled *Other People's Children: Cultural Conflict in the Classroom* (2006). Delpit argues that schools and teachers must be made aware of the disservice being done to many minority children when their home cultures are not acknowledged or integrated into instruction in the classroom. She puts it this way: 'Both student and teacher are expert at what they know best' (Delpit, 2006: 33). Although my students tend to appreciate Delpit's storytelling ability and respond positively to the frank tone of her writing, they often feel chastised by her admonitions. They want to argue with her theses, as they find her assertions simultaneously inspiring and problematic.

The provocative nature of the essays makes the text especially apt for the course, but most of the students in the class tend to be well educated middle-class white women, and they sometimes find it difficult to express their thoughts and feelings about being indicted as part of an oppressive system. So, I have developed a response assignment that culminates with the students writing a 'found poem'. Found poems, as a legitimate form for verse, emanated, at least partially, in the early 20th century from the impulses the Dada movement, which sought to deconstruct and de-contextualize existing materials in order to question assumptions about art and meaning-making. In this regard, the found poem reworks existing texts – often 'informational' texts, such as signage, legal documents, news reports or letters – reordering selected passages to render them in a poetic form. According to the website of the Academy of American Poets, we might think of the found poem as:

> the literary equivalent of a collage … consist[ing] exclusively of outside texts: the words of the poem remain as they were found, with few additions or omissions. Decisions of form, [however,] such as where to break a line, are left to the poet. (http://www.poets.org/poetsorg/text/poetic-form-found-poem)

For the assignment, I preview the book of essays in class, explaining that Delpit compels us to analyze our assumptions about the overarching aims of teaching. I also offer a simple introduction to reader-response theory, noting that it relies on the reader's tendency to make connections to any text by framing the reading with autobiography, a kind of response that is natural but often unacknowledged and unexamined. Then I ask the students to read the essays with their pencils in hand, noting any words, phrases, sentences or passages that 'stand out' for them. I consider the first step of this creative writing assignment to be ideation – a form of pre-writing idea generation. It is only after the students have created a 'bank' of generative language from the text that I explain how they will synthesize their responses to the reading by constructing a found poem. So, when they begin reading the text, the students are performing a familiar academic task: note-making – highlighting 'important' ideas. I purposefully do not tell the students, before they begin reading, that they will be writing poems, as I do not want them to read with the purpose of looking for 'poetic' language. I want them to read with the purpose of making connections with Delpit's ideas. The found poem, drafted as the last step in the process, serves as a synthesizing exercise, inviting the students to review their interactions with the ideas in the text and to organize the snippets of language they noted as they read in order to highlight a particular thematic concern. The final draft of the poem, though a creative reinterpretation of the arguments laid out in the essays, depends entirely on the language of the readings to render a snapshot of each student's transaction (to use Rosenblatt's terminology) with the text. The assignment also demands an iterative reading experience for the students, who must revisit the passages in the text that they underlined in their initial reading.

The assignment guidelines include these instructions:

As you read Delpit's text, have your pencil handy.

(1) Underline any passages that resonate for you for any reason.
(2) After you have read a section of the book, go back and examine the passages you underlined. What themes do you notice emerging?
(3) Write a response to the themes in your 'Reflective Practitioner's Journal'. You might think of it as a formal kind of journaling. In the response you are looking at your own life, examining what's going on for you and musing about how what is currently happening in your life may be reflected in the themes that emerge from the passages.
(4) After you have written your autobiographical response to the themes, go back to the text, using just the words you find on the pages, compose a found poem that joins together ideas, phrases, words, and images from the book. At the end of each line, insert the page number that those words came from in parentheses.

The students choose the themes they wish to explore, but the assignment asks them to provide 'evidence' of the key ideas they highlight by requiring that they appropriate the language of the text to support the themes (a form of citation).

An example follows of a response to this assignment (used with permission), in which the student author, Florence Corley Johnson, focused on the theme of 'voices'. The language of the poem comes entirely from Delpit's essays, although the phrases have been quilted together from different segments to unify the thoughts expressed by the poem. The writing here represents the student's first effort to generate a found poem from a scholarly reading:

Polyphony

In order to teach you, I must know you, (183)
    the diverse harmonies, the variegated rhythms, and the shades of tone, (11)
    the warm vital reality of children of color. (xiii)
We all carry worlds in our heads: (xiv)
With culturally clouded vision, (xiv)
We do not really see through our eyes
    or hear through our ears,
    but through our beliefs. (46)
It is painful to see yourself in the unflattering light of another's angry gaze. (47)
Issues of power are enacted in classrooms; (24)
It feels like secrets are being kept,
    time is being wasted. (31)
The college student of the 1970s, the panicked mother, (xv)
Headstrong, they think they know what's best for everybody's children. (21)
'Skills' or 'process' boxes –
The dichotomy is false. (46)
You can search for your own song, and
Harmonize with the rest of the world. (18)

Debriefing Johnson's response

I have used this assignment for several years, and I have never encountered a student who has been asked, in a course, to respond to an academic text in this imaginative way. My students are accustomed to making notes, writing reflections on readings, summarizing and analyzing for subtext, but they are not accustomed to writing poetry, in general, and certainly not as a response to scholarship. As is indicated by Johnson's articulation of the assignment, however, it is clear that this kind of learning task encourages the student to identify a leitmotif – a repeated theme in the text – and to construct a language collage that enacts their response to that theme. The creation of the poem relies on skills that graduate students already possess: reflection and textual analysis. But it asks them to reconsider what they recognize about themselves as readers, who filter what they read through personal lenses, 'making' the text as they read. The activity also demands that they revisit ideas in the reading that they noted but may not have examined deeply. The questions that guide the review of the student's note-making include 'Why did I notice this particular passage as I was reading?' and 'How do the passages I've noted fit together to characterize my inter-action with this text?' The process is metacognitive, asking the students to reflect on their thinking.

The final phase of this assignment is a staged reading, at which each 'poet' shares his or her piece, with the class acting as 'audience'. The reading also honors the student's effort to write creatively (which is often uncomfortable work, at least initially). Perhaps most importantly, however, reading the poems aloud offers the class another opportunity to discuss the variety of thematic concerns expressed in Delpit's essays. The poems act as provocative invitations to further discussions.

Example II: Reflective writing about service learning

I (Maureen) utilize service learning projects – designed to integrate volunteer/community service with course objectives – to offer students opportunities to put into practice the concepts they are encountering in courses. Service learning is an important component of an introductory course for pre-service teachers, EDU 500: Fundamentals of Teaching and Learning. Each semester, the students are assigned 20 hours of tutoring at an urban alternative school, a high school (grades 9–12) designed to address the needs of learners who have found it difficult to thrive in traditional public education classrooms. Each teacher in EDU 500 partners with an adolescent learner at the school, and as part of the assessment of their experiences the teachers develop case studies about the students with whom they work. This assignment reveals the teachers' levels of affective engagement with their assigned students. Creative reflection is a primary component of the case studies.

As one of the primary course texts, the teachers read Parker Palmer's (1998) *The Courage to Teach: Exploring the Inner Landscape of a Teachers' Life*, which examines the connections between teaching practice and the identity and integrity of the teacher. They are asked to reflect on the connections among Palmer's text, their tutoring experiences and their notions about entering the teaching profession. As a coda to their case studies, the teachers identify a theme from the Palmer text and then explore this theme and its connection to their tutoring experiences.

The following excerpt from one student's project illustrates the kind of connections the pre-service teachers tend to make as they write about their teaching.

Sample Reflection: Michael

The theme that struck me the most 'in the Parker Palmer reading was something I refer to as 'connectivity'. In the first chapter Palmer states, 'Good teaching cannot be reduced to technique; good teaching comes from the identity and integrity of the teacher' (p. 10). To me this basically means that, as a teacher you can't just go into class every day, go through the motions and expect to intrigue adolescent minds. Palmer also talks about knowing yourself as a teacher. Having a good sense of self-awareness in the classroom is the only way to draw connections. Palmer goes on to say, 'In every class I teach, my ability to connect with my students, and to connect them with the subject, depends less on the methods I use than on the degree to which I know and trust my selfhood – and am willing to make it available and vulnerable in the service of learning' (10). Palmer is saying that in order for a teacher to be successful – you must apply yourself and connect with the subject and the students. Connectivity is very important to me in the way I want to teach and the way I see myself teaching in the future; I want to be the kind of teacher who can make valuable connections with students.

As far as how this relates to my tutoring experiences, I feel this theme of connectivity came very easily for my student and me. From the first day we met we seemed to have a lot in common. We work very well together, always making time for casual conversation – the kind that never seems forced. I feel like he enjoys when I am there and that he doesn't mind doing his school work when we work together. This makes me feel like my early approach to teaching is working well and I would like to continue to teach this way throughout my lifetime.

Debriefing Michael's case study

'Meaning is made through narrative, and human beings need meaning to survive and thrive. Human beings desire to learn and to understand themselves, and they need narrative to achieve this goal' (Waxler & Hall, 2011: 2). This assignment asks pre-service teachers to make connections between the readings and their experience of experimenting with teaching philosophies that they have encountered in their classes, in a relatively low-risk environment. This opportunity to experiment is 'low risk' because the students on the course are not yet being graded on their teaching performance; rather, they are being evaluated on their effort to document the experience. Through reflective writing, Michael describes how Palmer's notions about 'connectedness' influenced his thinking about the completion of his tutoring hours at the alternative high school. His narrative, while still formative as a piece of writing, indicates to me, as his instructor, that Michael is learning to value his 'teaching self', which leads him to comment on the relationship he built with the student he coached. As Rosenblatt (1969) proposes, every student, as a reader, brings unique background experiences to what she is reading and learning; therefore, each student's experience colors his translation of the ideas encountered in course texts and discussions into a personal teaching practice. Each teacher's narrative is individualized – creatively personal.

Service learning projects that connect young teachers with struggling learners provide a practical application for the academic work of the classroom, opportunities for deep reflection and a bridge between theory and practice. Palmer's text offers views on the cognitive and affective dimensions of what it means to be a quality teacher. Framing a teaching narrative with the themes Palmer spotlights allows pre-service teachers to articulate connections between what they notice about their own efforts to inspire a reluctant adolescent learner and larger philosophies about teaching practice. William Cronon, in an essay for *The American Scholar*, underlines the importance of both noticing and understanding linkages as a critical component of the process of becoming educated: 'More than anything else, being an educated person means being able to see connections that allow one to make sense of the world and act within it in creative ways' (Cronon, 1998: 78). In their writing assignment, students create a narrative and derive meaning that is reflective of their lives and their development as teachers. Unlike more traditional assignments that compel students to parrot aspects of texts they read, assignments that privilege narrative forms of synthesis provide opportunities for students to create grounded meanings about their lived experiences and the ideas they encounter in course readings, allowing the possibility of enduring learning.

Conclusions

Adapting creative writing exercises and forms for courses that typically rely on traditional forms of academic writing, such as research-based summary and analysis, invites critical interaction with texts, while simultaneously encouraging personal meaning-making. Students do not expect classes that focus on disciplinary content – not the arts – to include arts-based learning strategies and, as a result, they sometimes struggle with the kinds of assignment described in this chapter. They may feel ill-equipped to write creatively about subject matter that is not presented as 'art' and being asked to do so often feels unfamiliar. The struggle to address the requirements of the assignments, however, is important to the process of developing a creative piece. In some regards, it is harder work, but, as Louis Rubin (1983) reminds us, it often generates greater satisfaction with the process and with the product. In retrospect, students tend to regard the creative work as both novel and memorable; in conversations we have with students about courses, these are often the assignments they point to as the most interesting and important. But even if students do not immediately perceive the import of developing a creative writing project that demands repeated interactions with a course text, as instructors we understand the efficacy of an assignment that engages the intellect and the imagination. The pedagogy is sound. Translating ideas from a course text, framing them with a personal perspective and generating aesthetic responses forces students to grapple with course concepts and forge unexpected connections, which has the potential to intensify the learning.

Exploration

(1) Students are not typically asked to respond in an imaginative way to an academic text they read. They are accustomed, perhaps, to making notes, summarizing and reflecting, but they are not accustomed to writing creatively about scholarship. An invitation to do so often feels fresh, novel and interesting.

(2) Specific applications of Louise Rosenblatt's reader-response theory invite students to develop critical and meaningful relationships with the texts they read, which, in turn, deepens their understanding of content.

(3) Readers 'make' texts as they read them, interpreting their reading through cultural and personal frames of reference. Working in creative ways to interact with a text, by extension, builds self-awareness and an understanding of the self.

(4) Creative writing assignments are particularly useful in helping students engage with texts that are simultaneously inspiring and challenging. The assignments ask students to read with particular objectives in mind and prime them for in-class group discussions. Transforming the ideas in a text by developing a creative response requires that students re-read and re-think.

(5) Offering students unexpected and creative strategies for interacting with difficult texts energizes the classroom and encourages a sense of community.

(6) Asking pre- and in-service teachers to translate their ideas about the texts they read in courses into creative writing pieces models a pedagogical method for engaging with readings that they may emulate in their own practice.

(7) Creative writing assignments build on academic skill sets that students already possess, but interacting with a text in an imaginative way enhances those skills, offering students a richer repertory of reading strategies.

(8) Creative writing has significant potential to assist students in synthesizing their understanding of course themes, as it often asks them to review content, to reflect on their understanding, and to develop an interesting 'artifact' of their learning.

References

Cronon, W. (1998) Only connect: The goals of a liberal education. *The American Scholar* 67 (4), 73–80.

Delpit, L. (2006) *Other People's Children: Cultural Conflict in the Classroom* (2nd edn). New York: New Press.

Emert, T. (2010) Talking to, talking about, talking with: Language arts students in conversation with poetic texts. *The English Journal* 99 (5), 67–73.

Harkin, P. (2005) The reception of reader-response theory. *College Composition and Communication* 56 (3), 410–425.

Jackson, Y. (2011) *Pedagogy of Confidence: Inspiring High Intellectual Performance in Urban Schools.* New York: Teachers College Press.

Keene, E. and Zimmerman, S. (1997) *Mosaic of Thought.* Portsmouth, NH: Heinemann.

Palmer, P.J. (1998) *The Courage to Teach: Exploring the Inner Landscape of a Teacher's Life.* San Francisco, CA: Jossey-Bass.

Rosenblatt, L. (1969) Toward a transactional theory of reading. *Journal of Literacy Research* 1 (1), 31–49.

Rubin, L. (1983) Artistry in teaching. *Educational Leadership* 40 (4), 44–49.

Waxler, R.P. and Hall, M.P. (2011) *Transforming Literacy: Changing Lives Through Reading and Writing.* Bingley: Emerald Group Publishing.

Commentary 2

Poetry by Heart

Paul Munden

As I work for NAWE (the National Association of Writers in Education), my focus is often on the overarching issues faced by those involved in Creative Writing. NAWE is the UK subject association that aims to further knowledge, understanding and enjoyment of Creative Writing and to support good practice in its teaching and learning at all levels. Much of what the organization does, for its 1500 members and the wider community, involves a familiar program of publications and events. Here, by contrast, I am writing about a specific new venture, that of 'Poetry by Heart', an initiative of the Poetry Archive (see www.poetrybyheart.org.uk). Led by Sir Andrew Motion, the project involves a national recitation competition for students aged 14–18. After a successful first year in 2013, it has government funding for a further two years, with the aim of re-establishing poetry memorization and recitation in schools.

For some, learning poems by *heart* smacks of learning by *rote*. That is perhaps compounded by its inclusion in the newly revised primary curriculum for England, and I imagine that many writers may be wondering why NAWE should choose to be involved in a project that appears to be resuscitating a long-gone tradition, seemingly counter to what we more often champion – students exploring poetry by writing poems of their own. The reasons for the tradition's demise are well chronicled in Catherine Robson's book *Heart Beats* (2012), but Robson also investigates why the practice remains compelling. Poetry by Heart – like its counterpart in the US, Poetry Out Loud – is beginning to add new evidence of how and why students (and their teachers) are engaged not only by the fun of a competition but also by the fundamental connection between poetry and memory.

NAWE's involvement is in running a series of Teacher Days, exploring how contemporary poets and teachers might work effectively together not just in supporting the competition but also in finding new ways for poetry to enthuse and be better understood. Supporting teachers in this way has of course been at the heart of NAWE's mission from the start, but it has often proved difficult. It is rewarding to be given a new opportunity on this front, with an innovative impetus.

Ted Hughes' anthology *By Heart* (1997) presents one of the best-known means of memorizing poems, but his use of visualized images is simply one means towards a complex end. Don Paterson (1999: xiv) suggests that 'The poem is a little mechanism for remembering itself' and Poetry by Heart helps teachers and students to get to grips with that machinery – both as readers and as writers.

Watching the finals of the inaugural competition, I was struck by something remarkable, a sense of the reciter *becoming the poet*, somehow enacting the poet's own tussle with content and form, melody and cadence. What better way for students to engage with the essence of poetry, experiencing it as something *created*. The step from here to Creative Writing – and back – is both clear and inviting.

Memorizing a poem is not a virtuoso irrelevance: it is a fundamental part of learning about poetry and learning *through* poetry, enabling its echoes to resonate increasingly with our ongoing lives. Preparing one of the Teacher Days myself, I decided to use a particular poem of my own, 'The generation game', which takes its title from the old television quiz show. I went to my bookshelves and failed to find it. After a momentary panic, I realized that I could remember the whole thing: the structure was intact and the conveyor belt of images still passed before my eyes. The poem ends with the line 'Whatever you remember can be yours' and that simple idea came home to me with new force.

Every poet involved in the Teacher Days has brought something new to the project. Alice Oswald, whose own performances of her hour-long poem *Memorial* (2011) give captivating evidence of memorized recitation thriving as a professional artistic practice, gave insight into the fractional but crucial pauses hidden within a poem's apparent flow. Vahni Capildeo spoke of something similar, a natural pendulum swing within lines, not relating to breathing, or grammar, but to verbal clusterings, something akin to musical bar lines (though more subjective). She made particular reference to the ambiguity of line breaks – the idea of *not knowing what comes next*. Mario Petrucci, in rehearsing recitations, challenged that notion of creative hesitance by asking the audience to call a halt whenever they feel the structure is 'lost'. This difficult but revealing exercise highlighted the way in which poems are tightly strung, like a racquet: the connections between every line, phrase and word can be felt across the structure as a whole. Learning a *whole* poem is conceivably the solution to remembering its parts.

I stress here, albeit very briefly, the subtlety of what has been tested and discussed. Far from being mechanical, the process of learning and reciting poetry by heart is all about investigating the minutiae of composition. It is also about an essential relishing of language. As Catherine Robson remarks: 'A child said to me once that she liked poetry because she liked the taste of the nice words in her mouth' (Robson, 2012: 165).

Interestingly, Robson (2012: 72) makes it clear that memorizing poems does not necessarily cultivate a general faculty of memory that can be applied to other learning. Poetry by Heart, however, makes a new case: it engages with poetry on a deep, detailed and personal level, enabling a poem's memorable power to take hold. Even more importantly, perhaps, it is concerned with finding personal ways to apply oneself to the task. That application is itself a highly valuable transferable skill.

As with the Creative Writing A-level, of high significance to higher education, Poetry by Heart is not confined to schools. We have already shown, through work at Manchester University, how Creative Writing lecturers can play an invaluable part in the project, extending our sense of match between memorization and comprehension, a match that suffered a temporary split at the time of Britain's postwar education reforms.

Creative Writing is all about the new, and yet sometimes, dare I say it, our approaches to the subject seem anything but. We slip into false distinctions between process and product, between writing and literature. Poetry by Heart has refreshed my sense of why each is understood through the other, adding new argument to why poetry is best approached through deep reading, itself a creative act. Most Creative Writing programs stress the importance of reading within their pedagogy, but perhaps with too much emphasis on a linear model: read, then write. Poetry by Heart has demonstrated – in a way that I did not fully expect – why *reciting* is such an important part of the equation: the reciter, like the poet, is encouraging metaphorical thought in the listener, passing the baton in an endless relay. The initiative has, ironically perhaps, found the vigor of innovation within a most ancient and unfashionable practice, one that I hope will now gain a big following in many quarters.

References

Hughes, T. (1997) *By Heart: 101 Poems to Remember.* London: Faber and Faber.
Oswald, A. (2011) *Memorial.* London: Faber and Faber.
Paterson, D. (1999) *101 Sonnets.* London: Faber and Faber.
Robson, C. (2012) *Heart Beats: Everyday Life and the Memorized Poem.* Princeton, MA: Princeton University Press.

Chapter 5

Creative Writing as Education in the Chinese Context[1]

Fan Dai

Creative writing had not featured in Chinese tertiary education until recent years. Creative writing in both Chinese and English started in 2006, when the Department of Chinese at Fudan University set up a master's program in creative writing and, contemporaneously, its English counterpart was established when a teacher with a Master of Fine Arts (MFA) degree in creative writing taught an elective course at Renmin University of China.

In contrast, creative writing programs have become increasingly popular in Australia, the UK and the USA since the 1990s. Among the multiple reasons that explain the phenomenon, Brien *et al.* (2011: 244) list 'self-awareness, confidence and creative thinking', which are 'fundamental to formal higher learning' (Harper & Kerridge, 2004: 2).

In 2009, Shanghai University set up its Center for Creative Writing (in Chinese); this was followed by the International Writing Center in 2010 at Renmin University of China. The former launched a master's program in 2011. Its MFA and PhD programs were approved in 2014, both being the first ones in the country. Other universities, including Suzhou University, Zhejiang University and Peking University, have also established creative writing courses and programs in Chinese in the last few years. In the meantime, two series of creative writing craft books, translated from English, were published in 2011 and 2012, while more are being translated. Among these books are *Immediate Fiction: A Complete Writing Course* (Cleaver, 2002), *Now Write! Fiction Writing Exercises from Today's Best Writers and Teachers* (Ellis, 2006) and *Teaching Creative Writing: Practical Approaches* (Walker, 2012).

Since there has not been a tradition of teaching creative writing at the university level, research regarding creative writing in China has so far focused on introducing the components and teaching methods used in the West and on the recognition of creative writing as an academic discipline (Ge, 2011; Ge & Xu, 2011).

Currently, creative writing courses taught in English as a second or foreign language are few and far between. Only two Chinese teachers have received an MFA in creative writing, one of them being myself, the other at Renmin University of China. The course offered by myself to second-year English majors, however, has been running very vigorously, in that there are three faculty members (two of them native speakers of English) holding MFA degrees who read and comment on each piece of student work; in addition, films, speeches and creative performances and related activities are employed to develop students' creative literacy. The Center of Creative Writing (in English) of the School of Foreign Languages, set up in late 2012, which became the Sun Yat-sen University Center for English-language Creative Writing in early 2014, is the only one that holds regular readings featuring writers of English, which often include the reading of one or two Sun Yat-sen student writers.

In September 2014 I offered a bilingual creative writing course to 15 undergraduates who were non-English majors as a core general education course at the university, having supervised four students who chose to write creative theses instead of academic ones as part of the requirements for their bachelor's degree. I am also supervising two Master's candidates who are writing creative work in English, which they will themselves translate into Chinese, and will write an essay to discuss the non-equivalent parts of the English and Chinese versions. From 2016 onward, I will supervise PhD candidates who will include creative work as part of the requirements for their degree in English and English literature.

In terms of teaching method, I combine the Western workshop model with my experiences of teaching English as a second or foreign language, but makes adjustments according to how a particular group of students respond to the teaching. The pedagogical framework I have developed since 2009 includes the following components: reading as a writer, workshops, peer correction/appreciation, teacher assessment (which includes comments and grading), revisions, summary lectures on each assignment, a creative project called 'Going Beyond the Boundary' and a final creative performance. Neither of the last two is graded.

The Freedom to Write

The creative writing course at Sun Yat-sen University focuses on non-fiction, so that students, as new writers, can turn to their own lives for inspiration. The assignments give only general guidelines, so that students have the most freedom to write. For example, the first assignment tends to be as follows: write about someone who is important to you; or write about anyone or anything interesting. There are no restrictions such as word limits.

The freedom to write appeals to students. One student, Die, wrote that the course let students 'write not just for tests' and work's sake but also 'for life's and experiences', while another, Xiao, pointed out:[2]

> Writing freely is fascinating. It is no longer manufacturing a standard article on a set title with a fixed structure in a very limited time, which was the exact thing I did in high school.... it frees me from the guilt of thinking about those 'useless' things, the seemingly ordinary incidents that stirred, thoughts on the basic questions of life that had sunk in the busy trend of living, things that one has to think through before writing. Thus, I'm no longer thinking for nothing.

Obviously, 'meaningful literacy' takes shape here, where the 'living, thinking, experiencing and feeling person' is at the center of the language learning (Hanauer, 2012: 108). As a result, students experience the joy of self-discovery through writing. As Xin recognized:

> I didn't realize that I could write a 3000-word story in English before. And I didn't realize that I had so much to say about myself and my friends and my parents before. And I didn't expect that I could make any progress this semester before it began.

Feng appreciated creative writing because it 'provide[s] us with a good chance to release our inner feelings, which we may have no chance to share or to release in life, as we may not be able to find a proper person to be our listener'.

Students' reflections show that no other course at the university gives them the opportunity to look back at their lives, to appreciate the little things in life that mean a lot to them. This course, therefore, fills a gap in their education. As realized by Hui, 'the most important thing I learn is to love life. Creative nonfiction requires us to write something about our life. And it urges me to pay closer attention to life than before.'

Yi echoes her peers and makes a connection to the learning of English:

> Not only I've learnt a lot in English writing, which makes me truly feel that I am making progress in English but also it gives me a chance

to rethink things that I had no time or was unwilling to think about before. It helps me figure out a lot of things. Now I see my life in a new light.

All these are in line with Brayfield's finding about creative writing leading to 'personal development, self-knowledge and awareness, self-expression and the development of their language skills. A creative writing class is the one place in the curriculum where every student is an individual and valued for that' (Brayfield, 2009: 185). This place is very much appreciated by Chinese students, who recognize it as something special in their education.

In her first assignment, Xin wrote about a friend she had lost contact with. The writing process reminded her of the lost friendship and she reconnected with the friend as a result. In fact, students frequently report the the mending of relationships with friends and family through their writing. Such 'therapeutic' effects have been recognized by scholars, as writing is 'a profound relief' (Silverman, 2009: 112) for the writer. Obviously, human beings tend to need to address 'the personal, therapeutical and affective aspects' through writing (Bishop, 1997: 143). Over the last three years of teaching, I have come to know multiple cases of improved or mended relationships resulting from creative writing, among every group of students.

Student Tian wrote a glowing comment: 'This course is one of the few courses I considered as really thought-provoking, meaningful and useful, and the kind of course which tertiary education should provide for students'.

Reading as a Writer

Throughout the course, students read established writers' work to learn narrative techniques. Experiences of hardship and misfortune are the frequent themes for such reading, so that students, typically about 20 years old, are exposed to aspects of life with which they are generally unfamiliar. For instance, in the essay 'In bed', Joan Didion depicts the world of someone who suffers from migraine through the tactful use of details and different voices, among other techniques, and shows how she dealt with it and even took advantage of it (Didion, 2009). Such readings prepare students for a future in which bad moments are inevitable and reassure them that people can pull through difficulties in one way or another. The combination of learning writing techniques and sharing experiences covers an aspect of education that the average course does not accommodate.

One student, Ying, reflected on the joy of discovering 'something worth reading' and of learning to write about her 'plain life and to write it down in a way that makes it not plain any more, which is also what I believe [is] "creative" – not the actual event itself but the unique view you have and the writing techniques you use'. This is a good indication that she not only had learned the necessary skills but also had learned to reinterpret her life.

I ensure that the reading materials are from different countries and cultures, so that students become aware of cultural differences and practices. For example, 'Being Brian' by Brian Doyle skillfully includes some facts of American life in general, such as how streets are named (Doyle, 2006). This makes students aware of cultural differences, an important aspect of writing for international readers.

The two native English-speakers who comment on the students' work for the course I teach often touch upon cultural issues. This reinforces students' cultural awareness. As Wei said, 'I may disagree with them a little, it still make us be more alert while writing – we shouldn't expect that our readers are only our classmates or only Chinese people'. Lan realized that 'it's ok to put Chinese elements into a piece because that shows who I am and what my culture has cultivated me into'. It is clear that writing also helps students understand their identity better.

Workshops

The workshop is very new to Chinese students as a technique in the teaching of creative writing. However, they quickly learn how to address the strong and weak points of the pieces in question. Since they write non-fiction, many of them find the workshop a good place for getting to know each other better. One encouraging fact is that they develop a strong bond among themselves from the close reading in preparation for the workshop.

Xing reported that she received warm messages from classmates after the workshop for the story about her partial loss of hearing. A number of students showed their concern for her through conversations and text messages. Yuan, an exchange student from another university, wrote about her workshop experiences two years after she took the course: 'I can't forget how the course affects my life and the feeling of being a family when sitting around as a circle in the workshops'.

This fills a void where students do not have a place to talk about their problems and find support. As Yang put it, 'after the workshop, we would found that something which was so serious and so hard to deal with became less of a burden. And those sad things [that] happened to us was not the only case. We were not alone.' In fact, for a while, too much workshop time was spent on experience-sharing, although I felt this to be very important

(Dai, 2011), due to the therapeutic nature of activities, but I soon found a balance for discussion between this and narrative techniques.

The close reading of their peers' work makes students more aware of how narrative techniques work. They feel good about helping their peers and in turn adopt a more critical stance to their own work through revision.

Therefore, the workshop plays two major roles: enhancing students' critical thinking and providing them with a platform to understand more about each other. Students enjoy the role of constructive reader, which they do not play otherwise, and they appreciate the opportunity to critique classmates' work and to get to know them better. As Feng described it, 'during the workshop we can share our experiences associated with the two essays with the whole class. We can share, discuss, debate … which makes me feel we are the masters of our own classes'.

It is not an exaggeration to say that the workshop is the vehicle that takes students to a place where every individual's experiences and opinions are valued.

Summary Lectures for Assignments

This component of the course is where creative writing meets the teaching of English as a second or foreign language. By citing extracts from their essays (with some context given), I demonstrate in the summary lecture how students have effectively used narrative techniques. All works are posted online so students can read what interests them, and they are able to discuss any issues arising with the essay authors. Such student interaction does not usually happen in other courses.

The summary lecture also notes the typical mistakes in the writings and invites students to suggest better expressions. More often than not, students make different yet similar suggestions, so they can see that the same meaning can be conveyed differently, with subtle changes. Such collective effort makes the error correction non-threatening and unforgettable.

The summary lecture gives every student an opportunity to shine and be proud of themselves. The student's name is given when an extract is used to illustrate good writing technique; no name is given if it is a weak expression. This creates a positive learning environment. As Yu reflected, 'This is the only course where everyone can feel good about themselves. I can never compete with others in other courses. But I can shine in this if I tell a good story.' This resonates with Zhao, who was thrilled because one of her titles was quoted. This motivated her to take creative writing seriously. She began to enjoy her study: 'not only [in the] creative class, I changed my attitude on other class. I did my homework more carefully. And I found I didn't hate English.'

Multiple Comments

Assessment (which in the context of this chapter includes critiquing and grading of students' work) remains a problematic area for creative writing (Weldon, 2009) and can even involve 'the most difficult' decisions for teachers (Uppal, 2007: 50). Giving specific comments on each assignment demands a lot of time. In order to ensure the quality of the assessment, the time the two assessors need for making comments on students' work is recognized as the equivalent of teaching one course; they grade four assignments by 30 or more students in one semester. As a result, along with comments in the summary lecture, students receive multiple responses for each assignment, significantly more than in an average writing class.

As is well recognized, comments on creative works are subjective, as they depend on the background and personal interests and limitations of the assessor. Students are often troubled by the sometimes different or even opposing opinions of the assessors. Chinese students, possibly more so than ones in most English-speaking countries, tend to take teachers' comments very seriously. They ask what they should do – whom to listen to when making revisions. This becomes even more complicated when they hear more different views from their peers in the workshop.

I see this a good occasion to tell them that it is their work, and they know better than others what will help them. The perspectives of more than one assessor push students to think independently. Although they experience the discomfort of not having straight instructions, they soon feel the joy of being an independent thinker and writer. Independent thinking encourages students to explore further what they want to do with their essays and become competent writers.

What Jin says is exactly what I would like to happen:

We listen to, but [do] not necessarily follow, responses from our peer readers and comments from teachers. We are not told whether our wok is 'good' or 'bad'. We have more freedom to present our thoughts and feelings, while at the same time it also means that we bear more responsibilities of finding out our own problems in writing and expressions and establishing our own style of writing. In this process, I've learned to be an independent thinker, who has own judgement towards an article and writing.

Revision

Revision in creative writing has not been received much attention from creative writing researchers. Among those who have worked in the area are: Bishop (2004, 2005), who (respectively) addresses revision at the sentence level and gives 50 tips for style revision; Goldthwaite (2004), who focuses her discussion on the alternate style of writing through revision; Gerrity (2004), who refers to her own experience to give specific examples of various instances of revision; and Cook (2004), who addresses revision at the punctuation level.

Students' revision in my course is informed by comments from the assessors and peers. As Dethier (2004: 7) points out, comments from teachers and peers should be based on 'logic, imagination, and reason, not obscure rules'. Therefore, students must sift through them and then highlight the changes made and explain the reasons for making them. This makes the revision process more conscious and students have to think very clearly.

Yang said of the role of revision: 'I can observe what I have written in a more objective view, jumping out of the identity of "the writer". Through revising I could reflect and summarize the most valuable experience I accumulated in this time's writing and the suggestions I got.'

Revision strengthens independent thinking and allows students to better assess which comments from various assessors are more helpful to them.

Creative Projects

At least three components of the course inspire students' creativity, in addition to the study of creative writing. One is the movie and speeches and creative/artistic activities the students are introduced to as supplementary learning materials. Another is the 'Going Beyond the Boundary' project. Still another is the creative performance at the end of the course.

The movies and speeches and so on are assigned as self-study materials for students to observe and appreciate the techniques of expression. For example, students were asked to watch closely a speech by Benjamin Zander on the TED website, 'The transformative power of classical music' (www. ted.com/talks/benjamin_zander_on_music_and_passion?language=en). They were told to observe his dress code, his facial expressions and gestures and so on, all of which contribute to his eloquence and has implications for the writing of details.

The 'Going Beyond the Boundary' project is done mainly outside the classroom. Every week, one or two students would go to class in the way they have wanted to but never dared to, due to social constraints. It encourages students to be creative without being outrageous. They are required to start the 'show' from their residential hall, which is about a 10-minute walk from the classroom, so they can feel the pressure from the inquisitive eyes of anyone on campus. Therefore, they need to make sure that their creativity catches attention instead of leading to negative consequences.

Students have a few minutes to explain the thoughts behind their appearance, so that they have both fun and learning to do. Since they take turns to do the project, they are in some kind of competition, yet creativity gives it a positive nature.

If the 'Going Beyond the Boundary' exercise sets students' imaginations free, the creative performance at the end of the course pushes the imagination and creativity to a higher level. Neither counts toward the final score for the course, but students' enthusiasm for these optional activities is evident, a good indication that they go for the creativity, not for the high scores valued in the educational system.

These two extracurricular projects, though demanding in terms of both time and energy on the students' part, are the highlights of the course. The creative performance leads students 'to a broad range of activities and jobs beyond the classroom' (Healey, 2013: 63). As Tian said, and his classmates would agree, there is a Lady Gaga in everyone.

Conclusion

The creative writing course goes far beyond writing and contributes to the overall education of the student. This echoes with the following arguments: 'Creative writing courses provide value-added relevance as a core requirement of the college curriculum' (Donnelly, 2012: 9); 'What creative writing has to offer in the classroom goes beyond the familiar production of student poems and stories to an enriched experience of the various activities that we engage in, in general, throughout English studies' (Haake, 2007: 15).

The pedagogical framework of the course allows a variety of creative activities for students to learn as conscious writers, to assert their creativity, to grow as writers and as compassionate human beings who enjoy beautiful relationships with those close to them.

Explorations

As this is only the fourth year of the course, its practices are not widespread, in that creative writing in English as a second or foreign language is very new; it takes time and evidence to prove its value and specify its role in tertiary education and it takes time to train teachers. In the research for the immediate future, the following issues should be further explored:

(1) *Chinese student experiences for doing creative writing.* In-depth interviews on their learning experiences should reveal more about what the course means for them.
(2) *Reading materials.* In addition to established writers' work, I intend to use my own work-in-progress and very well written pieces by previous students to make students feel closer to writers/good writing.
(3) *The role of the workshop.* Workshops have served not only as a platform for students to learn to critique but also to learn a lot more about their peers in the Chinese context. What more can be learned about students' workshop experience, as it is still a rare form of classroom teaching?
(4) *The assessors' experience.* While students benefit greatly from the assessors' detailed comments, is the experience of critiquing and commenting beneficial for the assessor?
(5) *Revision.* Qualitative research is needed to examine students' focus in the process of revision and see how it informs teaching.
(6) *Summary lecture.* This is the part of the course that is not frequently seen in its Western counterparts. What else can be done to make it more effective, including the aspect of language teaching and learning?
(7) *Creative activities.* A better structure than the current loosely organized one is needed for all the creative expressions beyond writing to enhance students' creative literacy.

All in all, the teaching of creative writing is a field that is yet to be further explored. Without a doubt, it has a lot to offer to Chinese students, as a practical course to learn writing in a second or foreign language and as one that contributes tremendously to the all-round development for students in higher education.

Notes

(1) The research findings reported in this chapter were from the project 'The Pedagogical Framework of Creative Writing', sponsored by China's 2013 National Social Science Foundation, project code 13BYY089.
(2) All students write an informal reflection paper about the course, and the student quotes used here (reproduced verbatim, without correction) are taken from that paper, which is not graded. All the students gave their permission for me to quote from them.

References

Bishop, W. (1997) Writing is/and therapy. In W. Bishop (ed.) *Teaching Lives: Essays and Stories* (pp. 143–156). Logan: Utah State University Press.

Bishop, W. (2004) A study in sentence style. In W. Bishop (ed.) *Acts of Revision: A Guide to Writers* (pp. 70–86). Portsmouth: Boynton/Cook.

Bishop, W. (2005) Contracts, radical revision, portfolios and the risk of writing. In A. Leahy (ed.) *Power and Identity in the Creative Writing Classroom: the Authority Project* (pp. 109–120). Clevedon: Multilingual Matters.

Brayfield, C. (2009) Creative writing: The frequently asked question. *New Writing: The International Journal for the Practice and Theory of Creative Writing* 6 (3), 175–186.

Brien, D.L., Freiman, M., Kroll, J. and Webb, J. (2011) The Australasian Association of Writing Programs 1996–2011. *New Writing: The International Journal for the Practice and Theory of Creative Writing* 8 (3), 238–263.

Cleaver, J. (2002) *Immediate Fiction: A Complete Writing Course.* New York: St Martin's Press.

Cook, D. (2004) Punctuation as editing. In W. Bishop (ed.) *Acts of Revision: A Guide to Writers* (pp. 91–106). Portsmouth: Boynton/Cook.

Dai, F. (2011) Writing, sharing and growing together – Creative writing in Sun Yat-sen University. *TEXT* (special issue, Creative writing in the Asia-Pacific Region), April. Available at http://www.textjournal.com.au/speciss/issue10/FanDai.pdf (accessed January 2015).

Dethier, B. (2004) Revising attitudes. In W. Bishop (ed.) *Acts of Revision: A Guide to Writers* (pp. 1–11). Portsmouth: Boynton/Cook.

Didion, J. (2009) In bed. In J. Didion *The White Album* (pp. 168–172). New York: Farrar, Straus and Giroux.

Donnelly, D. (2012) *Establishing Creative Writing Studies as an Academic Discipline.* Bristol: Multilingual Matters.

Doyle, B. (2006) Being Brian. In P. Sondra and M. Schwartz (eds) *Writing True: The Art and Craft of Creative Nonfiction* (pp. 227–234). Boston, MA: Houghton Mifflin Company.

Ellis, S. (ed.) (2006) *Now Write! Fiction Writing Exercises from Today's Best Writers and Teachers.* New York: Jeremy P. Tarcher/Penguin.

Ge, H. (2011) The academic status of creative writing studies as an academic discipline. *Journal of Xiangtan University (Philosophy and Social Science Edition)* 35 (5), 104–108.

Ge, H. and Xu, D. (2011) The outline of Chinese creative writing studies. *Exploration and Free Views* 6, 62–72.

Gerrity, M. (2004) Subterranean rulesick blues. In W. Bishop (ed.) *Acts of Revision: A Guide to Writers* (pp. 61–69). Portsmouth: Boynton/Cook.

Goldthwaite, M. (2004) From correct to effect: Revising and alternate styles. In W. Bishop (ed.) *Acts of Revision: A Guide to Writers* (pp. 51–60). Portsmouth: Boynton/Cook.

Haake, K. (2007) Against reading. In K. Ritter and S. Vanderslice (eds) *Can It Really Be Taught? Resisting Lore in Creative Writing Pedagogy* (pp. 14–27). Portsmouth: Boynton/Cook.

Hanauer, D. (2012) Meaningful literacy: Writing poetry in the language classroom. *Language Teaching* 45 (1), 105–115.

Harper, G. and Kerridge, R. (2004) Editorial. *New Writing: The International Journal for the Practice and Theory of Creative Writing* 1 (1), 1–5.

Healey, S. (2013) Beyond the literary: Why creative literacy matters. In D. Donnelly and G. Harper (eds) *Key Issues in Creative Writing* (pp. 61–78). Bristol: Multilingual Matters.

Silverman, S.W. (2009) *Fearless Confession: A Writer's Guide to Memoir*. Athens, GA: University of Georgia Press.

Uppal, P. (2007) Both sides of the desk: Experiencing creative writing lore as a student and as a professor. In D. Donnelly and G. Harper (eds) *Can It Really Be Taught? Resisting Lore in Creative Writing Pedagogy* (pp. 14–27). Portsmouth: Boynton/Cook.

Walker, E. (2012) *Teaching Creative Writing: Practical Approaches*. Cambridge: Professional and Higher Partnership Ltd.

Weldon, F. (2009) On assessing creative writing. *New Writing: The International Journal for the Practice and Theory of Creative Writing* 6 (3), 168–174.

Tracing Roots in a Foreign Language

Asma Mansoor

In Pakistan, English has a rather unique status. It may not be the language spoken on the streets but the constitution specifies it as an official language:

> (2) Subject to clause (1), the English language may be used for official purposes until arrangements are made for its replacement by Urdu. (Constitution of Pakistan, chap. 4: 251)

Yet Pakistani society is anything but bilingual. As a matter of fact, its cultural diversity makes it plurilingual, with diverse provincial languages shaping its linguistic topography. In Islamabad alone, one catches several strains of languages, all interbraided through code-switching and code-mixing. One hears English and Urdu words interspersed in Pashto conversation, and families conversing with each other in mixed strains of Punjabi, Urdu and English. Urdu is the national language, English a remnant of Pakistan's colonial past and the ethnic languages define one's roots. With such linguistic diversity available to my students here, it is little surprise that they generally do not have a very strong command of any one language, since they have to wade through multiple languages in order to convey their messages. The problem is compounded by class differences and a variegated educational canvas in Pakistan, where the children of the elite speak and write in English as if it were their mother tongue, whereas the majority of students studying in government-run schools display a wide range of responses toward English. A number of them can read and understand English but are not articulate in the language; a majority, however, can read English but cannot truly understand it. So how to teach Creative Writing in English at the university level to students who belong to linguistic and educational backgrounds that are poles apart?

The answer to this question is anything but simple and the ways of dealing with this issue are equally diverse. However, one of the interesting factors that has come to the fore is the way these students use the English language to retrace their ethnic and cultural roots, not merely through a personal and cultural anamnesis but also by discovering what is unique in their own culture. Therefore, my approach in teaching my students Creative Writing does not hinge on isolating them from their own culture and focusing on the foreign culture, with which most of them are unfamiliar; instead, I tell them to bring their own experiences and culture to their creative compositions. Some are uncomfortable with it, but others happily delve into the adventure. Why not write about the roguish, tardy *doodhwala*, who rides on his motorbike all day supplying adulterated milk provided by his emaciated buffalo – *bhains* – to rich families, rather than writing about a British milkman distributing pasteurized milk like clockwork every day, early in the morning, about whom they do not know anything.

The Creative Writing classroom, for my students, thus becomes a space where they get an opportunity to view and re-view their native environment. While critics may argue that this re-viewing of their native social scene should be done in their own language, since language is the means through which reality is constructed, my argument is that there can be no absolute reality and identity in today's hyper-real world. Others argue about why they should rewrite themselves in the language of the Other, their former colonial master. The answer to this objection is that English is entrenched within Pakistan's social and cultural canvas, and has become firmly assimilated within the linguistic infrastructure of the country over the nearly seven decades since Pakistan gained independence from the British. While a command of English may be a prerogative of the powerful Pakistani elite, it is now no longer a language of the Other alone; rather, it has been appropriated by the natives to serve as their own tool of expression, as my students do in a Creative Writing classroom or workshop. However, even as the students negotiate a vast spectrum of diverse cultural and linguistic resources, the language they use reflects a border crossing, as the English language is made to cross various thresholds, so that, in Derridean terms, their writings come to reflect the following conflict:

> We only ever speak one language … *(yes, but)*
> We never speak only one language …
> (Derrida, 1996: 7, author's italics)

Since there is no *'pure idiom'* (Derrida, 1996: 8, author's italics), this premise has enabled me to let my students navigate through a multilingual field to reconstruct their own world in the language of the Other, molding it, playing with it in ways they like and enjoy. In doing so, they are not letting the language of the Other shape their identity; as a matter of fact, they are using it to adapt to the world they are familiar with. So, when a student of mine wrote a horror story, she did not write about demon-infested mansions and castles, she wrote about a *ghote* in rural Sindh plagued by a lingering *churail*, with long hair and inverted feet. Another wrote about a handmade doll – *guriya* – that possesses a character in a *haveli*, which is a large mansion, so that she ends up murdering her family. Similarly, another wrote about her own mother's opulent village life, as the daughter of a feudal *chaudhary* from the rural Punjab, accoutered in a *ghaghra choli* and married off to another feudal lord twice her age. Another student, in a story entitled 'Princess', wrote about a *maharani* waiting for the arrival of her warrior groom after a battle with the Rajputs in 15th-century India, in the following terms (quoted with permission):

> The person I saw in the mirror today was very different from what I usually saw. The biggest difference was that I was smiling. I couldn't believe that he was actually coming back. After months of waiting, he was finally returning home from war. Victorious in his battle. My happiness had nothing to do with the victory of our troops. It was solely based on the fact that my husband was returning home. I hadn't seen him in many months. This was the first time after our *vivaah* that he had left me for so long. And when he was leaving I thought it would be a matter of days. But I was naïve. Wars did not go on for days in our region. They went on for years. I was lucky he was coming back so soon. At least that's what my mother in law told me. I was lost in these thoughts as I took off my *ghagra choli*. My *kaneez* helped me put on my *lehenga*, which I had specially gotten made to wear for him when he returned. I fixed my *dupatta* on my head, because I couldn't go into the main courtyard without covering my head. And I was so eager to meet him that I would go out to receive the troops, much to the disapproval of my mother in law. But I just could not wait.

As the example given above indicates, while delving into and out of multiple languages and multiple experiences based upon their native environments, these students engage in Creative Writing in English to re-extract the traces of their individual and collective history and culture from the palimpsest of memory. They then redraw it not merely to make it articulate again in a language that may not be their own, but in a language which they have, willingly or unwillingly, made their own. Antithetically, instead of the foreign language taking them away from their roots, it draws them toward their roots, making them revisit them from a different angle. In doing so, these students are not merely re-appropriating (Derrida, 1996: 66) and re-constituting the target language, they are revisiting their own heritage and activating it in a language that is now ingrained within their own cultural substratum. The results of this *melange* of the native and the foreign make Creative Writing in the context of English as a second language an intriguing site for further debate and study.

References

Constitution of the Islamic Republic of Pakistan. Available at http://www.box.com/shared/3vk516hrj7 (accessed 16 March 2013).

Derrida, J. (1996) *Monolingualism of the Other or, The Prosthesis of Origin*. Trans. P. Mensah. Stanford, CA: Stanford University Press (1998).

Chapter 6

Questions and Answers: Responding to Creative Writing Teaching and Learning

Craig Batty, Simon Holloway and Gill James (with Graeme Harper)

Because creative writing is many kinds of conversation – between writers and readers or audience, between writers and themselves, between the actions of writing and the results of writing, between the imagination and communication, and more – *Creative Writing and Education* is, as noted, based on conversations. This chapter attempts something else with that notion by using a Q&A format. In essence, the writers in this chapter took the following roles: I (**GH**) made statements and posed questions. Responding to these were Craig Batty (**CB**), Simon Holloway (**SH**) and Gill James (**GJ**). I have known Craig, Gill and Simon for varying lengths of time, though I have known all of them long enough to have an entirely comfortable conversation with them individually or as a group. Each at some point studied with me as a PhD student; each now works in a university, teaching creative writing.

The method of creating this chapter was not 'live' Q&A. I am located most of the year in the USA, Craig is located in Australia, and Gill and Simon are located in the UK. While it's entirely possible to have a live Q&A session that spans those time zones, it isn't always convenient, and I wanted the creating of this chapter to be convenient so that the interlocutors could relax into it. This Q&A was thus conducted via email and was therefore asynchronous.

Secondly, the method of creating this chapter was intended to be Socratic, or exploration via the elenctic method. The chapter does indeed start with a 'thesis', and the notion I had was that we would then pursue in Socratic form an examination of concepts and claims. However, I asserted the initial thesis and I believe it to be true. What then happened was that the conversation seemed to have that original thesis pervading it. This might simply be because all three interlocutors believe the original thesis to be true. Or it might be because the original thesis was too broad or vague.

More positively, though, it all might be because that original statement – 'Education in Creative Writing matters' – poses not so much a thesis (that is, something put forth as an idea) but rather a synthesis (a combining of ideas). In this sense, the statement might be a combination of thesis and antithesis, in that one of the most intriguing discussions of recent decades has been that associated with the considerable increase in creative writing courses in colleges and universities, and how this relates to more economically driven notions of importance of contemporary post-secondary education. In colleges and universities, formal education in a discipline or subject is put forward as essential to higher learning and, though informal learning is both acknowledged and promoted, there is no doubt that such sites of contemporary education deal in formalizing knowledge. What the opening statement below might represent, therefore, is an acknowledgment that while we might know that informal education is considerable, and even essential, for creative writers, the growth of formal educational opportunities is neither opposed to that nor unimportant.

Finally, as a matter of approaching spontaneity, the writers were asked not to adjust their responses when they read the responses of the others (which they only did toward the end of the Q&A period). This was partly me admitting that their responses were turning out more interesting than my questions! Thus, what appears in the following pages is the original, unadjusted responses of the individual interlocutors responding individually to questions posed by me – becoming a sort of asynchronous, accumulative expression of ideas. The three respondents each have different interests, and certainly different personal histories, but they all share an interest in, and active participation in, creative writing education.

GH: Education in Creative Writing matters.

CB: It is interesting that you say 'Education in Creative Writing' and not, for example, 'Creative Writing education'. So it certainly made me think in a variety of ways. 'Creative Writing Education matters' is perhaps a given: of course, people should be educated in the area and made to understand its benefits; educated about the power of Creative Writing, for the self, for others and for the world at large; yes it can be taught – at least, writing craft can be taught, and creativity can be cultivated. 'Education in Creative Writing' reminds me that not all writers can teach; not to be disparaging but, as we all know, some writers are oblivious to what they do (unless probed) or refuse to believe that there is a way of educating others about how to do it, making teaching situations awkward at best. It also reminds me of the lack of attention paid to teaching Creative Writing, where, apart from the odd book and a smattering of journal articles, there seems to be an assumption that it is 'just taught'. Lastly, this also reminds me that students in Creative Writing programs want an education: they want to be taught things, to receive content, to learn. They do not just want to 'do'. Too many times have I witnessed 'bad' teaching practice, where workshopping is seen as the only way of teaching. But how do students know what to say in a workshop? What are they looking for in a piece of writing? How do they craft a critique? They need to be taught content. They require an education in creative writing.

SH: It's interesting that the sentence says 'Education in CW' and not 'Education of CW'. Education matters. Creative writing matters. To me, the issue depends on how you define education. Writers are self-taught, in that the practice of writing informs other writing and, more basically, being alive is an educational experience which affects the perceptions and attitudes conveyed in and through creative writing. Many would say that 'reading' the world, coupled with textual reading and the compositional skills gained by seeing how others construct their work, make up a writer's toolbox – this starts as soon as any type of language is used, even pre-birth, and that type of education continues until death.

At the more formal level, as a teacher of creative writing in higher education I'm a little worried by the attitude of 'I've got a degree so I'm a writer', which seems to pervade the thinking of some students, regardless of how much actual writing is going on, and the institutional notion that the development of craft is all that matters. A writer lives, experiencing and interacting with that life, and writes. Craft helps (it's hard to write effectively without being able to craft that work) but the term 'education' includes an awful lot more than what goes on in classrooms, whether the student is aged 6 or 86. Any helpful tips, advice and skills offered can help, but the job of a writer is to write. Classes may help you to understand more about how to express yourself effectively, but teachers are not going to write, rewrite, edit and proof the text for you: part of a writer's education is to learn the amount of work, of all types, involved in that job description.

(One could interpret the statement differently, taking the word 'matters' as a noun rather than a verb, but the above would be pretty much the same!)

GJ: Education, in any discipline, isn't just about learning a set of skills and applying them. If it's really happening, then a deep understanding takes place.

Why educate? Won't writers learn simply by writing? After they've completed their 10,000 hours working at the craft, won't they have acquired all the skills they need? Or is there the possibility that they might have spent those 10,000 hours hitting their overburdened brain against the same concrete wall with never a sign of a breakthrough?

Education in creative writing can take many forms: autodidactic activity, through one-to-one mentorship to higher education programs, with many other possibilities in-between. Is a common trait that deep reflection that looks at both product and process? It asks what is happening, how it is happening, whether this can be streamlined and fine-tuned and whether the streamlining and fine-tuning are effective and productive. It guards against it being destructive. There is a constant cycle of action–research, similar to that used by teachers of all disciplines and many other creative practitioners in their creative practice.

I'm aware of an escalation that results from such reflection. I see it in my students' work and hope it is in my own. As they apply this deeply, critically reflective process, the writing becomes more creative, in that it creates more. It gets more to the point, it creates more vivid images in the consumers' minds and it communicates better. The last is perhaps the main point. Education in creative writing matters if it produces writing that communicates effectively. I believe it does.

GH: You seem to be saying that education is important to a creative writer only in certain circumstances?

CB: I think I would see it as education always being important to a creative writer, at all times, but perhaps in different 'shades'. From my experience of writing and teaching writing, the learning process never stops, and it is hard to 'switch off' and not be engaged in some kind of education. For example, reading a book about constructing a solid narrative structure is an obvious type of learning; but watching a film that employs such a narrative structure is also a type of learning, even if the film is viewed with friends at the weekend, or on a long-haul flight while drinking free wine. I often discuss with my students the notion of the 'writer–reader/viewer': those of us who read texts and view screens from the perspective of wanting to know how the work has been put together. We cannot read or view blindly; we are constantly seeking clues to bring to the fore the work of the writer: narrative cues, linguistic tricks, visual motifs and so on. At these times, we are always learning; we are always educating ourselves. And it is important to flag up that latter point: educating ourselves. I think we choose to do these things, or at least to want to do these things. When we make the choice to pursue our dream of being a writer, we are also making a long-term commitment to learning. Hopefully we get pleasure from it but, that aside, we are choosing to always be on the lookout for something that will help us with our own work. In this way, education 'wholesale' is important at all times.

SH: Again, it depends on what you mean by 'education'. If we are talking about a formalized set of classes, whether delivered over distance or face to face, then students might (or should) bring a set of expectations and desires with them. There are what institutions term 'transferable skills' that can be gained, certainly, but if the writer has certain specific goals in their learning then these can be achieved by and through formal educative means. The writer might, for example, want to look at their use of dialogue and speech, and this can be addressed by learning more about the use and effects of such things. In such a case, education is important, yes, yet it is only one way to address these concerns – there's no substitute for practice, and for the detailed, intricate reconsidering of that practice as part of the creative act. So much of writing is rewriting, after all. To me, the greatest benefit of formalized education in creative writing is the appreciation and knowledge of that reconsideration, the gaining and developing of skills with which a writer approaches a text in process and sees how to improve it. Whether this self-critical, self-analytical approach is currently being taught, or indeed whether formal education is the best place to learn it, is another question entirely.

GJ: I guess that might be true for a lot of things we learn. Don't we go through a cycle of knowing nothing, learning something, using that at first uncomfortably and then comfortably and then wanting to stretch ourselves and find out and be able to do more? So, at some points we're 'resting' or even 'wallowing' in it. At other points we're learning and going forward.

But I guess some commercial writers don't extend that cycle. They find something that works and they stick with it. And make a lot of money. But, good for them – maybe their publishers can then afford to risk something less mass market.

Maybe there also comes a point when you seek out some 'education' and what you get is disappointing. You think 'I knew that already' or 'same old, same old'. At that point, perhaps, one needs to look at a different form of education.

Education, anyway, has many forms. We can:

- follow formal lessons in formal settings;
- be mentored;
- watch and learn from other creative practitioners who are ahead in the game;
- learn with our students;
- learn though our networks and from our peers.

Interestingly, we become educated whether it is important to us or not. Perhaps it's only at that point in the cycle where we want to learn more that it seems important. It tends to happen anyway, whether we seek it out or not. And maybe the mass marketeers have to fight it.

GH: How much do you feel learning more about the action or process of their writing contributes to a student's creative writing and the results of it? Are there any dangers in learning more about those actions?

CB: This is a good question to ask, and one that I am constantly grappling with when talking to PhD students about the differences between practice-based and practice-led research. In some of my own academic work I have reflected on my practices and processes, but always with the aim of educating (that word again!) others – those who also want to write screenplays, or develop stories for screenplays. I do, however, think that there can be a danger in 'just looking inward' – and that relates to self-indulgence. At the end of the day, although it may be interesting to hear about what writer X does, and look at some of their draft work (for example), I think it is only truly interesting – and revelatory – if it says something beyond that writer's work. It needs to speak to the community of practice at large, otherwise who is ever going to benefit from it? There are often tensions when we speak of craft as research or craft as knowledge, but I believe that craft absolutely is research and knowledge. By reflecting on one's own work and understanding how it has been created – poetics, perhaps – what we are actually doing is deepening our understanding of craft. And this is where I think we can neatly and productively bring together self-reflection and the educating of others. If an Oscar-winning screenwriter talks about how they wrote their film, I want to learn something from it. I want to glean something that might help my own practice. If, instead, they talk about how they wrote their film because they want to enlighten themselves only, then why should anyone else be interested? So yes, I think students – anyone – can learn a lot from reflecting on their practices and processes, but I would be very cautious about them doing this merely for the purpose of helping themselves. If someone is going to generate knowledge and understanding, then it should be shared – especially in the academy.

SH: At times, students of creative writing can bring a certain resistance to the theories of writing (if we can call them that), a reluctance to accept that there is anything other than the spontaneity of creative action. Some come with the belief that there might be some magic that teachers can impart, a secret code which is known only to the few and makes everything 'work'. Yet to engage with an education in and of writing means hopefully that they are willing to investigate the nature of process, to inspect through close examination exactly what they do when they write and, by extension, how. As a teacher I would much rather a student produces a good piece of work and knows how to make it better than an outstanding text with no idea how they did it!

To some extent, this means breaking down the processes of inscription. A potential danger here is that in focusing on what is termed 'craft' the student gets taken so far away from the moments of insight and spark and recognition that they become mechanics rather than creators, that the joy of that discovered phrase is replaced by engineered expressions; it's vital that teachers and students allow the work to be individual, related to that writer's personal view, rather than manufactured homogeneity.

Writers are autodidacts, co-opting means and modes from their experiences of being alive as much as from their acts of writing, and the teacher's job is to provide them with the tools and opportunity to do this more consciously, making creative choices instead of automatic ones.

GJ: Learning more about how they write and how the creative process works certainly changes what our students eventually write. Naturally, so does every other experience they have. But perhaps the whole point of education is that we scrutinize what is happening and apply what we see in order to get a better handle on the process. We bring a focus to that process and attempt to unpick it.

Isn't this, though, what higher education is all about in any discipline and in fact doesn't our particular discipline do it rather well?

Maybe this scrutiny pushes us all toward experimentation. We say 'Okay, this is what we've observed. Now what happens if we do something else?'

Is there a danger? Maybe. This scrutiny of process and product certainly makes both reading and writing different. We rarely stop editing and critiquing or trying to work out how creativity happens. Final-year undergraduates and masters students complain that they lose their enjoyment of reading and spontaneity in their writing. They are in fact offered another way of reading and of writing. They can enjoy the text that they normally wouldn't want to look at because they are absorbed in the process of reading it critically as a writer. They write with more confidence because they understand the process better.

A further danger might be that we become too clever and a little jaded because we have become so aware. Yet that awareness itself keeps us looking for new possibilities. This is what we offer our students and ourselves as well.

GH: Let's change focus just a little. You've just woken up in a magical world where you are given a choice to learn one thing you don't already know about Creative Writing. What is that one thing you'll choose to learn, and why?

CB: I'll be honest here and say that, for me, it would be learning about all the 'literary greats'. Because my area is screenwriting, and all of my studies and training have taken place in an interesting space somewhere between creative writing and film/media studies, I feel that I do not have as strong a sense of 'the greats' as many of my creative writing contemporaries. I know all there is to know (okay, maybe an exaggeration!) about screenwriting – from gurus to pedagogy – and have a strong understanding of film, media and cultural studies. I feel that I am able to make interesting connections between, for example, Robert McKee and the Frankfurt School; Syd Field and semiotics; perhaps even Christopher Vogler and liminality! In the greater sense of creative writing, however, I will be honest and say that I know more about practice and pedagogy than I do about 'literary theory'. So if I were in a magical world where I had the chance to learn more (is a university supposed to be that anyway?), something about great prose writers and associated 'theory' would hit the spot. I also know very little about poetry, so that could be an interesting learning curve. That said, because I generally do not tend to 'get' poetry – nor possess any ability to write it – I doubt whether I would feel confident in learning about the field. Then again, they say that failure is one of the most exciting things about learning....

SH: I'm not sure I like the sound of this magical world: part of the pleasure comes from finding things out as you go along, and to be given knowledge in one go might be confusing and distracting....

Having said that, I'd like to know more about writerly choices: Do we make them consciously or are they automatic? How does one lead to others? How much is 'play', that is, happy accident, and how much is previous action/experience leading one to choose the 'right' option, regardless of conscious action? Is there such a thing as a happy accident?

If when I'm writing I receive a casual word from a loved one, or happen to hear a particular color shade mentioned on the radio, then that color or word can find its way into the work, leading to other actions, other words. A poem can be restructured around that color: 'maroon' carries connotations which 'indigo' doesn't, for example. Was this always going to happen? Have I now written a different poem?

I'm interested in how many of the choices writers make are made because of immediate stimuli, and how many are, if not predetermined, then at least more likely, based on writers' experience, history, culture and so on. Or, to put it another way, how much does chance play a part, if at all, or are we just following the paths and patterns that we were always going to follow, but perhaps in a slightly different way?

GJ: A truly magical place would take me away from the daily round and give both time and brain space to learn this new one thing that I don't already know.

My playwriting colleagues talk about 'subtext'. I kind of get it when I hear them explain it to the students. Then it goes away again.

'Tell me,' I say. 'Explain it in plain English in a way that a confirmed novelist can understand.'

'You understand it already. You must be using it in your stories.' At this point they go away shaking their heads.

Maybe. There is dialogue in fiction and it carries some of the role that it also plays on the stage. And if I know how to construct the latter, won't it also enhance the former anyway? So it would be useful. Plus I want to have a go at another genre. I know a little but I need to experience it to understand fully.

So I'd like this magical space to give me the opportunity to put in the time it will take. Maybe, if my playwriting friends are right, and I've got it to some extent, it won't take the full 10,000 hours they say creative practitioners need to learn their craft.

It's highly likely that in the course of doing this I'll discover other things that I don't know but didn't know that I didn't. And so it goes.

GH: Magical worlds aside, what do you think you might know about creative writing education in five years that you do not know now?

CB: Wow, that's an interesting question! I guess by then we will know a lot more about the discipline – bearing in mind that it is still a relatively young discipline in the academy – so it might be somewhat of a steep learning curve. I think we will know a lot more about why students choose to study Creative Writing, and what they got out of studying it. There are statistics available about employment, satisfaction and so on, but I think in five years' time we will know even more about 'what happened next'. It will be really interesting to know, for example, how many students went on to get published, how many moved into teaching, how many decided to work in related areas such as public relations, advertising and communications. It will also be interesting to know how they feel about this – whether, for example, they saw Creative Writing as a great way to prepare for these industries, or whether they felt that they had 'failed' as a writer by working in these areas.

For my own professional practice as a lecturer and supervisor, I think – or hope – that I will also know more about how to better 'educate'. I think that my experience by then will tell me much more about what has worked and what has not, informing my education practice for the better. I think, also, that I will know a lot more about the wider context of Creative

Writing education, and with perspectives on it from different cultures and communities, which again will hopefully make me a much better and more informed lecturer and supervisor.

SH: I'll know nothing, and the nothing I know then will be as nothing compared to the nothing I know now. There's so much to do. Hopefully in five years' time the conversations, debates and arguments that are going on will have been further developed, so that a critical mass of writings will emerge. The current progress in creative writing education – of which this book is a great part – will I hope have continued to the point where writers, educators and students might agree on more than they disagree on: though let's not get to a point of consensus, because such things are not only dull but proscriptive. We need to challenge ourselves, our teaching, our writing and most of all our students, so that the subject can benefit from all the expertise and practice going on.

In more precise, personal terms I'd like to think that I'll know something more about the reasons why writers make the decisions they do: there must be more to the challenge of creativity than the difference between primary, instinctive or automatic choices (system one), and the secondary, deeper or consciously reasoned decisions (system two), as outlined by Daniel Kahneman in *Thinking Fast and Slow*; why do I pick the words I do, I wonder, and how can I transfer the knowledge of those choices to other (student) writers in a way they can understand? Of these actions, and of so many others, I feel that I know nothing. My nothing is more than others' nothing, but I'd like to get to the point where I know something....

GJ: I might know a lot more that I know now. I suspect I'll get the sense that I know even less of the whole, a smaller proportion of everything that there is to know. As with writing itself, the more you find out, the more you realize there is to find out. A lifetime is nowhere near long enough. Thank goodness. We're never going to get bored.

There are trends of course. Creative writing is beginning to be used as a valid response to show understanding in other disciplines. In a way, it becomes education by creative writing. It's being used to explore history, dementia and the future in my institution.

Neuroscience is looking at what happens when we read and when we write creatively. It's discovering the mechanics of it all and seeing a pathway to empathy. But actually, didn't we already know that? I guess in five years I'll be more aware of how all of that works.

Creative Writing is part craft, part science, part art and to a large extent something else indefinable. This indefinable quality no doubt has something to do with how the other three combine. We may have a better handle on what that is.

A sure thing though: many questions will be answered by then but many more will be asked.

GH: If someone who had not taken a course in creative writing, never attended a creative writing class, not really read anything about creative writing education, asked you for your best advice, what would that advice be and why?

CB: Assuming that they had a passion to write – and it is really obvious when someone has, compared with someone who just thinks it sounds like a good idea – I would recommend (1) attending some short courses or evening or weekend classes, just to see how they feel about things, and (2) reading some craft books, to see how they respond to the idea of learning about Creative Writing. I think this is important because it emulates, in some way, what they will experience if they do decide to pursue things. I would also advise them to consider the best way of them writing and learning to write. Some students suit a three-year degree, whereas some students best suit short courses and industry master-classes. We have to think about the educators here, too, in the sense of 'Do we want students in our classes who will constantly challenge everything we say and criticize the readings we set?' (I say this from experience!) Conversely, some students do not like high-profile workshops and master-classes; they feel like those running them are mainly giving anecdotal advice and that they are not actually learning anything. So new writers need to understand the different types of Creative Writing education landscape. Finally – flippantly – if someone said they had never taken a course in Creative Writing, never attended a Creative Writing class, nor ever read anything about Creative Writing education, I would say, 'Why not?!'

SH: Write. Keep writing. Write some more. Read everything you can get your eyes on: books, magazines, newspapers, billboards, the sky, the look on people's faces, the shapes of buildings, the sound of aircraft, the taste of vegetables, the smell of children, the touch of skin. Take those readings and add them to your store. Accept the perfect, individual wonder of these readings of human existence, of your own individual voice.

Write all the time. Read what you've written and see what you think of it. Try to discover what you want to say, and how you want to say it. Find someone you can trust enough to show them your hidden percep- tions and hidden voice and ask them to read your writing. Listen very closely to what they say. Watch their eyes. Join a writing group. Learn to give and take criticism, knowing that it's that particular text that's being commented upon, not the author. Read your own work again, and then write again.

Be accurate in how you express yourself, precise in the use of your experiences and understandings. Practice the skills, techniques, tools and tricks of writing to help you in this. If you want to, enroll in a more structured course, perhaps even at university, as long as it inspires you and you trust the folk teaching you. Read 'How to...' books if you must, but don't expect them to tell you 'How to', because, practical and helpful though they can be, they are not you. Never let anyone tell you that the way you see the world is wrong. Trust yourself. Thicken your skin. Accept disappointment. Celebrate tiny victories, for as long as you need to. Above all, keep writing. There are no short cuts, no easy options and no one will write your texts for you. Writing is work. Get it done.

GJ: I would tell this person that they might like to take an interest in this topic. I would tell them to try it for themselves first: read a little and then write a little. Talk to people who have attended a creative writing course. Find out what they learnt and how they learnt it.

I'm presuming this person is curious about creative writing education. 'How does that work?' is the frequent question we are asked. 'How can you learn to write creatively?' 'How can anyone be taught?'

I presume we're not being evangelical. But if we are I might say, 'Try writing about the world to find out about it.' So we're back to education by creative writing.

I would invite this person to write. Then look at what is written. Reflect on it deeply. What happened in this writing process? How has something that works been created? How? What's out of kilter? What needs to be done? How have others achieved this? Can you share this with others?

Maybe I would encourage sitting next to symbolic bamboo and writing haiku, for this somehow, for me, epitomizes the learning process for creative writing: stimulus, response, deep and crucial reflection. Learn about this process by engaging in it.

I am a little in awe of this person because I know few people who never ever attended a creative writing class. This feels like an act of charity.

My best advice though? That has to be: try it. See if it works.

Exploration

(1) **GH:** Isn't it time now for more international conversations about the practice of creative writing?

(2) **CB:** Creative Writing education can take place in any form and at any time. It can be formal or informal; active or passive; explicit or tacit. Creative writers are 'learning' all the time.

(3) **CB:** While many argue that talent cannot be taught, what can be taught are craft and context. Creativity can be taught, or at least harnessed. As for talent, that needs to be executed and used in the right ways – and that can be taught.

(4) **CB:** If Creative Writing can develop its own research methodologies, then so can it develop its own pedagogic practices. There is no 'right' or 'wrong' way to teach the subject, which does not make things easy, but it does make things exciting.

(5) **SH:** Creative Writing takes place at different times and in different places. It is more than the actions of holding a pen or typing at a keyboard: the education of the author is continuous, and everything she or he learns forms part of the creative process.

(6) **SH:** Education is inevitable. It is more than the conscious acquiring of knowledge about a particular subject at a particular time in a particular place: when we take part in the world we add to our store of understandings.

(7) **SH:** The creative choices we make are our own. They are more than cultural, sociological, circumstantial: with conscious or practiced decision-making we can instill in a text something of our own individual interpretations of human life, our own imaginings and perspectives.

(8) **GJ:** Creative writing learning often involves a form of action research, of which deep critical reflection is an important component.

(9) **GJ:** As we move on, we put in our 10,000 hours plus into the craft in a process that isn't just craft but that is in part science also and in part art and actually one where these three elements blend in such a way that any pedagogy or methodology here is totally different from any other in any other context.

(10) **GJ:** Learning pathways project into the future, into the great unknown, where the only certainty is that we are going into expansion: the more we know, the more we find out we have yet to discover.

Commentary 4

Against Carefulness

Katharine Coles

Teachers of poetry writing know we can teach precision and craft, if perhaps not to all students then to many. We teach them how to control tone and the importance of choosing precisely the right word not only for its denotations but also for its connotations, via which meaning resonates through the poem. We teach them exact rhyme and the subtle differences between different kinds of slant rhyme. We teach them how to distinguish between words that are essential on any number of levels and those that aren't, and how to build both individual metaphors and metaphors that work across an entire poem.

All of these are important skills for poets to have. But the discipline inherent in developing care can often lead to the wrong kind of carefulness, especially in the context of the evaluative workshop. When students demonstrate precisely the competencies to which we have led them, they are praised – first by their fellow students, then by their teachers. And when they err, whether because they haven't mastered the skills we've taught or for other, better reasons, they are corrected – perhaps even berated. Praise and blame occur publicly, so by the end of a given discussion everyone in the room knows who 'liked' a poem (and precisely what they liked) and who didn't (likewise); everyone knows who 'won' and who 'lost' for that class period – by which I mean, finally, whose work was praised and whose not, by other students and especially by the teacher.

A possible way to think generally about the tension between the need to master technique while at the same time taking risks is to distinguish *care* from *carefulness,* aiming for the former while trying not to tip over into the latter. This is a distinction that can also carry over into the classroom: if we are to encourage risk-taking, we must be committed to caring for our poems, for each other and for each other's work, while avoiding being so careful that we are unwilling to risk making mistakes. I would make a similar distinction between courtesy and propriety. Courtesy implies attentiveness and care, best practiced within the context of a generous honesty in which the practitioner is as honest with herself as with the other and as forgiving of the other as of herself. Propriety attends more to form than to context and content; one may practice propriety reflexively, in the absence of, even instead of, attentiveness, care, generosity and honesty.

I've spent enough time over drinks with poets who teach to know their most common lament by heart: that many of our students' poems, even (or perhaps especially) those that are perfectly good, by which I mean competently constructed, may still be missing something – texture, yes, but most of all that quality that makes the best poems feel like white-knuckled adventures; that brings readers face to face with what is uncertain, surprising, thrilling, even heart-stopping; that enacts encounters with something about the world or the self that was unrevealed until that moment and yet that is so resonantly true it pulls a reader up short. Our common complaint is that the typical 'workshop poem' seldom does this. Indeed, a poem whose primary attention is to carefulness is unlikely to be the poem I've just described. In order for a poem to become such an adventure for its reader, it must have been an equal adventure for the poet, in the act of its composition. And to become an adventure, it must embrace risk.

Please don't mistake me. I am not one who likes to grouse about the 'workshop poem', which I see not only as a necessary stage in the student's progress toward writing better, riskier, more individual poems, but in fact as a high achievement of creative writing programs. It's a symptom of self-hatred among teaching writers that they view with contempt the accomplishment of helping thousands of students a year become 'merely' competent in the practice of their art. Such poems result from hard work and hard teaching; their relative abundance right now is a result not of the workshop's failure but of its success, not of its lowering the ceiling but of its raising the floor. Even in themselves, such poems often offer pleasures, if milder ones than those described above. This very success allows them to compete for our admittedly scattered attention, but they don't displace excellent poems or prevent them from being written now any more than they ever have.

Still, if we concede that one real difference between a student who is merely good and one who is excellent is the ability to balance discipline with risk, with uncertainty, even with a kind of recklessness, we are wrong to write off the ability to embrace risk as among the skills we categorize as wholly unteachable (ear, anyone?). If we could help our good students learn to tolerate, perhaps even to embrace, disciplined risk, might we help them become a bit better than good? And if we can open this possibility in the workshop for our good students, might we be able to accomplish even more with those who are already inclined toward the white-knuckled?

I believe we can. In my own efforts along these lines, I have developed two specific strategies for running my workshops and have begun to give my students exercises to help them embrace risk. Paradoxically, the first workshop strategy and most of the exercises are designed to shift the poet's attention away from herself and onto the work – to displace, temporarily, the risk in writing in an attempt to help the poet embrace it.

The first workshop strategy, which I call the analytic (as opposed to the evaluative) method, is aimed at simultaneously increasing the seriousness of the workshop while minimizing the writer's personal or psychological vulnerability within the workshop setting. For a detailed description of the techniques employed in the analytic method, which can be used in either prose or poetry workshops, see Coles (2006). In brief, the technique employs not evaluation but close readings that reveal what is happening and how the piece before us makes it happen. The difference may seem subtle, but its effects are not. The class shifts its attention away from the activity of picking a piece apart in order to find things to praise or blame, and toward a collaborative effort on the part of the readers in the room to experience the piece as fully as possible *as it is*, and to make that experience visible to the writer. This method also emphasizes and makes visible the responsibility of the reader in producing a finished 'version' of the work through the act of reading. Thus, it helps the writer understand the importance of opening rather than forestalling opportunities to let the reader intervene, wonder, puzzle and play in the piece – and also how far the writer can productively go in opening such opportunities. Doing so – which is risky – is rewarded by the gift of the reader's attention and collaboration, the gift of her care for the poem, and through the poem for the poet.

I've been teaching some version of the analytic workshop for nearly 20 years. Within the last year or so, I have begun to develop a corollary workshop strategy, which involves explicitly inviting and encouraging risk-taking. One simple but surprisingly effective way to do this is to set aside a portion of the first class or two to talk about vulnerability and risk as they are at play in the writing of poetry and in the activity of the workshop. Despite what incredibly risky, vulnerable spaces workshops are (or maybe precisely because they are so), this is a conversation we hardly ever have out loud – as if, like Clint Eastwood staring down the barrel of a gun, we can minimize the weapon's effects if we pretend it's not there.

In my graduate poetry workshops, I introduce the topic by bringing in podcasts of people in various professions talking both about how important it is to take risks and about how difficult and painful such risk-taking can be. (The TED radio hour has a wonderful program on this very topic, and all of the participants have also given full-length TED talks that are on line at www.npr.org/ted-radio-hour.) I note that it's inherently uncomfortable, not only for the students but also for me, to listen to strangers talking about their most deeply vulnerable or embarrassing professional moments – especially to do so in a group, especially in a new group comprising poets one wishes to impress. From listening to, say, a surgeon and a sociologist and a biologist talk about their experiences with risk, we move on to talking about how and why what we do is risky. We begin with what we do in the workshop, move on to what we do on the page and end with how one relates to and exerts force on the other.

During this conversation, two things happen that the students aren't used to. First, as I implied above, I am taking my own risk in talking about this at all, given that it's a topic we have all for years tacitly agreed not to bring to each other's attention. Also, by listening with my students to strangers talking about vulnerability, I admit that the experiences of those strangers might apply not only to my students but also to me. I am asking us all, including myself, to take the stories to heart. By making my own vulnerability present and visible, I intentionally step out of the role that is both given to and often carefully cultivated by me: that of invincible teacher fully entitled to the last word. I take my place alongside the students in a difficult but deeply worthwhile endeavor, in which the risk is worth whatever embarrassment or pain it might produce.

Perhaps laying the groundwork in this way would be sufficient. But I see it as tantamount to making a commitment that I will continue to take risks during the workshop – that I will not always withhold my own readings to the end, that I will not only challenge their readings but will invite them to challenge mine, that I will admit to being uncertain, persuadable or even wrong in my readings. Through these strategies and others, I work to keep the language of risk and vulnerability front and center throughout the workshop and invite students to take their own risks, both in their readings and, ultimately, in their writing. Though I remain firm in my commitment not to praise or censure poems in the workshop, I do often praise the students' *readings* of poems, most particularly when those readings are themselves risky, when they are generous in their efforts to account for elements of the poem that might seem at first to be unaccountable, or when they engage and account for risk-taking in the poem under discussion. Essentially, the only thing I will praise a writer for in front of the rest of the class is risk-taking – and I praise it when it fails as well as when it succeeds. Sometimes, I even offer a reward (usually a book) to the student everyone agrees took the biggest intelligent or potentially productive risk in a given class, whether the risk paid off or not. Rather than competing to pile up praise and avoid censure, then, by the end of the class the students, at least most of them, compete to reach beyond themselves.

Not all of them will succeed, of course – certainly not all the time. But then I don't always succeed either. That's why we call it *risk*: there are things at stake, and one of them is failure, even public failure. The point is that for writers, both students and teachers, the most important habit to cultivate is arguably that of extending ourselves, a gesture that is inherently risky, whether we are making it in our classrooms or at our desks. Since we are bred in the bone to seek safety, whether physical or emotional, this gesture never becomes easy; it's one we have to develop consciously throughout our working lives (and I would suggest our personal lives as well, since for writers the two spheres deeply intersect). But how many more of our students might succeed – and in how much larger ways – if we, as teachers, intentionally set out not only to create occasions for risk-taking on their parts but also to model it for them in our own writing and in our teaching? In this perhaps more than in any other pedagogical practice, teachers must walk the walk. If we practice caution, if we keep ourselves safe from our students, we are only teaching them to do the same in their relationships with each other, with readers and with us.

Ideas into Action

- *Care versus carefulness.* One tension that can exist in a creative writing workshop is that between the desire to instill craft and technique, on the one hand, and to encourage risk, on the other. The ethic of care can create an environment in which over-carefulness is unnecessary.
- *Courtesy versus propriety. Courtesy* is important to this ethic, *propriety* less so. One may always be courteous while also being honest, while certain forms of propriety may forestall honesty.
- *Praise and blame.* A workshop designed around public evaluation (praising and blaming) necessarily inhibits risk-taking, both in writing and in workshop. Since pretty good (i.e. 'workshop') writing is often competent but careful while the best is both technically excellent and risky, the praise/blame model may actually impede students in becoming the best possible writers.
- *The analytic method.* Rather than relying on evaluation, the analytic workshop focuses on closely reading poems, with the goal of describing how they operate to build poetic experiences for the reader. The poet watches careful readers 'build' readings of the poem at hand based on

what is provided on the page to get an idea of what the poem is actually doing. Attention is displaced from the poet and what the poem has done that is praise-worthy or blame-worthy onto the poem, the reader and the act of reading.

- *The language of risk.* Another strategy that encourages risk-taking is to introduce the language of risk and vulnerability into the workshop in an overt recognition that risk and its attendant vulnerability are inherent in what we do. This conversation not only acknowledges but honors and rewards risk, while foregrounding the hard truth that taking risks is the action that is most likely to lead to both dramatic failures and spectacular successes.

- *Teacher as model.* Introducing the language of risk and vulnerability explicitly into the class also opens a space for the teacher to act as a model for risk-taking behavior. This modeling may be the most important thing the teacher can do to help students embrace risk.

- *Risk-taking and play.* It might seem that exercises are inimical to risk-taking. Indeed, the exercises I give in the context of encouraging risk-taking don't necessarily appear to be directly related to risk-taking

Box 1 Engaging and manipulating the texts of other writers

Cento
The cento is a poem made from sentences or lines drawn from a single other work (*Frankenstein*, say, or *Paradise Lost*, or an article from the *New York Times*) or from a body of works (Shakespeare's sonnets, the articles in November 1957's *National Geographic*).

Erasure
An erasure is a poem created by erasing most of an original text. The new poem is what remains when the text has been erased. The remaining words may inhabit precisely the same positions that they did when the larger text was present, or not. Some or all of the larger text may remain slightly or entirely legible. (See Jen Bervin's erasure of Shakespeare's sonnets, *Nets*; Ronald Johnson's erasure of *Paradise Lost*, *Radi Os*; and Janet Holmes' erasure of Emily Dickinson's poems, *The Ms of My Kin.*)

Once they've erased another writer, I ask them to fill the spaces in the erasure with words and commentary of their own to create a dialogue with or meditation on the original text.

After the students have performed erasures on the texts of others, I ask them to select poems of their own to erase.

at all. In nearly every case, they involve engaging and manipulating the texts of other writers (Box 1) rather than working from one's own generated text and/or personal experience. The idea is to displace risk temporarily from the poet as a writer and person, to depersonalize the task of writing, in order to encourage risk-taking on the level of language and meaning-making in the form of poetic play. Of course, editing, deleting and selecting are, in the end, both skill-based and personal, even deeply so. By the time the poet is finished with a given exercise, the result is often startlingly individual and revealing, even to the poet.

References

Bervin, J. (2010) *Nets*. New York: Ugly Duckling Press.
Coles, K. (2006) The elephant in the room: Addressing content in the short story workshop. In G. Harper (ed.) *Teaching Creative Writing*. London: Continuum Books.
Holmes, J. (2009) *The Ms of My Kin*. Bristol: Shearsman Books.
Johnson, R. (2005) *Radi Os*. Chicago, IL: Flood Editions.
The TED Radio Hour. www.npr.org/ted-radio-hour.

Chapter 7

Interpretation, Affordance and Realized Intention: The Transaction(s) Between Reader and Writer

Nigel McLoughlin

Since Stanley Fish's paper 'Interpreting the *Variorum*' first appeared in 1976, it has had a great influence on reader-response criticism. It has been part of a movement toward centralizing the experience of readers, the interpretive strategies readers use to make meaning, and the socially constructed nature of language more generally. The arguments contained in 'Interpreting the *Variorum*' have been seen as problematic for the discipline of stylistics (Fish, 1979; Paton, 2000; Smith, 1978). Cognitive stylistics (sometimes also called cognitive poetics) is based around a set of theoretical approaches which attempt to explain and model the cognitive processes through which readers make meaning from texts. It incorporates theoretical approaches from cognitive science, psycholinguistics and linguistics and applies them to the interpretation of literary texts. This can include consideration of mental scripts and schemas (Cook, 1994), the ways in which cognitive metaphor theory (Lakoff & Johnson, 1980; Lakoff & Turner, 1989; Turner, 1987) and blending theory (Fauconnier & Turner, 2002) can be applied to texts, or, as in examples I consider later, how 'text world theory' (Werth, 1999; see also Gavins, 2007) might allow us to analyze the mental spaces constructed through the act of reading the text in a particular context.

Text world theory offers a way of analyzing the relationship between mental 'worlds' produced as readers integrate information in the text with their contextual knowledge in order to generate a stable representation of the world of the text. This considers the 'world-building elements' (people, things) that make up the text and the processes that act upon them, and how they are integrated into a holistic mental world. It also maps the types of movement into different worlds, by allusion to past or future worlds for example, or through modalized propositions which offer insights into characters' wishes and beliefs, for example, which create separate worlds in which these wishes and beliefs might be realized (for a broad introduction to a number of different approaches, see Stockwell, 2002a).

This chapter examines the arguments Fish makes, offers ways in which cognitive stylistic analysis may address Fish's concerns and finally identifies any common ground between Fish's arguments and stylistics generally, and cognitive stylistics in particular. In so doing, the chapter considers how such analyses can be of benefit to the educational development of creative writing students by examining how such approaches may deepen their understanding of how texts are processed by readers, and what the evidence suggests may be ways of manipulating readerly processes for authorial goals.

Fish's basic arguments in 'Interpreting the *Variorum*' may be summarized as follows (Fish, 1980a):

(1) Formalist analysis 'flattens' the text and makes the temporal or serial aspect of language and text disappear (147).
(2) Formal structure does not exist independently of the reader's experience (147).
(3) The focus of description should be the reader's experience rather than any structures in the text (152).
(4) Through interpretive strategies, the reader 'realizes', both in the sense of 'makes real' and in the sense of 'understands', the author's intention (161).
(5) Interpretive communities are those who share the same strategies for 'writing texts, for constituting their properties and assigning their intentions' (171).
(6) An author makes an utterance on the basis of assumptions about strategies employed by a reader rather than on the basis of what is 'in' the text. These assumptions are in turn based on the strategies the author would employ when confronted by such an utterance (173).

Fish argues that there are no objective linguistic structures, only subjective ones. In the introduction to his essay 'Interpreting "Interpreting the *Variorum*"', Fish states that interpretive communities will agree among themselves what constitutes a 'fact' and by extension a 'structure' (Fish, 1980b: 174). Fish is right in that all structures that we perceive are the result of perceptual strategies we employ. Because our perceptual systems tend to function in basically the same ways for the vast majority of us, we tend to agree on our perception of those structures. With regard to language, such perceptual strategies are required for us to perceive even the most basic structures. Phonemes are perceptually classified with clear boundaries, which can change depending on: the language spoken (Werker & Lalonde, 1988); the rate of speech (Summerfield, 1981); and the surrounding phonological and lexical context (Ganong, 1980). Part of language acquisition is the use of interpretive strategies to decide where word boundaries are (Johnson & Jusczyk, 2001).

We have socially constructed inferences, which we understand but which exist beyond what is said. Because of this, we can understand 'it's warm in here' as a request to open a window, when the context signals it. Speakers of a language agree on what constitutes, and what functions as, basic linguistic structures within that language. I agree with Fish that 'intention and understanding are two ends of a conventional act' (Fish, 1980a: 161). That act takes place in language, usually where both participants are familiar with, and broadly agree on, what the 'interpretive community' of those who use the language consider to be the 'rules' of that language. They generally agree what particular 'structures' are used for and the set of meanings that those 'structures' generally afford.

So, in effect, even though linguistic structures arise out of interpretation, whether they are 'real' or 'socially constructed' is a moot point among the community who use them. The community behaves as if they are 'real'. Fish slips into this behavior on several occasions, for example he says: 'a reader is invited to place [the significant word or phrase] first in one then in another structure of syntax and sense' (Fish, 1980a: 154). If, as Fish asserts, these structures do not exist, then readers must create the structures into which they can insert the word. The fact that it is possible to describe the structures a reader creates in terms of syntax and sense, and understand these descriptions in reliable ways, demonstrates that language users construct very similar structures in similar circumstances. Further, they socially construct agreed sets of possible affordances and meanings that are generated prototypically from what they agree to see as structure. This will influence what the author is likely to try to achieve through the use of that agreed structure, or through novel variations of language structure that may challenge the agreed use. This is not to say there cannot be some disagreement, and misunderstanding, but the disagreements and misunderstandings are usually limited within certain bounds. Fish acknowledges as much in his chapter 'What is stylistics and why are they saying such terrible things about it?' when he says:

> The structure with which the stylisticians are concerned is a structure of observable formal patterns, and while such patterns do exist they are themselves part of a larger pattern, the description of which is necessary for the determination of their value. (Fish, 1995: 108–109)

In order to illustrate what he feels is wrong with formalist analysis, Fish presents several ambiguities, which he refers to as 'syntactic slide[s]' (Fish, 1980a: 147), which are resolved across a line break. Fish asserts that formalist analysis of the text results in a masking of what the reader is experiencing, by focusing on a 'correct' interpretation, which may not necessarily be agreed by other readers. A cognitive stylistic reading of the lines concerned will bring out the reader's experience, foreground the temporal and serial aspects that Fish asserts disappear in stylistic analysis, and provide an explanation for what the reader experiences.

One would predict that such explanations can be very helpful to creative writing students in offering a structure and a vocabulary through which they can understand and analyze the reader's experience. This is important for two reasons. Firstly, creative writers are always the first readers of their own texts, and any means of understanding how they function as readers, and what the processes of reading actually entail, will be helpful to them as readers of their own texts by allowing them to better understand how their interpretive processes integrate with their perceptions of linguistic structure to yield the effects that they do. Secondly, by understanding the mechanisms by which it is thought that these perceived structures may relate to interpretations, the student may be better equipped to devise texts which deploy certain structures in novel ways and to experiment deliberately, while having some theoretical understanding of the likely effects on the reader. Such experimentation and analysis on the part of writers may also inform the theories they test through the need to explain surprising results and the manifestation of unintended meanings, which may require some change to the theory to be made in order to accommodate the new knowledge generated with regard to perceived structure and meaning.

The first of Fish's examples considered here occurs in Milton's 'Lawrence, of virtuous father virtuous son':

He who of those delights can judge, and spare
To interpose them oft, is not unwise.
(In Fish, 1980a: 149)

The word 'spare' at the end of the first line quoted is lexically ambiguous. It can mean 'refrain from' or 'forbear to'. At the end of the utterance the reader is left not knowing whether the lines are a warning to refrain from delights or an approbation of judicious indulgence in them. There is psycholinguistic evidence to indicate that both senses of an ambiguity are activated initially and resolved by contextual cues subsequently (Swinney, 1979). Where the context favours both, the most common meaning tends to be initially chosen (Rayner & Frazier, 1989). If the meanings are equally common, then the ambiguity may well persist without final resolution, as it does here. In terms of text world theory, the effect of such ambiguity may be described as giving rise to two possible text worlds at the same level – one where the delights are warned against, one where they are approved – and the reader is then forced to toggle between these, as no clear resolution emerges (for an example of text world theory in action, see McLoughlin, 2013; for an in-depth treatment, Gavins, 2007, is exemplary).

Such an analysis does what Fish asks and analyses the experiences of the reader as they attempt to make meaning in real time. Further, it offers the potential to include Fish's interpretive communities as part of the analysis. For example, those who view Milton as a devout and temperate man may settle on 'refraining from delights' as the meaning. Others, who perhaps view Milton primarily in terms of his beliefs in personal freedoms, may construct the meaning 'one should make time for delights'. Yet other readers, perhaps those who see Milton's closing lines as transferring judgment to the reader, may resist settling for one meaning and maintain both meanings as important and integral features of the text. However, readers are also capable of holding in mind these three possible intentions without settling on a final choice. Such analysis demonstrates for the writing student the interplay between context and structure, and how different effects can be achieved or may be favored through manipulation of the relationship between the structural features of language and what is allowed into context and what is withheld. This provides a principled way to examine and explain the interpretive moves the reader carries out in terms of different sets of cognitive processes and their relation to the linguistic structure.

Contextual knowledge is processed along with lexical meanings and syntactic structure in order to generate the overall meaning of the text. The meaning generated can and does change as the reader encounters the words in series. A classic example of this occurs in certain reduced relative clauses, such as 'The horse raced past the barn fell', where one meaning is constructed up until 'barn' but a new meaning must be constructed when one encounters 'fell'. This typically results in a need to go back and reanalyze. There are also texts that withhold sense – nonsense verse, for example, even where it is syntactically regular, such as 'Jabberwocky' (Carroll, 1871). We cannot claim to make *sense* of them, because even though the structure is capable of making sense, the words that are strung on the structure lack lexical meaning. Sense is also difficult to make where meaningful words are combined on an 'illegal' structure, such as 'fell past raced the pig the cow'.

Fish's argument that intention is known as soon as it is recognized, and it is recognized when sense is made, and sense is made as soon as possible

(Fish, 1980a: 164), is in line with psycholinguistic theory. Research has shown that initial sense is made as soon as the (perceived) structures afford closure; that this may be influenced by expectation and prior context; and that reanalysis occurs if there is later found to be an irresolvable conflict with subsequent contextual or linguistic cues (Rayner *et al.*, 1983; Tanenhaus *et al.*, 1989; Taraban & McClelland, 1988). The experimental data support the idea that different senses and meanings can emerge in temporal series and change as the text is presented. This can be exemplified by an analysis of another example Fish uses, which focuses on a structural ambiguity, which again is situated at a line break, this time in Milton's 'On the late massacre at Piedmont':

> Their martyred blood and ashes sow
> O'er all the Italian fields where still doth sway
> The triple Tyrant: that from these may grow
> A hundredfold, who having learnt thy way
> Early may fly the Babylonian woe.
> (In Fish, 1980a: 153)

The structural ambiguity here is whether the adverb 'early' acts to modify 'learnt' or 'fly'. The former will imply a meaning that those brought up in faith may escape the coming woe, while the latter will imply that those who have seen what God is capable of will flee quickly from his wrath. Because of the introduction of the line break, the latter meaning is initially constructed because the eyes need to perform a longer 'return sweep saccade' (Liversedge & Findlay, 2000: 10) back across the line, allowing time for 'who having learnt thy way' to be activated as a unit of sense, and because readers know that lines of poetry often function as a unit of sense, the adverb is initially assigned to the following sense unit, modifying the verb 'fly'. Reanalysis may also take place because part of the contextual knowledge about the author conflicts with this reading.

Such structural ambiguities afford different interpretive communities the opportunity to construct different readings, depending on contextual knowledge and personal beliefs about the nature of God, or beliefs about what poems are meant to do. It is possible to use cognitive stylistic analysis to help understand and explain the cognitive processes the reader uses in order to make meaning from the utterance, and to suggest possible ways in which different interpretive communities may construct different meanings from the text, and how these may be preferentially accessed and why. It is interesting that in the example above 'thy way' can be understood as meaning how God has treated the Waldensians. However, Fish argues:

'This is not the conclusion we carry away' (1980a: 154). An interesting question which may be raised at this point is: who is the 'we' in this instance? It appears that Fish assumes we all belong to the same interpretive community at that point, possibly because certain biases and cultural and autobiographical knowledge related to Milton are being assumed in the reader of 'Interpreting the *Variorum*'.

Reading as a poet, I 'realize' – to use Fish's parlance (1980a: 161) – Milton's intention as using the line break in order to play off the afforded meanings in both poems. Because the reader must perform a longer saccade across the line break, it is a useful place for a poet to insert structural or lexical ambiguities. At the line break, while the longer saccade is in progress, to reach the start of the next line, the reader will have longer to process the information to that point, and thus the reader will be forced to hold active any ambiguity, at least until after the saccade is complete, and new information is added.

Students of creative writing (particularly poets in this instance), having been made aware of these effects, and the ways in which they can influence how they use their line breaks, stanza breaks and other pauses, may be encouraged to usefully apply this knowledge to purposefully experiment with likely cognitive effects in the reader, as a deliberate artistic strategy within their work. In the case of prose writers, perhaps, switches between alternate plot-lines or for dramatists changes between speakers and scenes might provide opportunities to use space and pauses in equivalent ways. Cognitive stylistic analysis also provides an appropriate theoretical framework and a set of vocabulary which can be used by students to discuss the use of craft for certain cognitive effects when contextualizing their work in the critical commentaries which tend to accompany assignments.

Fish's notion of interpretive communities has received just criticism for not being fully explained, in terms of either the origin of interpretive communities or how they may change (Toolan, 1990: 130). The fact that a collection of individuals will engage in readings which are stable 'because they will see (and by seeing make) everything in relation to that community's assumed purposes and goals' (Fish, 1980c: 15) is problematic, because, as the human sciences have shown us, human beings tend to vary across a statistical distribution (and not always a normal distribution) with regard to almost every measurable quality in terms of perception and belief. So, at the very least, such communities must be 'radial categories', with individuals varying across a number of different axes. It may be that most individuals may be classified as belonging to more than one interpretive community; and it is possible to expand the notion to include an interpretive community of 'English-speakers' who interpret utterances as arising from the structures that exist for them; who have developed and use strategies to 'decode' these perceived structures; and who draw socially agreed denotations and connotations from them. It could further be argued that such an interpretive community is constructed through the processes related to language acquisition, such as phoneme recognition, the development of word boundary recognition and parsing competence.

Interpretive communities may develop from training or political views. Fish gives one clear example of this where he refers to those readers who impose a 'Christian exegesis' on texts (1980a: 170). Perhaps some of the most easily identifiable interpretive communities are those who construct resistant or politicized readings of texts from particular perspectives, such as feminist or Marxist readers. However, there will also be significant individual and sub-group variation within these radial categories. As Sara Mills (1992) demonstrates, it is possible to belong to more than one; or to sit in the radial space between two or more; or to construct a new interpretive community out of elements of others.

Mills' reading of John Fuller's poem 'Valentine' (quoted in full in Mills, 1992: 195–197) demonstrates how two very different interpretations may be constructed from the same text. Mills chose to analyze the poem because it caused a polarized discussion along gender lines when it was taught at a summer school she attended. Most of the males, she reports, found it humorous and read the poem according to what she says is its dominant reading: that of a light-hearted address from the poet to the object of his affection which uses innuendo and playful images. However, the females felt more angered by the poem, perhaps because it invites a reading from a perspective of male power and objectifies the female. Mills uses a Marxist feminist contextualized stylistic approach to analyze the poem, through which she produces a reading which in many respects runs directly counter to the dominant one, and in which she demonstrates the potential within the language for much more ambiguity and, through that, its affordance of a very sinister reading indeed.

In part, this is generated by the images that Fuller uses. For example, the voice of the poem talks of having the object of his desire in his power, and seeing her eyes dilate. The dominant reading reads the dilation of the pupils as being due to desire, but the pupil of the eye also dilates when one is afraid, so the potential exists to read against the dominant account and the contextual knowledge affords a more sinister possibility. This is not the only image in the poem that affords this ambiguity. The object of the speaker's affection is visualized being chased up a tower screaming and being made to cower. The dominant reading is taken to be that such 'violence' is merely playful, but the potential exists for it to be read (as Mills does) to signify the wish to frighten and subjugate the object of desire and to have power over her.

What such analysis demonstrates for the writing student is that intention is not fixed and, as Fish says, is 'realized' by the reader, and can be 'realized' according to the reader's particular reading strategy (and the political context of their reading), and that the language affords such constructions of perceived intention and meaning through its heavy dependences on the context or contexts within which the utterance is perceived by the reader to occur. This is might be particularly said of literary critics, who are trained to foreground what may be backgrounded, or unconscious in the text; and by being aware of this, writers may be more sophisticated readers and more in control of how their 'intent' might be 'realized'.

However, interpretive communities need not be so clearly marked. Fish (1980a: 168) outlines two interpretive presuppositions for his reading of 'Lycidas': that the reader is familiar with both Milton and pastoral poems. However, if the text is presented as a completely anonymized text to someone unfamiliar with it, the reader will still be able to extract much of the same basic meaning from it, even though their reading may not be quite as rich, because there are things that will be missing from their background and contextual knowledge.

A similar example of how differing cultural knowledge may lead to different 'realizations' of a poem may be given with regard to Seamus Heaney's 'Mid-term break' (Heaney, 1998: 12). In the poem, a large number of white things are mentioned: snowdrops, ambulances (white with a red cross), nurse's uniforms, bandages and candles. However, a Northern Irish Catholic will know that, traditionally, young children are buried wearing a white shroud, in coffins lined with white material. In the case of very young children, the coffin itself is also white. So, when those who possess that specific cultural knowledge read the poem, the overpowering image is complete whiteness except for the poppy bruise and the red cross on the ambulance. Many people will share the knowledge related to the ambulances, nurses, candles and bandages but not the shroud, coffin and lining. They may picture the child in a suit, or a uniform, and picture a brown coffin. There is nothing in the linguistic structure of the text to indicate the color of the coffin or the burial clothes; it depends entirely on the contextual knowledge. Readers from these different communities are constructing different texts from exactly the same utterance.

These differences can be explained by cognitive stylistics in terms of the mental picture evoked by the interaction of cognitive processes and cultural contextual knowledge in each case, thereby providing ways of understanding how interpretive communities may originate and change. Text world theory, for example, could therefore be used to describe the differences in the text worlds constructed by each reader. In this example above, the two text worlds constructed will be populated by subtly different world-building elements. The aim is not to merely identify that different readers construct different meanings; we know that they do. The aim is to identify the factors that influence that, and find cognitive models which can explain how it happens. Such models may help the student better understand how readers construct meaning, and the mechanisms through which the construction of meaning may be influenced by the linguistic choices of the writer.

When discussing how interpretive communities are made up, Fish seems to fall into the trap of which he accuses others – that of flattening the text. The temporal dimension that Fish so prioritized in the early part of the essay seems to have been overlooked. Fish gives no consideration to the various points within the temporal processing of the text when the interpretations begin to diverge and how readers find themselves moving into different interpretive communities over the course of the textual utterance and why that might happen. This leads to my main argument with Fish, especially in relation to the 'cruxes' he analyses: why should we read a text roughly the same way up until an ambiguity and then suddenly find ourselves in different 'interpretive communities' if the linguistic structure itself (socially constructed or not) did not afford such differentiation? There seems to be no dispute among readers with regard to the vast majority of meanings, and even where there are cruxes that afford choices of meaning, readers must recognize the choices of meaning available in order to choose between them. Psycholinguistics suggests that one possibility for readers settling on a preferred interpretation is the varying contextual weights each reader may give, dependent on their experiences and viewpoint, to the meanings afforded by the perceived structure.

In the preceding arguments and analyses it has been demonstrated that stylistics is capable of foregrounding the temporal aspects of texts and foregrounding the reader's experience of making and choosing meanings. Even if readers construct the 'structures' rather than the structures being 'real', one can still use cognitive stylistics to analyze these agreed 'structures' and how they give rise to meaning(s), even if one has to begin by acknowledging the fact that they are constructed using perceptual and interpretive strategies. Given that Fish acknowledges that there is an author 'hazarding projection' (1980a: 173) and that projection, since it takes the form of an utterance, must have some linguistic structure, 'real' or socially constructed, from which members of a language community are capable of creating meaning(s), then stylistics can accommodate Fish's view as one which does not lie outside its disciplinary aims. This is expressed by Stockwell as:

a rigorous account of reading that is both individual and social, and genuinely recognises the text as an intersubjective phenomenon and the literary work as a product of craftedness and readerly cognition. (Stockwell, 2002b: 92)

This accommodation is particularly useful to creative writing students in that it allows a way of analyzing and contextualizing the perceived 'authorial projection' in terms of its 'realized intention', thereby acknowledging the cooperative venture entailed in making text, and the complex relationship between writers, readers and writers as readers, while also drawing on pre-existing literary, cognitive and linguistic frameworks, which can inform such discussions, and place them within a theoretical context.

Exploration

(1) Cognitive stylistics may prove useful to creative writers because it offers a set of theories and models through which it is possible to understand the cognitive strategies of the reader and different ways of reading.

(2) Models such as text world theory can provide a detailed examination of cognitive effects engendered by linguistic structures and their effects on the reader in real time.

(3) Cognitive stylistics may offer insights into the ways in which interpretive communities are formed and operate.

(4) It can also offer an alternative view that can account for tolerance of ambiguities and readers reading from the viewpoint of several interpretive communities simultaneously.

(5) This is useful to the student writer because, through learning how language structure influences readers' cognitive models of the text, they can learn to manipulate those structures and thereby the reader's cognitive processes.

(6) Fish's realization of the 'author hazarding projection' and the 'realization of the author's intent' can influence emergent creative writing theory that seeks to focus on the experience and strategies of both writer and reader.

(7) Focus on the cognitive processes engendered through the processing of text can also suggest some interesting new exercises for textual production that can be used to teach students about language structure and creative textual structuring.

References

Carroll, L. (1871) Jabberwocky. In *The Complete Works of Lewis Carroll* (p. 153). New York: Modern Library (1936).

Cook, G. (1994) *Discourse and Literature: The Interplay of Form and Mind*. Oxford: Oxford University Press.

Fauconnier, G. and Turner, M. (2002) *The Way We Think: Conceptual Blending and the Mind's Hidden Complexities*. New York: Basic Books

Fish, S.E. (1976) Interpreting the *Variorum*. *Critical Inquiry* 2 (3), 465–485.

Fish, S.E. (1979) What is stylistics and why are they saying such terrible things about it? Part II. *boundary* 28 (1), 129–146.

Fish, S.E. (1980a) Interpreting the *Variorum*. In *Is There a Text in This Class? The Authority of Interpretive Communities* (pp. 147–173). Cambridge, MA: Harvard University Press.

Fish, S.E. (1980b) Interpreting 'Interpreting the *Variorum*'. In *Is There a Text in This Class? The Authority of Interpretive Communities* (pp. 174–180). Cambridge, MA: Harvard University Press.

Fish, S.E. (1980c) Introduction or how I stopped worrying and learned to love interpretation. In *Is There a Text in This Class? The Authority of Interpretive Communities* (pp. 1–21). Cambridge, MA: Harvard University Press.

Fish, S.E. (1995) What is stylistics and why are they saying such terrible things about it? In J.J. Weber (ed.) *The Stylistics Reader: From Roman Jakobson to the Present* (pp. 94–116). London: Routledge.

Ganong, W.F. (1980) Phonetic categorization in auditory word perception. *Journal of Experimental Psychology: Human Perception and Performance* 6 (1), 110–125.

Gavins, J. (2007) *Text World Theory: An Introduction*. Edinburgh: Edinburgh University Press.

Heaney, S. (1998) Mid-term break. In *Opened Ground: Poems 1966–1996* (p. 12). London: Faber and Faber.

Johnson, E.K. and Jusczyk, P.W. (2001) Word segmentation by 8 month olds: when speech cues count more than statistics. *Journal of Memory and Language* 44 (4), 548–567.

Lakoff, G. and Johnson, M. (1989) *Metaphors We Live By*. Chicago, IL: Chicago University Press.

Lakoff, G. and Turner, M. (1989) *More Than Cool Reason: A Field Guide To Poetic Metaphor*. Chicago, IL: Chicago University Press.

Liversedge, S.P. and Findlay, J.M. (2000) Saccadic eye movements and cognition. *Trends in Cognitive Sciences* 4 (1), 6–14.

McLoughlin, N. (2013) Negative polarity in Eavan Boland's 'The famine road'. *New Writing: The International Journal for the Practice and Theory of Creative Writing* 10 (2), 219–227.

Mills, S. (1992) Knowing your place: A Marxist feminist stylistic analysis. In M. Toolan (ed.) *Language, Text and Context* (pp. 182–205). London: Routledge.

Paton, F. (2000) Beyond Bakhtin: Towards a cultural stylistics. *College English* 63 (2), 166–193.

Rayner, K. and Frazier, L. (1989) Selection mechanisms in reading lexically ambiguous words. *Journal of Experimental Psychology: Learning, Memory, and Cognition* 15 (5), 779–790.

Rayner, K., Carlson, M. and Frazier, L. (1983) The interaction of syntax and semantics during sentence processing: eye movements in the analysis of semantically biased sentences. *Journal of Verbal Learning and Verbal Behaviour* 22 (3), 358–374.

Smith, B.H. (1978) *On the Margins of Discourse: The Relation of Literature to Language.* Chicago, IL: University of Chicago Press.

Stockwell, P. (2002a) *Cognitive Poetics: An Introduction.* London: Routledge.

Stockwell, P. (2002b) Miltonic texture and the feeling of reading. In E. Semino and J.V. Culpepper (eds) *Cognitive Stylistics: Language and Cognition in Text Analysis* (pp. 73–94). Amsterdam: John Benjamins.

Summerfield, Q. (1981) Articulating rate and perceptual constancy in phonetic perception. *Journal of Experimental Psychology: Human Perception and Performance* 7 (5), 1074–1095.

Swinney, D.A. (1979) Lexical access during sentence comprehension: (Re)consideration of context effects. *Journal of Verbal Learning and Verbal Behavior* 18, 545–569.

Tanenhaus, M.K., Carlson, G.N. and Trueswell, J.C. (1989) The role of thematic structure in interpretation and parsing. *Language and Cognitive Processes* 4, 211–234.

Taraban, R. and McClelland, J.L. (1988) Constituent attachment and thematic role assignment in sentence processing: Influences of content-based expectations. *Journal of Memory and Language* 27 (6), 597–632.

Toolan, M. (1995) Stylistics and its discontents: Or getting off the Fish 'hook'. In J.J. Weber (ed.) *The Stylistics Reader: From Roman Jakobson to the Present* (pp. 117–135). London: Routledge.

Turner, M. (1987) *Death Is the Mother of Beauty: Mind, Metaphor, Criticism.* Chicago, IL: Chicago University Press.

Werker, J.F. and Lalonde, C.E. (1988) Cross-language speech perception: Initial capabilities and developmental change. *Developmental Psychology* 24 (5), 349–355.

Werth, P. (1999) *Text Worlds: Representing Conceptual Space in Discourse.* Harlow: Longman.

Chapter 8

Movement, Maps, Mnemonics and Music: Teaching Fiction and Poetry Writing Using Sight and Sound

Gail Pittaway

Literary terminology is littered with visual and aural references but so often in the teaching of writing or the analysis of texts, attention is placed more on the cerebral than on the sensual elements of language. We refer to an image in analysis, but the critical process of identification blocks our ability to recognize the visual range of the meaning of a word. We note the 'music' of a line of poetry, but lose the rhythm and color of a stanza in the disinterment of its parts.

In my teaching of creative writing in New Zealand for the last 20 years, a great deal of time has been spent in getting my students to see what is great about great writing. Have I done them a disservice in only introducing them to the canon? I have included reading and research components in their assessments, in recognition of the value I place on extending their knowledge and range, and they have produced thoroughly beautiful work for me to read. But sometimes this has not been enough to achieve better writing results, and even I have become bored with being clever and well read. Sometimes we simply need to rediscover play, to delight in more unexpected ways into writing, to extend our boundaries and stretch the membrane of our imaginations.

Over the last few years I have been working to introduce more experiential, even sensory elements as stimulus materials to the creative writing classroom. Having begun my working life in the secondary school system, the context of my work is now within the tertiary sector, teaching creative writing within a Bachelor of Media Arts degree, at all levels of a three-year degree, in a polytechnic in New Zealand's fourth largest city, Hamilton. My students are in the communication stream and planning to major in journalism, public relations, advertising or moving image. For some electives, these students are joined by photography, music, painting and sculpture and graphic design students. We also offer postgraduate, project-based qualifications, an honors program and a Master of Arts. In all this teaching I have increasingly felt like one of those lonely monks or abbesses of the Dark Ages, upholding the Lindisfarne of learning, protecting the endangered manuscripts of the canon from the barbarian at the door. This was a justified stance to take in the days before technology dominated education. Then I was educating students in the Great Tradition, as well as using the readings as model texts to inspire student writing, essentially using a literary approach to knowledge transmission.

That all changed as the next shift was made in the academy. Creative writing occurred in computer laboratories, online, virtually or as a mixture of both. Technology is now irrevocably a part of the landscape of learning and while it makes opportunities for writing easy to arrange, and provides structures and models for the students to follow and experiment with – such as the A4 page, email, Word documents and PowerPoint presentations – it also provides unnecessary distraction and encourages a minimalist approach to the written text. Word counts, assessment amounts and time allocations are all measured out in linear, temporal ways that are not always conducive to creativity. Students are writing, oh yes; but is it worth the time spent on the process? As Deleuze and Guattari (1996: 49) might ask, where is the 'chaosmos'? When confronted with a blank screen, as opposed to a blank page, the temptation is now to click over to Facebook and check in with the peer group, rather than work toward creating ever more beautiful syntax.

Faced with a student body with an increasing ignorance of the canon but a growing range of technical skills, it seemed timely to adjust the overtly reader/writer approach, which was becoming frustrating to manage, and to attempt to diversify both the content and delivery of the creative writing class, building on several strategies and stimulus activities which had worked in the past. In addition, I researched ways of enhancing the students' writing opportunities by giving them prompts which were not literary but more varied in sensory and intellectual appeal. At all levels, the students still have to produce a portfolio of original writing but do so now in response to a wider range of opportunities to write, such as responding to music, drawing maps, looking into or out of paintings and photographs by altering the point of view or perspective, or simply moving – from going outside to getting on buses, or walking down the high street to an art gallery or museum. This changed approach has had a beneficial effect not only on classroom atmosphere – now one of expectation and anticipation – but also on invigorating the students' writing, my own teaching, theoretical reading and even my own writing. At the end of this chapter, in 'Exploration', I will share some of the ideas and activities which seemed to work with my classes. I have been grateful for the cooperation of my writing students in allowing me to use their work and to participate in focus groups about their writing.

Learning Theories and Styles

From a theoretical point of view, creative writing intersects with a variety of models: sociological, biological, educational, cognitive, cultural, aesthetic, creative and ludic. Writing is in itself both a physical act and a by-product of cognition. As Susan Stewart notes in her extended essay *On Longing*, 'Handwriting is to space what the voice is to time…. Writing contaminates; it leaves its trace beyond the life of the body' (Stewart, 1993: 7).

Those of us who are writers as well as educators know that, like teaching, writing is itself a site of learning, at times painstakingly physical, not fast enough to keep up with the mind, at others pure joy in the play of discovery.

In the latter part of the 20th century, Dewey (*Experience and Education*, 1963), Piaget (*The Origin of Intelligence in the Child*, 1953) and Vygotsky (*Thought and Language*, 1962) all contributed to our awareness that learning is a multifaceted process, arising through the biological development of the brain, with social interaction and physical experience. Deleuze and Guattari developed a theory of qualitative multiplicities (Deleuze & Guattari, 1987: 30), which has been developed and adapted by educationalists as a theory of multiple literacies, where knowledge acquisition is deemed to happen in many ways, simultaneously (Masny & Cole, 2009: 2–4). More recently, a theory of multi-literacy, sometimes called the New Literacy Studies, focuses more on the acquisition of technical skills for learners – their versatility with media in particular (Kress & van Leuwen, 2001).

In teacher training today, three important theories of learning dominate. One is Kolb's theory of experiential learning, from which the other two concepts developed. Kolb (1984: 41) identified two contrasting processes for learning from experience – thinking and watching – with levels developing through concrete experience, reflective observation, leading to abstract conceptualization and active experimentation. The interactions and combinations of these elements of learning, occurring not necessarily in that order, give rise to the four main styles of learning he describes as diverging, assimilating, converging and accommodating.

From Kolb's basis, two more recent developments are applicable to teaching older learners. VARK theory recognizes that all students have differing learning tendencies – visual, aural, reader–writer or kinesthetic styles, which can also be described as active, reflective, theoretical or pragmatic learning styles (Fleming & Mills, 1992). The other is Lazear's 'Eight ways of knowing', which asserts that eight basic multiple intelligences are: verbal/linguistic, intrapersonal, interpersonal, naturalistic, visual/spatial, bodily/kinesthetic, logic/maths and musical/rhythmic (Lazear, 1999). To this list Gardner (1999) has added a ninth intelligence: existential, being the capacity to think deeply about questions of human existence.

Yet most of the teaching and learning in the academy occur with the focus upon reading and writing, including for creative studies and practice.

Social Theories

Social and cultural theorists have popularized a generational approach to learning in Western culture: the Seniors before 1925; the Builders, 1925–50; the Boomers, 1951–64; and then Generations X, 1965–80, Y, 1981–94, Z, 1995–2009, and now Alpha, or α, since 2010. As with astrology, those whose births fall between divisions are described as being on the cusp (McCrindle, 2010). As an aside, one unexpected result of the Christchurch earthquake in 2010 is that many statistical figures for New Zealand are dated before 2009 in contemporary data research, as Christchurch was the base for the national census agency. In 2009, Generations Y and Z made up 30% of the populations of New Zealand and Australia (McCrindle, 2010: 1). Generation Alpha (α) or that 1% of the population born since 2010, will only increase the trends for earning and learning of its antecedents. Each generation will be technically educated to a higher level than previous generations from 1900 up to 1980. The world experiences of the Generations Y, Z and upcoming Alpha are or will be dominated by the internet, cable television, globalization and environmental awareness, along with notions of cultural and religious tolerance. Peer opinions or trends are identified as the dominant influences for the later generations, of Y and Z, as opposed to the respect for authority of the Builders' generation, or respect for data and facts of the Boomers (McCrindle, 2010: 2); for the Alpha generation it is a little too early to summarize the trends, apart from technology and globalization.

Taking all of this into account, then, it became clear to me that I was a perpetrator of a major generation gap, and that the application of more varied approaches to teaching creative writing seemed an educational imperative. So what were some of the strategies, new or emboldened, that were used in these classes and, importantly, did they effect any changes in classroom management, productivity or quality of writing? What other effects were there from shifting away from what I used to do, to making changes, apart from the point that it was certainly more fun for me, the teacher?

The Classroom Environment: The Site of Learning

The most important single alteration I made was very simple: we changed rooms. If you were to go into a primary school classroom on any working day, you would be overwhelmed by the variety of stimuli presented: every possible wall, board or window is festooned with color, words, posters, collages. In secondary schools, the classrooms have become more specialized and the emphasis is perhaps more on charts, posters or maps, but it is still visually stimulating. In tertiary institutions, however, creative writing classes are called generic and are put into generic classrooms, or generic computer laboratories, where students might encounter a fire drill poster as the most vibrant piece of artwork adorning the walls. Here, the concept of the site of learning, that intersection between educator, learner and the discipline, is treated as a functional one, usually determined by a functional officer – usually the department secretary liaising with the time-tabling committee. It is often out of the hands of the educator to choose or manage this site.

Over the last two years, my second-year writing class (which develops writing in memoir, poetry and short fiction) has been housed in a large computer laboratory in an open-plan space that is shared with a drop-in center for the graphic design students. We are lucky to have a computer laboratory for editing, but with so many students bringing laptops to class perhaps this was not the most suitable place to work. With computers and a printer in the room, the focus is likely to be on product or production but, after all, two-thirds of the class time will be more about process, while in a workshop environment critique, discussion and reflection must also have their place. Furthermore, having design students urgently printing out their typographical projects is not conducive to supporting a student who has never written a poem before, reading out one on personal grief, or another reading from a short story on taking to prostitution to pay off the student loan – items to be shared in an atmosphere of trust or at least one free of interruption!

Movement

It seemed a matter of urgency, in the first place, to change the site where the creative writing class happened, to make it safe from interruption or disruption, flexible enough for silence, reflection or discussion. So we moved to what was usually a meeting room, with no computer but a range of plain tables that could be arranged in a central boardroom format or separated; the doors led to a small courtyard and so no other classes moved past. Another bonus of this was that the meeting room was often used for lunch meetings, and there would sometimes be a plate of fresh sushi left over, or of chocolate brownies, or one day plates of sandwiches and cake. In an act of unashamed opportunism I allowed everyone to eat – but only one thing at a time and then to write about each, using 'sweet' and 'savory' as prompts. This didn't generate many memorable pieces of writing but certainly improved teacher–student and student–student relations early in the course.

Here is an excerpt from one piece of 'savory' writing from a student I shall call Morag, from that exercise:

'What's an indoor picnic without cucumber sandwiches?' The shrill voice of my brother's fiancée rang through the hall. 'What do you mean there's no cucumber? How are we supposed to have sandwiches without cucumber?' As if she could hardly believe we were still confined to the use of ration books from week to week.

'Let us not forget that we are in the midst of a famine, my dear.' My brother rested his arm affectionately around her shoulders then led her away. Always the bearded voice of reason, my brother.

We are timetabled for one four-hour class a week, which has given plenty of time for outings, viewings, writing discussions and afternoon tea, with individual drafting and editing usually occurring in the last hour or sometimes two. Without simply presenting a list, I'd like to offer ideas on some of the most successful activities for developing content as well as inspiration for the class. At the time of writing, this project is ongoing, with more classes to work with later in the year, and over summer school. But from the small group in semester 1 in 2013, and classes in semester 2 in 2012, it's clear that the application of movement, music and mnemonics to creative writing has been successful in getting students writing with energy and imagination.

Another move that proved productive was to go on field trips, in particular to see exhibitions of painting and photography. As Professor Jeri Kroll said in a keynote address at the 2009 conference of the Australasian Association of Writing Programmes, there are 'multiple sites of knowledge hidden within the allusive world of ekphrastic writing' (writing in response to paintings) (Kroll, 2010). She looked closely at W.H. Auden's response to the Bruegel painting *The Fall of Icarus* in his poem 'Musée e des Beaux Arts' and also referred to Graeme Harper's 2007 discussion of the 1840 Danhauser painting of Franz Liszt performing to an audience, which explores the generative interaction between music, painting and audience (Harper, 2007: 93–96).

'White Cloud Worlds' (see www.whitecloudworlds.com) was an exhibition of fantasy, science fiction and speculative painting and design, curated by one of the leading artists of the Weta Workshop stable in Wellington – the designers of costumes, landscapes and props for Peter Jackson's two trilogies of films *Lord of the Rings* and *The Hobbit*. A touring exhibition of such work offered a chance to introduce not only a visual dimension to writing but also images that were strongly narrative in nature, or revealed strong points of view. Students were issued with a response sheet on which to jot down or sketch immediate responses. What is happening? What has just happened or is about to happen? To whom? About what? Two of the strongest efforts came from responses to images of women – one mysteriously masked, the other a pure heraldic image of a woman warrior, which elicited a long prose piece which began in this way:

> The world spins for a few seconds as I struggle to regain my bearings. It is impossible to see anything through the thickness of the smoke and heat of the battle. All I can see are the bodies of my men and their horses strewn in front of me.
>
> Suddenly in the distance I see a pillar of light streaming down from above. Silhouetted against this bright light is the dark figure of a man in full body armour astride a magnificent black stallion his red standard flapping in the breeze.

The student, Helena, later commented, 'I was surprised by the way this story came out – I don't usually like action stories or fantasy but the title of the painting, Valour, and the woman with sword and armour just made it happen'. Interestingly, another field trip was to another exhibition, this time of photographs by the photojournalist Brian Brake, which was less successful in evincing imaginative work – the realism was too explicit. However, as an exercise in point of view writing, it was worth the short excursion.

Memory, Maps and Other Images

A strategy that I've used before is to get students to draw a map of a place they know well, from memory, from at least three years ago (at 19 or so they are so young that it seems like a long time ago, when so many of them were still at school). Then they can either write a story or write down a list of possible stories they associate with the subject of the map. My favorite story from this year's class, and never told before, was from Thomas, who drew the floor plan of his secondary school, a Roman Catholic school, then wrote a true story of how he and two school mates were nearly expelled for blasphemy. As altar boys they abused their privilege by regularly breaking into the tabernacle which housed the Host biscuits intended for use in the Mass and snacking on them. One of the boys even brought cheese to eat with the biscuits but they realized the store was dwindling and so eventually confessed before they were discovered. It was the map exercise which drew this memory out.

I'll share a few more exercises using images. One that I have refined came first from New Zealand poet Lauris Edmond, who used to encourage people at workshops to remember photographs and write from them. I get my students to bring photographs to use, then work through a sensory-based diagram (Figure 1, top left) of recollection and collection of memories and insights based on what is in the photograph as well as its context, in time, place, even history (Figure 1, bottom).

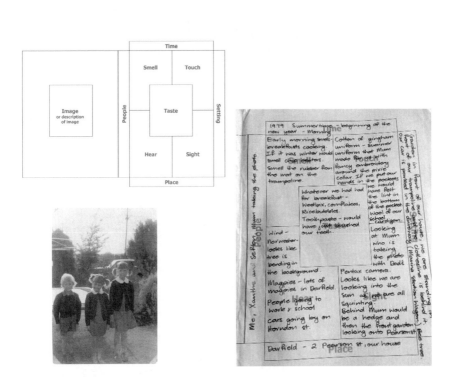

Figure 1 Writing from a photograph. Students used a photograph to prompt sensory memories, to form the basis for a piece of writing, the plan for which is shown top left

Another exploration of image with intertextuality comes from another New Zealand poet, Michael Harlow, who encouraged participants at workshops to superimpose elements of nature, such as leaves, stones or flowers, over existing poems, then mine the vocabulary that is contained and write a new piece using only those words. One that suits the time of year of my poetry class is to use autumn leaves over poems about autumn. Figure 2 illustrates the technique with John Keats' 'Ode to Autumn'.

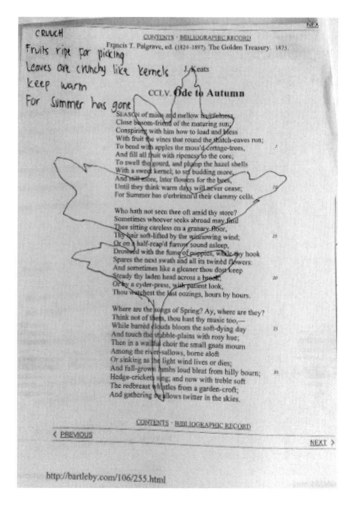

Figure 2 Intertextuality – leaf molding

Here's a draft from Katrina, who used an autumn leaf placed over William Blake's 'To autumn':

The sun runs in the morning's veins
The thrilling song of summer roves
Singing of the air, her joy.

Now the bright sunlight breaks
The clouds run forth;
The tune of her blood is in the autumn.

And my own offering from Keats' 'Ode to autumn':

Summer
Your store
Has run. Sleep now
With the mossed fruit
And think what wind-laden clouds
Will touch your skies.
Mourn where you watch
How the garden dies
And rest asleep a while.

Music

Music has been less successfully utilized in these classes, for several reasons. Listening and aural skills take more training and tend to be prejudiced to preferred genres and styles. One training task we tried was to listen to talk-back radio for about 15 minutes and then continue a monologue in the voice of one of the speakers. It was hard not to use clichés, we all agreed. Even when the class went to a lunchtime classical concert, a first for all of them, and with a 'blank page' instruction to respond to the experience, the responses were all about the audience, or the interplay between musicians. None were abstract responses to the sounds of the music. As a warm-up one day, I suggested everyone think of a song for which they could remember the tune and one verse and chorus, and then write a parody on a completely different topic, such as a friend's birthday or a political event. Even more fun, we sang them to each other – 'My head will grow warm', homage to a beanie hat, to the tune of 'My heart will go on' from the film *Titanic*, which just about brought the house down, closely followed by my own parody of

'Danny boy', about the leaders of our current National government, led by John Key, privatizing our main hydropower Might River Power, based in Huntly, just up the river from my home:

> Oh Johnny Boy, you've really blown it this time
> You've gone and sold our assets down the drain
> The winter's here and all the river's filling
> And in the meantime the power's on the wane.

Ludic Theory

Finally, this leads me to reflect on the importance of play in creativity, the ludic and mimetic elements, so often lost in the process as the learner matures (Kolb & Kolb, 2010). Party games such as 'Consequences' (see Exploration, point 9) or longer writing games such as writing a short story in three postcards, or playing Scrabble and then using the words generated on the board, all make writing fun. Also good starters are sending people out to eavesdrop in malls or on buses, and come back with three lines or concepts they overheard or observed, or to look at a building out of a window and construct a secret activity that occurs within. So, too, on a suitable day, is a bout of pareidolia (seeing shapes and signs in natural or man-made objects, such as cloud-gazing), writing mnemonics for other writers and themselves to remember, even something as simple as WED, 'write every day'; each of these could be offered as a warm-up but some turn into larger pieces or better pieces. Students still learn how much writing and rewriting must occur before a good idea becomes good writing.

There was an additional benefit to this multiple literacies experiment: the field trips with exposure to art, music, photography, the world of nature or the city around them were not activities that the majority of the students would have chosen for themselves. They tend to access music, movies, television, radio, news, weather through social networking sites such as Facebook, Tumblr and YouTube, giving them exposure to the dominant orthodoxy of popular culture in all its often facile faces. Against this new system, iterations of art or high culture are seen as complex, challenging, even subversive. We had not rejected the canon but refreshed it and introduced risk. The old can become the new. The dogged application of play, fun, food, movement, mnemonics, maps and music has been rewarding for all participants, so that Koestler's adage rings true:

> Creative activity could be described as a type of learning process where teacher and pupil are located in the same individual. (Koestler, 1964: 96)

Exploration

(1) Contemporary students tend to be visual and kinesthetic learners, rather than only reader/writer in style.

(2) Peer influences are a dominant trend for recent generations, who work happily with technology, also in collaborative and collective activities.

(3) Students learn through experience more effectively than reading about experience; there are multiple literacies to learning.

(4) Pay attention to where your class is writing; the space needs to be quiet enough for reflection, but have possibilities for you to make noise or move around.

(5) Use paintings or photographs as prompts for writing, and give students guiding questions to get them looking closely. Then invite them to write from inside the image. Or use poems as images and place leaves or hands over passages of text, to extract words and phrases to be rearranged.

(6) Use sound as a prompt – read together about John Cage's 1952 composition, 4'33", then experiment with listening to the sounds of silence. Or eavesdrop on passengers on buses, trains or customers in queues and use as scripts or dialogue.

(7) Play music to the class or invite students to bring music to listen to while they are writing, in response to the mood.

(8) Maps and plans are extremely useful. Use Google Earth to find places you have only heard of but never found before; or draw a map or floor plan of a place you know well and list the ideas for stories you recall.

(9) 'Consequences' is a party game where all participants are given a page of blank paper and something to write with. Each writes on one page to each prompt, then folds the page over and passes it along, so no one can read what has been written already, and all add a new prompt on a blank part of the page. Common prompts are: Name ... [person A]; Meets ... [person B]; At ... [a place]; Activity [what are they doing?]; Person A says ...; Person B says...; And the consequence is.... Then everyone reads out what is on the piece of paper in their hand.

(10) For experiments with found writing, use newspapers (photographs, headlines, classified or personal advertisements). Or read about constraint writing, for example *Damascus*, by Richard Beard, (2005), and attempt a short story using only one source.

References

Beard, R. (2005) *Damascus*. London: Vintage.

Deleuze, G. and Guattari, F. (1987) *A Thousand Plateaus: Capitalism and Schizophrenia*. London: Athlone Press.

Deleuze, G. and Guattari, F. (1996) *What Is Philosophy?* New York: University of Columbia.

Dewey, J. (1963) *Experience and Education*. New York: Collier.

Fleming, N. and Mills, C. (1992) Not another inventory, rather a catalyst for reflection. *To Improve the Academy* 11, 137–149.

Gardner, H. (1999) *Intelligence Reframed: Multiple Intelligences for the 21st Century*. New York: Basic Books.

Harper, G. (2007) Editorial. *New Writing: The International Journal for the Practice and Theory of Creative Writing* 4 (2), 94–95.

Koestler, A. (1964) *The Act of Creation*. London: Hutchinson.

Kolb, A. and Kolb, D. (2010) Learning to play, playing to learn: A case study of a ludic learning space. *Journal of Organizational Change Management* 23 (1), 26–50.

Kolb, D. (1984) *Experiential Learning: Experience as the Source of Learning and Development*. Upper Saddle River, NJ: Prentice Hall.

Kress, G. and van Leuwen, T. (2001) *Multimodal Discourse: The Modes and Media of Contemporary Communication*. London: Hodder and Arnold.

Kroll, J. (2010) Living on the edge: creative writers in education. *TEXT: Journal of Writing and Writing Courses* 14 (1).

Lazear, D. (1999) *Eight Ways of Knowing: Teaching for Multiple Intelligences*. Andover, MA: Skylight.

Masny, D. and Cole, D. (2009) *Multiple Literacies Theory: A Deleuzain Perspective*. Rotterdam: Sense Publishers.

McCrindle, M. (2010) *Engaging with Generations X and Y*. Parramatta: Australian Leadership Foundation.

Piaget, J. (1953) *The Origin of Intelligence in the Child*. New York: Routledge and Kegan Paul.

Stewart, S. (1993) *On Longing: Narratives of the Miniature, the Gigantic, the Souvenir, the Collection*. Durham, NC: Duke University Press.

Vygotsky, L. (1962) *Thought and Language*. Cambridge, MA: MIT Press.

Commentary 5

Don't Look Now: Exploring Smellscapes and Soundscapes Helps Writers-To-Be

Sieneke de Rooij

The Overpowering Visual Aspect

As a creative writing teacher, I often work with students taking their first course in creative writing. These newbies in the world of writing classes have frequently been writing for years, hiding their texts in their notebooks, too shy to show them to readers yet also utterly convinced of their own talent.

In many of their stories and poems, I've found they predominantly use descriptions of a visual nature. They write about color and texture, size and measurements, light and dark. They can tell you what their characters look like and what they wear, what their house and street look like, their workplace and their colleagues. The visual aspect is easily accessible to most people, and when you haven't been made aware of this writing automatism, you simply don't notice it in your text. In fact, the visual in texts by inexperienced writers can be so strong that I have come to believe that I can help them reach a deeper level in their writing by forcing them to use the sources of their other senses. I have to do this at an early stage of the course, or they risk settling firmly in their habit of writing mainly from the visual sense and neglecting the power of sound, smell, taste and touch (and emotional feeling).

So what happens when I tell my students to use all their senses except their vision and later, when writing, to write without any visual aspects? What does it do to them and their texts if they are forbidden to use their most accessible sense?

To help my students find more variation in their writing, I created some lessons and assignments in which I forbid any visual input from entering a text. (A hard task indeed, and most students subconsciously sneak in some color anyway, but if they try very hard the results are much better.) I put a ban on writing about anything that can be seen, and focus on smell and sound to access memories. These memories can later be used to write a family history or can they can be raw material for poetry and prose.

I choose to concentrate on smell and sound because of their undisputed power of projecting people into memories and physical recollections. (I am a great lover of smell and sound myself; it's hard for me to resist buying an old sleigh bell or a strange herb.) The process of working with smell and sound, prompted from reality and continued in imagination, leads to a completely different set of memories and experiences. The effect is that texts become much more varied and profound. These texts also have more impact on readers, which can be heard in the feedback rounds.

Smellscapes

I start a first workshop with the aid of my home-made Ol'Factory (in Dutch it's called the *Olfactotheek*, but the English name turns out to be more fun). This is a collection of smells with historical value to most people, which I use to help them to access memories. The Ol'Factory is a little suitcase filled with small jars. Each contains some 'stuff': fluids, grains, solid matter. Most cannot be recognized visually. The collection was created after an ample poll among students, relatives and other writers. All smells are powerful and unique. To name a few: a well known 'smell for elderly ladies' that remind people of their grannies instantly (in the Netherlands, this is 4711 or Maja soap); sherry; a particular brand of baby shampoo that everyone recognizes; *trassi*, a sharp and rather unpleasant-smelling ingredient of the Indonesian cuisine which is traditional in the Netherlands; cinnamon and nutmeg spice cake; copper polish; a classic old-fashioned aftershave that our fathers used in the 1950s and 1960s; a medicinal disinfectant odor; a sharpened pencil; and so on.

The jars are unmarked. My students go around in silence and smell. They do not have to determine the scents, just let themselves drift away in any memories or associations. I encourage them not to speak, but the jars do provoke a lot of laughter, sighs, nodding and scribbling. The fact that they don't have to know what they smell is liberating – it makes them free to pursue their own thoughts.

After that, they sit down in silence, and write in reaction to prompts I give them. I read at a slow pace, with time for note-taking, but not too much, to keep some pressure on:

A fresh scent, a sharp scent, an old scent, a new scent.
A scent from my childhood, a scent I never smell anymore, a scent belonging to grandma.

A white scent, the scent of an animal. A black scent, a grey scent.
A scent from another world; a scent from the future.
A scent I have forgotten, a scent I don't know. A scent that reminds me of....

Then they have a list, which they may quickly edit (in no more than three minutes).

Everyone reads their list out loud. Discussing our results afterwards, we are often surprised at some scents that seem important to several people – freshly mown grass, bread baking, apple pie, seashore – as well as some very personal, unique and interesting descriptions that emerge from this exercise. 'This is poetry already!' one of my students once remarked. How true. After that remark, we wrote titles for our lists. 'What I still miss' made a list into a poem. When we have worked the lists into new texts, usually some very original poetry emerges.

Soundscapes

Another great help in leading writers away from the visual aspect is the use of old, real-life sounds. My favorite collection is the Library of Vanished Sounds. The version in English is at http://www.nps.nl/nps/radio/supplement/99/soundscapes/bibliotheek (click on the WAV links). Many sounds are typically Dutch; others are more universal and some are British.

I give my students the assignment to stroll around in this Library and explore various sounds, then choose one to work into a short text about a main character who is confronted with this sound. (In Family History writing courses, they can use this exercise to write a scene for their own project.) Listening to sounds without seeing visual images brings you much deeper into the listening experience. Many people find this activity quite addictive and can hardly choose.

Students' new texts resulting from this assignment are interestingly different. Overall, writers as well as readers or listeners hear much more intensity in the text's atmosphere and much more emotion, both in reading aloud and in reading silently. Physical sensations such as goose-bumps are often reported. Readers can bring associations to mind much more easily. Feedback is more about emotions: melancholy, nostalgia, *Weltschmerz*. More readers experience physical sensations of fear, excitement, breathing, as their bodies react more to text where sound is strongly incorporated. Old car horns, steam whistles, planes taking off in the Second World War, the London Blitz, a teletype room and the auction master at top speed at the fish auction in Urk in 1936 can do that to you.

The texts themselves have a film-like impact, like in the opening scene of a movie that gently slides you into the story so easily or grabs you with great force.

Last but not least: writers report much more introspection during the writing process and more concentration while writing.

Working with sounds from real life (as opposed to musical inspiration) is an inspiration for students to continue to focus on sound and smell. (Of course, the same can be experienced with the sense of touch.) Some of my students presented me with new scents for the Ol'Factory and made me smell rifle grease and Brylcreem for the first time. And did you know that dead ladybirds give off a *very* specific odor?

Conclusion

To show rather than tell you about some of the results in my students' texts is complicated, as they have all been writing in Dutch. But I can give examples of what some of my students in a Family History writing project have been doing differently from before.

One woman wrote a scene about a walk in the dunes along the North Sea, using almost exclusively bird sounds to describe the experience of the main characters. She used some bird guides for the description of the sounds, to bring in a lot of variation.

'Daddy, daddy,' Wim cried. 'We heard the Ghost of the Dunes!'

And, indeed, the Dutch text really does make you hear ghosts in the dunes.

Another woman wrote about two people leaving on a ship. They have been waiting for a long time in the cold wind for the ship to leave, grabbing the icy railing. Eventually, the deck starts vibrating and at the same time the steam horn gives off a deafening, rumbling sound. Their bodies start trembling with excitement as they can feel their feet searching for new balance.

A third student describes a little girl, sitting under a staircase with her mother and little brother. All around them, things come crashing and crumbling down. Outside, noises change faster than she can understand. Inside, she hears her mother's voice, praying softly. And the neighbor is still playing his accordion.

The next story is about a boy and his mother on a train platform. He can see nothing; we understand that he is surrounded by legs, suitcases, coats. All the sounds echoing in this large railway station frighten him and his mother's voice cannot reassure him. The shrill whistle of the train about to leave makes him jump; a woman is crying for her child; planes fly over the station. 'Just keep close to me', his mother keeps repeating.

When we discussed these texts to give feedback, I asked my students to comment in two ways on the text read out loud: to describe to each writer what 'film' they saw in their mind, and to tell them about the voice they heard. All students commented on how much more feeling they had for the main characters, and how they felt they knew them very well already. Apparently this writing with a reduction in visuality, but entering the worlds of hearing, feeling and smelling, brought them all closer to the people and their lived experiences.

Then there is the great side-effect of association. Sounds and smells easily trigger memories of other sounds, smells, taste and experiences. So when we (in Amsterdam, looking at the historic windmill from my window) talk about windmills turning in a good breeze, we also start hearing children running on their clogs, on cobblestones. And the next moment you are smelling pea soup! This may sound like a cliché, but it is simply how the mind works.

After a few experiments in writing without the visual with quite different groups of students, I am convinced that we, as teachers, can help our students bring more depth to their work in this way. Sometimes I even throw in a sixth sense for fun, an idea which may open up whole new worlds of imagination.

I am sure that many of you have tried, but if not: take a fun risk and do compel your students from time to time to leave all this seeing alone and observe in different ways with other senses. Increased introspection in the writing process is, in my opinion, one of the most productive long-term effects. *Don't look now; come to your senses* is a fertilizer for writers who are just starting to work their land.

Chapter 9

Redesigning the Lecture in a Cyber World: A Creative Writing Case Study

Kevin Brophy and Elizabeth MacFarlane

It seems that universities are riding waves of government policy-driven and technology-driven change over which they have little control and whose outcomes are uncertain. The recent rise of massive open online courses (MOOCs), combined with a global eagerness for bringing subjects online or into blended physical–virtual environments, has the potential to change our practice of education, the conceptualization of the university, the academic workforce and the very architecture of university campuses.

In 2011, York University introduced 11 new blended courses (offered partly online via the internet or on social media and partly on campus through face-to-face teaching). It planned for 75 more, ranging from first-year to masters-level courses in 2013–14 (Dehaas, 2012: 54–55). York University is not unusual. Dehaas and others suggest that the possible consequences of shifting so much delivery of educational content online could be fewer senior lecturing positions and a growth of lower-level tutoring jobs (Wright, 2013: 38). It will almost certainly mean fewer large lecture theaters being built on campuses (Dehaas, 2012). The advent of MOOCs is alarming or an exciting impetus, depending on one's view.

But what exactly is a MOOC? Jon Baggaley, a British education psychologist, points out that there are many forms of MOOC and no single definition can encompass them. For instance, some commentators have distinguished between the cMOOC and the xMOOC, with the xMOOC based upon behaviorist learning principles and the cMOOC developed along more 'connectivist' or social approaches to learning (Liyanagunawardena *et al.*, 2013: 216). In essence, and with some cynicism, Baggaley writes that the point of commonality might be that 'MOOCs tend to be simpler and more impersonal than earlier forms of online education: no teachers, no supervisors, no fees or entry requirements' (Baggaley, 2013: 368).

There seems to be a natural fit between the entrepreneurial spirit of the MOOC and that ongoing experiment, often initiated by neo-conservative education policies, aimed at commodifying and commercializing tertiary education as a retail business (see Brown, 2013; McGettigan, 2013). New outsourcing businesses acting as proprietary providers of multimedia MOOC materials are fast appearing. Udacity was formed by a Stanford professor in February 2012, Coursera in April 2012 by two other Stanford computing professors, edX in May 2012 by Harvard University and the Massachusetts Institute of Technology. In Australia, the University of Melbourne was the first to adopt the Coursera model. With 10 subjects on offer, over 600 lectures videoed and more than 214,000 students enrolled, it looks to be an immediate and spectacular success, although one with no clear business plan (see http://le.unimelb.edu.au/moocs), and the usual low completion rates – less than 20% (Baggaley, 2013: 372).

In this swirling experimental environment, we continue to teach at the University of Melbourne. In our case, it is creative writing, a discipline that sits somewhere between the vocational-instructional or practice-based arena of tertiary education (e.g. law, medicine, engineering and mathematics) and the more critical, conceptual, developmental and cultural arena (art, litera-ture, philosophy, history, cultural studies, sociology). Creative writing as a tertiary education discipline moves, perhaps surprisingly easily, between constructivist theories of activity-based learning (Biggs & Tang, 2009: 19–21) and approaches that allow for the phenomenography of students' considered and altered perceptions of the world (Marton & Booth, 1997). At the University of Melbourne, we deploy a range of teaching methods in different classroom situations: there are some lectures to whole-subject cohorts, mainly delivering historical overviews, theoretical and cultural contexts, craft-based analysis, close readings of selected texts, or reflective talks and readings from experienced and well known writers; some subjects are delivered as seminars that combine mini-lectures, discussion of readings, and workshopping; there are tutorials where students apply critical frame-works and writerly concerns to selected texts; and there are workshops where students are guided through discussions of each other's work in progress. Characteristically, in our creative writing subjects students spend a lot of time talking with each other – connecting with each other.

It seems, then, that creative writing, as a discipline, should welcome the new virtual world, where words can be unlimited, communication can be instant, creativity can flow and the keyboard still reigns. It seems to be an opportunity to move away from the apparently tired old model of lecture and tutorial. Indeed, the virtual world has given rise to a new theory of learning, 'connectivism' (Siemens, 2009), which holds that learning is essentially distributed across networks and takes place through unrestricted nodes of connection between students. These networks in a virtual system can be so vast and complex and ever changing that no single student or teacher can hope to cover a whole 'curriculum'. Despite excitement around this new conception of learning, there is no clear evidence that the MOOC or that virtual learning spaces have opened us to a wholly new way of learning, or are effective educational tools. Noting that the developers of MOOCS are themselves computer scientists, not educators, Jon Baggaley writes: 'All that has really happened is that solid educational principles have been replaced by a mass communication model with very few principles' (Baggaley, 2013: 370).

MOOCs typically, for example, rely upon peer feedback and student-to-student commentary or discussion, in accord with new collaborative, connectivist versions of learning. However, when student-to-student interaction is unsupervised, and when the interaction is not framed by careful instructional design and clear goals, it can be educationally counterproductive. In their assessment of the success of CCK08, an early connectivist MOOC conducted through the University of Manitoba, Canada, Jenny Mackness and co-authors reported on the experiences of students invited to become 'autonomous' learners who found themselves set adrift in unstructured networks. Students complained of 'appalling [online] behaviour', 'patronising and teachery posts', 'trolling' and im-possible divides in expertise among students. They concluded that 'whilst connectedness was afforded by technology, it did not necessarily ensure interaction.... [T]he dynamics of connectivism are perceived [in this report] as both enablers and inhibitors of learning' (Mackness et al., 2010: 270).

The low completion rates that still bedevil the model might be largely due to students discovering fairly quickly that learning is not happening for them in this interconnected, massive, virtual world. In a recent literature review, Nikolaos Vernadakis reports that there is a large body of research showing students in online classes are less satisfied with their experience than are their 'traditional' colleagues (Vernadakis et al., 2012).

As these new electronic learning environments inevitably emerge and spread through education systems, the occasion of the live lecture (still an important part of our creative writing educational toolkit at the University of Melbourne) that once stood at the center of the academy now finds itself heading to the margins. Some commentators are breathing loud sighs of relief at the apparent demise of the lecture. 'The bitter truth', Moshe Vardi writes in a recent educational newsletter editorial, 'is that academic pedagogy has never been very good. It is well established that a professorial soliloquy is an ineffective way of teaching' (Vardi, 2012: 5). He pictures lecturers as self-important professors 'monologuing' to large classes. Karl Smart from Michigan University echoes many others in referring to 'a passive lecture model' (Smart *et al.*, 2012: 392), dependent on an expert teacher filling the minds of students with information. When we turn, however, to the difficult matter of evidence on whether lecturing is or is not educationally effective, the picture is not clear cut. In their study, for instance, Schwerdt and Wupperman reported on a comparison between mathematics teachers who adopted the traditional 'sage on the stage' approach and those who followed an in-class problem-solving small-group teaching style. They concluded:

> traditional lecture style teaching is associated with significantly higher student achievement. No support for detrimental effects of lecture style teaching can be found even when evaluating possible selection bias due to unobservable teacher characteristics. (Schwerdt & Wupperman, 2011)

Student achievement in that study was measured by exam performance, which is a limited measurement of learning, so it is possible that other dimensions of learning were actually more advanced by the small-group problem-solving approach. Nonetheless, in general, there is no clear evidence that lecturing has failed to teach or has prevented learning.

In fact, it is not even clear what the term 'lecture' actually refers to. In an acerbic review of theories of learning styles, Marianne Jennings reflects:

> It is a fascinating intellectual challenge to realize that an entire body of research and literature [dating from the 1960s] that concludes the lecture is a flawed means of instruction began without a definition or an acknowledgement of the wide variety of approaches used by lecturers/ sages. (Jennings, 2012: 192–193 n. 5)

Those who have worked in a university or studied at a university will know that lectures take place in a variety of settings, not always in an amphitheater, and that lecturers can engage students in question-and-answer exchanges, in small-group or paired exercises and in electronic quizzes. Screens with PowerPoint, animation, document projection, internet and video have brought a stream of new visual possibilities to lectures. As a live occasion, the lecture can take the form of analysis, hypothesis, argument, narrative, explanation, confession, meditation, sermon, comedy routine, dialogue, summary, provocation, demonstration, celebrity keynote address, extempore performance or a carefully scripted reading (Chilwant, 2012). There is no formula and, beyond there being (usually) a single figure in front of a group for 50 minutes, it remains an unpredictable and versatile format. It is so variable that it makes little sense to dismiss the lecture wholesale as an ineffective educational method.

The lecture as a live event, however, is under severe threat, and not just because at any lecture a significant number of students are texting, emailing or Googling on phones and laptops. We know that students are increasingly disengaging from campus as employment, social life and entertainment compete for their time. A report from the University of Melbourne found that over the five years 2004–09 there had been a decline in students experiencing 'a sense of belonging' to the University (James *et al.*, 2010: 40). Additionally, in increasingly cost-effective undergraduate courses, academics across the system find they are teaching larger and larger numbers of students, who in turn find it increasingly difficult to avoid becoming alienated early in their tertiary experience (Ramsden, 2003: 147).

Perhaps most significantly, lectures are now routinely captured as audio-with-PowerPoint screencasts or as video on virtual sites attached to subjects, a development that makes it possible for students to go back over the lectures and to watch lectures at a time and place of their choosing. Anecdotally, this virtual availability of the lecture has decimated physical attendance at the occasion of the lecture itself. From our experience, attendances at captured lectures declines to less than 50% of enrolments if attendance is not checked and related to eligibility to pass the subject. There is no plausible justification, however, for insisting on attendance when the essential elements of the event have been captured and can be delivered to students' electronic devices. What might be the solution to this declining lecture attendance? Is there a problem? Is it enough to leave students to look at or listen to a lecture via electronic capture? Could we do away with lecture theaters entirely (ironically just as undergraduate enrolment in creative writing is ballooning) and deliver lectures direct to camera? What effects might this have on student learning?

We have seen above that the MOOC, an entirely online experience of learning, does not seem to satisfy students, judging from non-completion rates and the range of other problems. This situation has led some educationalists to propose the 'flipped' classroom: students watch lectures at home then come to the campus to do their 'homework' in class, that is, their thinking about, analysis, investigation and critique of the material covered in the lecture (Sams & Bergmann, 2013). For creative writing, this offers an opportunity to continue with the general presentation of common lecture material via social media, while foregrounding for students guided in-class discussions of ideas and texts, and the testing of skills through face-to-face workshopping. The flipped classroom further prompts for us a move toward coherent links between lecture content, student activities and assignments. In the past, lectures have not been tied closely enough to what we ask students to do in the course of subject and what assignments they are given. Upon reflection, this coherence can ensure a more ethical presentation of subjects to students.

In debates over whether a lecture-based teaching method is more effective or appropriate than a learning-styles teaching method (Jennings, 2012), case method (Ardalan, 2015), learner-centered method or problem-solving method (Biggs & Tang, 2009), two elements of the education environment seem to fall outside the usual vision. Firstly, there are ethical dimensions to the situation. For the course provider the ethical considerations might be:

- the curriculum has well researched and relevant content;
- the expectations are appropriate given the 'level' of the subject;
- the curriculum content and the activities required of students during the semester inform the assessment tasks;
- criteria for grading assignments (assessment) are published to the students and the marking reports show how the student has performed against each of the criteria.

Sometimes the alignment of assessment with curriculum and with the activities of students during a course is presented as an educational strategy that encourages 'deep' learning (Biggs & Tang, 2009: 22–26). We would prefer to see this as a way of meeting basic ethical standards in education. Whether a student takes a 'deep' or 'surface' approach to learning is then legitimately a decision for each individual student.

Secondly, we hold that learning cannot actually be measured. Student satisfaction can be measured, exam performance can be measured and facility at essay writing (or poetry, fiction or script writing for that matter) can be more subjectively measured. But none of these 'measures' in any comprehensive or secure sense is a measurement of learning, although they might make us more or less confident that learning has taken place or that skills are present. There are some things we know, experientially, about learning: it changes us; it takes time. We cannot put our finger on exactly when it did change us but at a certain time we might realize we have internalized a body of knowledge, a way of thinking and perceiving, a way of continuing to develop and a set of skills (Sennett, 2008). Learning happens across a wide spectrum of phenomena, including the nervous system, mind, memory, muscles, daily routines, social worlds and the attention we give to further learning. Learning is subtle, transforming and relatively slow to happen in adulthood, especially in the complex settings of university courses. We know its fundamental ingredients are curiosity, imitation and experimentation, combined with some system of checking on one's progress (commonly called feedback, formative or summative). This holistic (and phenomenographic) conception of learning means that any subject and any assessment task can hope to detect only a sample of the student's learning and potential. The beauty and the challenge of creative writing as a tertiary discipline in undergraduate programs is its complexity. It is partly vocational (skills and practice based) and partly an intellectual and artistic orientation (partaking of the range of conceptual and critical possibilities across the humanities). The lecture will never be adequate as a teaching method in creative writing, but equally the workshop cannot be sufficient. Both, however, we consider important to the range of educational experiences students need and expect. We do not think it would be sufficient to abandon lectures in favor of workshops; nor would it be worthwhile to continue to lecture in the traditional modes when there are so many other modes of delivery possible now through social media, virtual networks and portals.

From the two points made above, and considering the emerging virtual environments for education as we have described them, we suggest that innovations in education must keep in mind the ethical contract between institution and student, as well as the varied, subtle nature of learning, without over-committing to new theories of learning that privilege models of learning that are too narrowly conceived.

Our innovation – our response to the new educational environment, driven largely by falling attendance at lectures but also by the university's enthusiasm and support for e-learning – has been to reshape a short-fiction course at second-year level in the Bachelor Arts at the University of Melbourne. 'Short Fiction' has an enrolment of about 150 students each year. The subject runs for 12 weeks, with lectures on history, interpretation and technique delivered through the first six weeks. The second six weeks focus more upon students workshopping their drafts of stories. We are planning a range of changes, including:

- video versions of nine lectures that outline a history of the short story, common elements of craft (plot, character, prose style, dialogue, ellipsis, imagery, focalization), the emergence of graphic fiction, detailed readings of selected stories and some interviews with writers;
- online 250-word responses to weekly reading material and lectures;
- a timed online 'exam' in which students produce an analytical essay in response to stories they have not seen previously;
- prepared questions to take to seminars in response to lectures;
- guided exercises in offering peer feedback to drafts of stories online.

These changes were in preparation for teaching the subject in late 2014 (August to November).

Our interest here is in reflecting upon the experience of filming and packaging the lectures. This has become a varied and challenging exercise, far beyond the simple one we envisaged of filming lecture delivery in a lecture theater. We have done this, filming the lectures as they were delivered in the last 'live' version of the subject in 2013. One interesting diminution of the lecture once it goes online is that the questions inserted into the live lecture format, inviting students from the floor of the theater to offer brief responses, and the moments of pause when queries or criticisms regarding ideas are invited, can no longer be part of a filmed lecture format. As it turns out, however, the filmed lecture might offer exciting new possibilities in graphics, cut-aways and edits (allowing, for example, the inclusion of graphic fiction and interviews with writers). Finding a balance between lecturer-on-screen and displaying the PowerPoint slides has been another editing issue.

We have also filmed the delivery of lectures as more intimate occasions in our offices. This exercise exposed us as less than professional performers in front of the camera. The technology seems to demand of us a level of 'performance' that is not demanded in a live lecture theatre. For instance, the leveling of the gaze upon the camera (the viewer) and the pacing of a filmed script delivery are skills not learned easily. Without these skills, the office-based 'lecture' looked stilted and strange on screen. We have, in addition, found ourselves going beyond office and lecture theater, out on to the campus, out to sites beyond the campus, to filmed versions of fictional scenes, and finally on road trips to contemporary writers for interviews on topics being covered in the lectures. These extensions to the video lecture material were not envisaged in the planning, but the natural versatility of the lecture and the portability of current digital equipment made all this possible. As a result, we do not have, as we thought we would, a simple archive of lectures to present to students on virtual sites but rather a series of modules in various formats that students are able to range across, watch repeatedly and delve into as they go through the semester. We can envisage at this point that the notion of lectures will be replaced by an unfolding of shorter digital presentations of topics, events, ideas and issues as material that will inform the reading of texts and the discussions taking place in on-campus seminars during the semester.

An unexpected element of this exercise in replacing live lectures with screen-based delivery has been the discovery of how varied on-screen material can be, perhaps more varied than the traditional lecture has always been. At the same time, we have achieved a clearer awareness of what has been lost in abandoning the live lecture: the live lecture is an opportunity to ask direct questions of students; it is the place to bring yesterday's current events into the context of the ideas being discussed, and to make those many minor and spontaneous adjustments to content as you present; and it is nearly always the occasion for students to come up to the lecturer afterward to reflect upon certain points. The live lecture challenges the lecturer to keep developing and critically re-evaluating the material being presented. All of this is lost when the lecture becomes (relatively) fixed as a video. The fact that in this subject we will also be replacing the lecture with time in on-campus seminars, however, means that we can retain elements important to the live occasion: question-and-answer time, critical discussion, students' responses informed by their viewing of the 'lecture', occasional passion in discussion, and the live cohort experience when students are together in a classroom.

This project aims to blend social, individual, synchronous and asynchronous possibilities for learning. The digital, virtual environment, for instance, allows students to find their own personal time for tasks, fitting them to a busy life and allowing for individual differences in the pacing and organization of learning. This values not just the presence of technology in our lives but the individualized, private aspect of learning. The image of a student with a book in a corner of a library might not be very different from that of a student with an iPad on her knees in a corner of a busy café. Both point to the immense world of individual curiosity privately pursued.

At present, three Australian universities with a team of five academics as a 'reference group', with a grant from the Australian Learning and Teaching Council, are working to develop a series of webinars, case studies and resources for blended synchronous learning (see https://blendsync.org) in recognition of the potential for students to be part of an interactive cohort while not necessarily being within geographic reach of each other. This use of technology serves an educationally social purpose, putting students in contact with professional, scholarly and artistic communities. With our project, students will have access to this technology but will also attend timetabled seminars on campus. We can envisage, though, that, in time, even this campus-based attendance might take on virtual forms, for it is not possible to predict in detail future developments in communication technology. An important reason for retaining synchronous elements in our subject relates to the fact that learning is progressive across time. We hope to provide ongoing guidance, by pacing the students' activities across a common schedule of attendances and tasks. We know that this might not suit the pace of learning for all individuals, but we hope that moving through a common experience with a cohort will be accepted as a necessary stimulus to the kind of adult-based and profession-based learning at which we are aiming. It is possible that the low completion rates for MOOCs, as mentioned above, have a lot to do with an almost complete commitment to the asynchronous potential in this form of learning. Students can in such a model become too isolated as individual learners, and find that because they do not belong to a peer group moving though the material at the same time as they are, there is no useful cohort experience for them. We will be feeling our way through the apparently opposing values embedded in synchronous and asynchronous elements of this educational environment, acutely aware that we do not have comprehensive answers or solutions.

Once this subject has been conducted in its hybrid environment, we intend to survey students on their evaluation of the experience, and continue to reflect on how the changes we have made affect the ethical contract with students and student opportunities for learning.

We are aware that once the internet, social media and communication technology are integrated into the experience and delivery of education, the fact that technology keeps changing will mean that there will never again be one settled model of teaching in the academy.

Our commitment is to honor the ethical contract between institution and student by articulating the relation between content, tasks and assessments. Recognizing the wide spectrum of phenomena involved in learning, we aim to continue to present material not just intelligently and well based in research, but in ways that are as varied as technological and human resources allow. Although we envisaged this project as a step toward bringing 'Short Fiction' into the MOOC world, its half metamorphosis into a hybrid environment might, for a creative writing subject, be its most educationally effective form.

The traditional lecture (if there is such a thing) will not entirely disappear, but it is likely that it will become less central to education in the academy. We envisage it now as one tool among many for delivering content and engaging students. We aim to recognize and exploit the versatility of the lecture by bringing it into contact with new media and new digital platforms – as far as our present skills allow. On the one hand, we can see that the lecture might become unrecognizable in its new, virtual and modular forms in our subject; on the other hand, it might make its own form of recovery organically, through the schedule of on-campus seminars still central to the subject.

Exploration

(1) If the traditional lecture or mini-lecture during seminars remains part of the delivery of a creative writing subject, how does its content relate to assessment tasks? This question challenges the content of lectures and asks what it is that is being assessed in a creative writing subject.

(2) If the traditional lecture remains part of the delivery of a creative writing subject, how can lecturers inject into the lecture program its possibilities as debate, argument, information-delivery system, confession, performance, inspiration and provocation?

(3) What are the justifications, or reasons, for 'capturing' lectures electronically for later use by students? If students prefer the electronic version, then is there any point in delivering new live lectures each semester?

(4) Has the lecture always been a difficult and problematic course-delivery method for creative writing? Perhaps creative writing is the very subject where doing is more important than talking about doing.

(5) If the lecture is to be abandoned in favor of online delivery, what useful aspects of the live lecture are lost and how can they be reinserted into the delivery of a subject?

(6) What might it mean to understand the educational relation of teacher to student as an ethical one? Is there an ethical method of teaching?

(7) How balanced must a creative writing education be between practicing skills and learning to adopt and critique theoretical ideas?

(8) Whose responsibility is it to engage deep learning – the teacher's or the student's? Should it matter to course designers if students see their subjects as a means to an end rather than as deeply engaging experiences?

(9) Can learning be measured?

References

Ardalan, K. (2015) Using entertaining metaphors in the introduction of the case method in a case-based course. In M. Li and Y. Zhao (eds) *Exploring Teaching and Learning in Higher Education* (pp. 69–96). Berlin: Springer.

Baggaley, J. (2013) MOOC rampant. *Distance Education* 34 (3), 368–378.

Biggs, J. and Tang, C. (2009) *Teaching for Quality Learning at University*. Buckingham: Open University Press.

Brown, R. with Carasso, H. (2013) *Everything for Sale: The Marketisation of UK Higher Education*. London: Routledge.

Chilwant, K. (2012) Comparison of two teaching methods, structured interactive lectures and conventional lectures. *Biomedical Research* 23 (3), 363–366.

Dehaas, J. (2012) Where did the prof go? The debate over whether to put more lectures online. *Maclean's* 125 (16), 54–5. Available at http://www.macleans.ca/education/uniandcollege/where-did-the-prof-go-2 (accessed January 2015).

James, R., Krause, K. and Jennings, C. (2010) *The First Year Experience in Australian Universities: Findings from 1994 to 2009*. Parkville: Centre for the Study of Higher Education, University of Melbourne.

Jennings, M.M. (2012) In defense of the sage on the stage: Escaping from the 'sorcery' of learning styles and helping students learn how to learn. *Journal of Legal Studies Education* (29) 2, 191–237.

Liyanagunawardena, T.R., Adams, A.A. and Williams, S.A. (2013) MOOCs: A systematic study of the published literature 2008–12. *International Review of Research in Open and Distance Learning* 13 (3), 202–227.

Mackness, J., Mak, S. and Williams, R. (2010) The ideals and reality of participating in a MOOC. In L. Dirckinck-Holmfeld *et al.* (eds) *Proceedings of the 7th International Conference on Networked Learning* (pp. 266–274). Available at http://www.lancs.ac.uk/fss/organisations/netlc/past/nlc2010/abstracts/PDFs/Mackness.pdf (accessed 18 November 2013).

McGettigan, A. (2013) *The Great University Gamble: Money, Markets and the Future of Higher Education*. London: Pluto.

Marton, F. and Booth, S.A. (1997) *Learning and Awareness*. Upper Saddle River, NJ: Erlbaum.

Ramsden, P. (2003) *Learning to Teach in Higher Education*. London: Routledge.

Sams, A. and Bergmann, J. (2013) Flip your students' learning. *Educational Leadership* 70 (6), 16–20.

Schwerdt, G. and Wuppermann, A.C. (2011) Is traditional teaching really all that bad? A within-student between-subject approach. *Economics of Education Review* 30 (2), 365–379.

Sennett, R. 2008 *The Craftsman*. London: Allen Lane.

Siemens, G. (2009) What is connectivism? Week 1: CCK09. Available at http://docs.google.com/Doc?id=anw8wkk6fjc_14gpbqc2dt (accessed 18 November 2013).

Smart, K., Witt, C. and Scott, J. (2012) Towards learner-centred teaching: An inductive approach. *Business Communication Quarterly* 75 (4), 392–403.

Vardi, M. (2012) Will MOOCs destroy academia? *Communications of the ACM* 55 (11), 5.

Vernadakis, N., Giannousi, M., Tsitskari, E., Antoniou, P. and Kioumourtzoglou, E. (2012) A comparison of student satisfaction between traditional and blended technology course offerings in physical education. *Turkish Online Journal of Distance Education* 13 (1), article 8.

Wright, P. (2013) News from the Net: Organising casuals in the US. *NTEU Advocate* 20 (1), 38.

Chapter 10

Originality and Research: Knowledge Production in Creative Writing Doctoral Degrees

Jeri Kroll

Writers in the academy over the past two decades have been debating the concept of creative research and what forms can best embody results, often focusing on aspects of creative higher degrees (Brien, 2004; Harper & Kroll, 2008; Krauth, 2011; Smith & Dean, 2009). In particular, they have explored what methodologies facilitate this re-imagined species of research and what kinds of knowledge it can produce in the context of doctoral education. Scott Brook, co-editor of the special issue *Beyond Practice-Led Research* in *TEXT: Journal of Writing and Writing Courses* (No. 14, October 2012), argues 'that the notion of practice-led research had achieved something like a "practical consensus" within university creative arts programs' (Brook, 2012: 1), working against further development. This chapter suggests that, nevertheless, focusing on what has become the standard thesis for a higher qualification in creative writing,[1] which (on some level) involves a process where 'making the work becomes inseparable from what is produced' (Carter, 2004: 11), can still yield fresh perceptions by encouraging candidates, supervisors and examiners to conceive of the doctoral dissertation as a whole. No matter whether it is presented as separate bound works (e.g. novel and exegesis or critical commentary)[2] or as an intertwined one-volume thesis where research and fiction support one another *in situ*, it builds complex layers of meaning. This hybridity necessitates flexible guidelines that allow myriad forms of knowledge production by candidates who undertake a degree that, by definition, should 'provide training and education with the objective of producing graduates with the capacity to conduct research independently at a high level of originality and quality' (Flinders University, 2013a).[3]

Supervisors must help candidates to discover research pathways sourced from one or more university disciplines: Creative Arts, Creative Writing,

Cultural Studies, English, History, Postcolonial and Women's Studies, among others. In fact, interdisciplinary projects require a wider perspective and foreground the question of what constitutes not only research but also originality. Concomitantly, writers in the academy must maintain profiles as practitioners while arguing for the validity of their own creative research in Australasia and the UK, articulating in various modes (e.g. research statements, refereed journal articles, catalogues, prefaces, festival appearances) what contribution to knowledge their work has made. The audience for these 'arguments' that disseminate new knowledge can comprise artistic peers, the academy, government auditing bodies and the various 'publics' who critique and consume art-forms.

In an effort to provide direction, Australasian universities have addressed the question of the symbiosis between creative and critical components in doctorates to varying degrees.[4] Many institutions echo the guidelines of Flinders University in South Australia, advising that

> students can make a case that part of the original contribution to knowledge of the PhD comes from the relationship between the two parts of the thesis. Alternatively, students can integrate the creative and critical portions of the thesis into a coherent whole and present it bound as one work. (Flinders University, 2013b: 2)

The University of Melbourne highlights this symbiotic connection too:

> Examiners should note that the dissertation and the creative work should be considered as complementary, mutually reinforcing parts of a single project. **The candidate may argue, however, that the relationship between the two parts contributes to the originality and creativity of the whole.**[5] (Melbourne School of Graduate Research, 2011)

The University of Western Sydney states:

> There is an appropriate and substantiated interface between the creative work and the dissertation [which as a whole is] a substantive original contribution to knowledge. (http://www.uws.edu.au/writing_and_society/postgraduate_study)

UK institutions take a similar approach. Bournemouth University, for instance, calls the creative artefact 'the practical element', which, together with the exegesis, comprises 'the outcome (or thesis)'; as a whole, it must make 'a contribution to knowledge and understanding embedded in practice' (http://www.bournemouth.ac.uk/courses). The 'Creative writing research benchmark statement' from the National Association of Writers in Education (NAWE, 2008: 13) notes in section 104, 'Defining principles': 'The process of acquiring knowledge in the discipline of Creative Writing ... highlights an active interrelation between the two' doctoral components. The phrase 'active interrelation' suggests something which can be demonstrated through 'separate text[s]' or an integrated product ('Notes about UK degrees' – NAWE, 2008: 14) and which, therefore, can be evaluated for the purposes of awarding a degree through an educational institution.

Whether stakeholders in the creative writing discipline name this connection 'symbiosis', 'interface' or 'active interrelation', they emphasize that this project, conceived from a passion for writing, and born after the journey of postgraduate study, always has to acknowledge its two parents – artistic practice and research. Examiners need to be sympathetic to the variety of thesis models that this family history makes possible and, in addition, to the types of knowledge that they generate. The hybrid doctorate complicates the supervisory role because it requires the production of original work. Supervisors must also tutor candidates, therefore, about how to interpret the criterion of originality. In sum, this chapter considers the effects that flow from having practice and research driving the search for new knowledge in the context of higher education. After discussing the nature of the hybrid creative thesis and exploring definitions of research and originality, this chapter turns to conceptions of craft and art. Finally, it considers the modes of knowledge that the creative writing doctoral degree makes possible. It concludes that doctoral candidates can generate a range of outcomes, among the most important being critical knowledge based on literary and cultural contexts and craft knowledge based on the art-form and its methodologies.

Originality in Research and Practice

'Originality' is a potent and yet slippery term. Applied in the academy, originality's meaning is embedded in conventional definitions of research, a practice driven by questions to which the researcher assumes no one yet knows the answers. These definitions appear in the publications of stakeholder organizations at international, national and local levels. In its online *Glossary of Statistical Terms*, the Organisation for Economic Co-operation and Development (OECD) defines research as follows (under its UNESCO definition of 'research and development'):

Any creative systematic activity undertaken to increase the stock of knowledge, including knowledge of humanity, culture and society, and the use of knowledge to devise new applications. (http://stats.oecd.org/glossary/detail.asp?ID=2312)

A more specific definition of 'experimental development' can also be applied to creative practice:

> Experimental development is systematic work, drawing on existing knowledge gained from research and/or practical experience, that is directed to producing new materials, products or devices … or to improving those already produced or installed. (http://stats.oecd.org/glossary/detail.asp?ID=908)

In addition, the OECD defines 'applied research' in its *Frascati Manual* (OECD, 2002: 30).

These developments that 'increase the stock of knowledge' or produce 'new materials, products or devices' might lead to improved processes or products that can be granted patents. The US Patent and Trademark Office explains on its website that 'any person who invents or discovers any new and useful process, machine, manufacture, or composition of matter, or any new and useful improvement thereof' can apply for a patent (http://www.uspto.gov/patents/resources/general_info_concerning_patents.jsp#heading-4). 'New' seems to be a synonym for 'original'. The term 'original' appears in the 2006 edition of the *Australian Code for the Responsible Conduct of Research*, which explains that research is 'original investigation undertaken to gain knowledge and understanding' (National Health and Medical Research Council, 2006: 10), while Excellence in Research for Australia (ERA) publications emphasize the idea of creativity (e.g. ERA, 2012). The UK's Research Assessment Exercise of 1998 through to the Research Excellence Framework of 2008 and 2014 at one point focuses on the idea of generation or birth, the 'bring[ing] into existence' (Macquarie Library, 1981) of something that did not exist before, saying that research involves the 'generation of ideas, images, performances, artifacts including design, where these lead to new or substantially improved insights' (see http://www.ref.ac.uk). It is worth noting that ideas cannot be patented; these must be actualized in a product that has to be sufficiently different from others in the same category. Stakeholders such as government employees, academic staff and members of peer-review bodies, among others, are involved in deciding what is original or new for the purposes of research assessment as well as the granting of patents.

In the contemporary world, a plethora of individuals, organizations and groups pass judgment about originality, but not every culture equates originality with creativity. In fact, 'imitation is a long-established, deep-rooted form of cultural transmission' (Sawyer, 2006: 24), although it has lost legitimacy in the developed nations. Yet recent studies reveal that in the academy apprentice postgraduates in the creative arts and humanities feel pressured to eschew imitation and often to produce new work in isolation. The originality of the thesis topic provides a case in point, since 'there is a fundamental distinction between the way students in science and science related disciplines identify a doctoral topic and the way it is defined within the humanities and social sciences' (Neumann, 2003: 57). As part of a laboratory team, students might develop (if not be given) a problem to solve and will have assistance in selecting methodologies. Creative arts students, however, find themselves trying to pin down an amorphous definition of 'originality and uniqueness' (Sinclair, 2004: 24). Contemporary research on creativity and its relationship to originality, however, calls into question the myth of the isolated genius (Boden, 2004: 14–15; Sawyer, 2006: 61; Sennett, 2008: 22; Sternberg, 2003).

Some recent debates about how to define key terms such as 'creativity' and 'originality' center upon when the outcomes of a creative process occur (the moment of creation and completion) or when those outcomes are recognized as being original (Andreasen, 2005: 14–17). The etymology of words such as 'create', 'genius' and 'inspire' underline this temporal disjunction. For example, 'the Latin *creare* ... means "to produce, make, or create"' (Andreasen, 2005: 6), which does not consider what happens to the created product after the moment of inception. The history of the Latin *genius*, 'derived from the Geek *ginesthai*, which meant, "to be born or come into being"' (Andreasen, 2005: 6), further complicates understanding of creativity, conflating an individual's muse (inner god, genius) with the ability to create. The Latin-derived verb 'inspire' overlaps in some ways with 'genius', as it signifies 'to breathe into' (Sawyer, 2006: 12). Writers whose work has been discovered or rediscovered after their deaths demonstrate these contradictions. As exemplary cases, Andreasen (2005: 14) notes John Donne (and the Metaphysical poets), Emily Dickinson and Vincent van Gogh – and one could add William Blake and Gerard Manley Hopkins to the list – whose current reputations rest on 20th-century advocates.

One of the proponents of a systemic understanding of creativity is psychologist Mihayl Csikszentmihalyi (1990, 1996, 1999). He defined the state of flow, or the loss of consciousness and total immersion experienced by individuals focused on a particular task, which can be anything – artistic, technological, athletic, scientific – they find enjoyable for its own sake. More to the point, he has investigated how 'cultures as systems of inter-related domains', comprising 'a community of people who share ways of thinking and acting, who learn from each other and imitate each other's actions', foster creativity (Csikszentmihalyi, 1999: 315). Once certain individuals have absorbed enough of the domain's 'knowledge, tools, values, practices' (Csikszentmihalyi, 1999: 314), they may be capable of generating 'a novel variation in the content of the domain', which those 'gatekeepers' ('the field') who belong to it recognize as novel (Csikszentmihalyi, 1999: 313). This description applies on the micro level to the collegial university creative writing program and on the macro level to literary cultures.

R. Keith Sawyer's 'sociocultural definition of creativity' (Sawyer, 2006: 286) develops Csikszentmihalyi's concepts by reflecting upon how society facilitates and evaluates artistic and scientific work as well as what might be patentable. Producing 'a product that is both "new and useful" … for some domain of activity' (Sawyer, 2006: 286) is possible only when the creator has 'domain-relevant skills' (Dacey & Lennon, 1998: 81) and possesses knowledge of the works that comprise that domain (Boden, 2004: 22). Sawyer suggests that the judgments that publishers, critics, awards panels, gallery managers, book reviewers *et al.* make about creative work form a 'consensus of people that are experts in that creative domain: the field' (Sawyer, 2006: 123; see also Boden, 2004: 10). The field 'determines whether a product is novel and appropriate. If the field decides that the product meets these criteria, the product enters the domain, where it is preserved and disseminated to other members of the field' (Sawyer, 2006: 123). Doctoral examiners perform the function of field experts, assessing the stylistic, critical and generic content of the thesis as a whole and determining whether it is in some sense an original contribution to its domain.

Candidates undertaking higher degrees, including those who come to the academy as professionals, need to immerse themselves, therefore, in the discipline's intellectual and aesthetic knowledge base in order to know what questions have not been asked before and what their project might produce that deserves the label 'original'. In fact, part of the doctoral project might include seeking the right questions for their professional practice and facilitating the construction of an informed argument about originality addressed to peers and the culture. Being able to disseminate results is part of the verification of originality. Csikszentmihalyi (1999: 313) refers to 'the ability to convince the field about the virtue of the novelty one has produced', while Strand (1998: 32) talks of 'publicly verifiable outcomes', which directly or indirectly might benefit the community. 'Benefit' is a diffuse term, but original research does not have to be limited to practical applications. Creative arts research can impact upon the community in innumerable ways and the community, in turn, participates in evaluating and ultimately accepting its outcomes. Sawyer expresses this interaction by asserting that: 'Innovation involves both the creation of a new idea, and the implementation, dissemination, and adoption of that idea by an organization' (Sawyer, 2006: 287). One could extend the notion of an organization to encompass a field of activity (e.g. the literary or visual arts culture) or, indeed, a culture as a whole.

To summarize, researchers must discover something original or must reinterpret existing knowledge to produce new insights and communicate them so that the relevant disciplines move forward. In applied research in hard science, the value of a new method of vaccine delivery, say, can be statistically demonstrated to peers and the community. In the social sciences, both quantitative and qualitative research can also produce outcomes that stakeholders recognize as original, such as studies that reveal the effect of indefinite mandatory detention on refugees. This type of work points not only to future directions in research but also can form the groundwork for public policy. This chapter later returns to examples of original outcomes in creative writing research

Knowledge and Art (or Craft)

In order to understand themselves as creative writing researchers, students and supervisors need to ask: what is knowledge and what is craft? Is craft a particular form of knowledge? Does craft generate knowledge in artistic works? This chapter now turns to what knowledge and craft meant historically and the way in which they are understood in contemporary culture.

In Ancient Greek philosophy, the two terms employed are *epistêmê* and *technê*, loosely translated as knowledge and craft, although in Plato's as well as Aristotle's writings (Macdonald Cornford, 1963; Randall, 1960) craft and art, which are both said to be subject to rules, are sometimes used interchangeably (*Stanford Encyclopedia of Philosophy*, 2014). In Plato's *Republic*, for example, Plato calls medicine both a craft and an art (Macdonald Cornford, 1963: 22–23). The discussion in Chapter III centres on how the commander (an expert in seamanship) and the doctor (an expert in medicine) must study their respective disciplines so that they possess knowledge and experience in order not only to function effectively but also to allow the craft or art to achieve 'its own greatest possible perfection' (Macdonald Cornford, 1963: 22). Training in requisite skills, honed through practice, must be underpinned by knowledge: 'even Aristotle refers to *technê* or craft as itself also *epistêmê* or knowledge because it is a practice grounded in an "account" – something involving theoretical understanding' (*Stanford Encyclopedia of Philosophy*,

2014). For those who attempt to define research in creative writing higher degrees, this connection between knowledge (or theory) and practice grounded in skill gained through training can heal what Sennett conceives of as 'modern society's ... historical inheritance': rifts or 'fault lines dividing practice and theory, technique and expression, craftsman and artist, maker and user' (Sennett, 2008: 11).

In the 20th century, Michel Foucault's use of the term *epistêmê* has gained currency, meaning the historical 'systems of thought and knowledge ... [that] define a system of conceptual possibilities that determines the boundaries of thought in a given domain and period' (*Stanford Encyclopedia of Philosophy*, 2013). How one creates this body of knowledge, judges it and communicates it is the province of epistemology. Creative writing academics have been engaged in determining what modes of knowledge are possible when practice is at the core of knowledge creation. They must also consider the necessity of theory, which helps practitioners to understand – give an 'account of' in Aristotelian terms – their practice. Clarifying the researcher's assumptions and setting them within a framework facilitates communicating (or disseminating) results. Giles Deleuze, in conversation with Michel Foucault, likens 'theory [to] a box of tools.... It must be useful. It must function. And not for itself' (see Foucault, 1972). So must theory or theories be involved in the hybrid doctoral thesis.

It is worth emphasizing that the ancient Greeks' fluid boundary between craft and art is not only philosophical but also linguistic. *'Poiein* ... the parent word for poetry [means] "making"' (Sennett, 2008: 24) and so poetry requires craft skill. Sennett goes on: 'Plato formulated this aim as the *arête*, the standard of excellence, implicit in any act: the aspiration for quality that will drive a craftsman to improve' (Sennett, 2008: 24); therefore, 'there is no art without craft' (Sennett, 2008: 65). The intensive training of apprentices in a workshop is replicated in the postgraduate environment, where candidates, who arrive with a degree of skill in 'making', aspire to improve technically, intellectually and aesthetically. They ground themselves in domain knowledge while engaging in the hard work needed to actualize initial inspirations; they strive to attain 'know-how' or *savoir-faire* (Lacan as cited in Hecq, 2012: 34), which entails 'a practice that *knows* what it is doing' (Hecq, 2012: 34). Part of the reflective practitioner's 'knowing' involves revisiting research questions in a heuristic process determined not by a conventional, scientifically biased research trajectory, but by arts practice. Producing an innovative creative and critical thesis is how candidates finally demonstrate that they 'know' in all of these senses. Harking back to Carter, 'making the work becomes inseparable from what is produced' (Carter, 2004: 11).

The Creative Thesis: Types of Knowledge

The demonstration of knowledge production takes various forms in the creative thesis. Criteria requiring the thesis to be 'publishable' or achieve 'high quality' or perform at 'an international level', that it reach 'current art-form industry standards', 'sustain critical examination' and 'display mastery'[6] are commonplace. These terms refer in the first instance to the creative work but the overarching criterion for a doctorate stipulates that the thesis makes that 'original contribution to knowledge' as a whole, as discussed at the beginning of the chapter. 'Publishable' does not guarantee high quality, given the market-driven mentality of major publishers, which are loath to take on risky work, which in fact might be ground-breaking (Fisher, 2012). 'High quality' as a denominating term is vague, although it does suggest that those in a position to judge (supervisors, examiners, publishers and critics) – in other words, experts in the field – will recognize the creative work's value. 'Current art-form industry standards' could mean that the work could be published given a sympathetic economic climate or it could mean that, as an apprentice manuscript, the writer has demonstrated acceptable skills. Terms such as 'mastery' and 'competence' also suggest the latter; the work is appropriate stylistically and structurally for its genre. Indeed, supervisors and examiners might find it easier to summarize the contribution of the thesis as a whole, including the critical element; this strategy takes the pressure off the creative work, which does not need to be 'cutting edge'. What the above criteria do not clarify is how either the components or the whole help to generate knowledge.

Many critics have debated the dynamics and naming of the practice-led research loop employed in the creative and performing arts (Bolt, 2004; Brien *et al.*, 2010; Cohen, 2010; Harper & Kroll, 2008: 6; Haseman, 2006: 98; Kroll & Harper, 2013; Smith & Dean, 2009). That ongoing debate is outside the scope of this chapter, but what can be asserted is that artistic practice drives the creative work even if practice is not the primary investigative mode. Suitable critical and cultural theories ground the methodologies. Under the practice-led research umbrella, candidates might undertake feminist, historical, postmodern and postcolonial studies, while also pursuing qualitative research (e.g. interviews with practitioners and audiences) or quantitative research (e.g. statistics about program numbers and market trends and surveys of examination guidelines). Creative writing research encourages candidates to engage with multiple points of view. In fact, the working rhythm candidates establish between creative and critical work will shift and rebalance, modifying the original research questions or throwing up new ones, but always foregrounding the heuristic dimension of 'making'.

Given this mutability, supervisors and candidates should discuss what types of knowledge production might occur. Bournemouth University (2011), for example, lists eight types of contribution, including 'aesthetic development', 'generic methodological innovation', 'new theoretical development' and 'new critical positioning of praxis'. Creative writing research faces the challenge of clarifying the concept of originality in two main areas: disciplinary or critical knowledge; and craft (technical or praxical) knowledge. Acquiring disciplinary knowledge (about contemporary poetry, for example, or about new media developments) helps students to contextualize their projects, giving them a sense of 'historical embeddedness' (Dacey & Lennon, 1998: 245). T.S. Eliot conceptualized the apprentice period as a time when individuals by themselves must perform this educative function, learning about the past (which is still 'living'; Eliot, 1919: 30) to uncover what work remains to be done. In the communities of practice formed during postgraduate study, students undertake this task with supervisors and peers. Gaining this type of knowledge facilitates the creative project's claims to advancing scholarship in the field, or of adapting or transforming to some degree the chosen genre, or of dealing with a subject in an innovative way that leads to new insights.

The second type of ongoing work that candidates can undertake improves craft knowledge; this might involve stylistic studies of texts, as well as intensive revision of creative products under supervision or mentorship – 'new models of practice' or 'new understanding of practice-led processes', for example (Bournemouth University, 2011). It leads to 'understanding [craft's] theoretical base' and refining its practical application in order, as Plato says, to seek 'its own greatest possible perfection' (Macdonald Cornford, 1963: 22). Following are two indicative examples of knowledge contributions.

The thesis of a Flinders graduate (PhD, 2012), Dr Sharon Kernot,[7] demonstrates a range of possibilities. Before and during postgraduate study, she worked as a social welfare officer for an anti-poverty organization based in a low socio-economic area. Her novel *Underground Road* (Wakefield Press, 2013) explores, among other subjects, what effect gambling addiction and mental illness have on those living in a disadvantaged community. Media coverage of the novel might lead those with the ability to design government policy to address isolation, financial stress and depression, and also enhance public understanding of the links between poverty and gambling. The exegesis, 'Writing poverty – The reflexive practitioner: Social welfare worker and creative artist', analyses not only the factual research necessary to embody these issues and how the subject of gambling addiction has been dealt with in contemporary fiction, but also the ethics of writing about one's workplace, drawing on current debates in life writing. This thesis, therefore, demonstrates enhanced critical understanding of contemporary 'non-fiction novels', as well as sociocultural insights into the writer's responsibilities. Here, the interface not only occurs between craft, art and knowledge in the thesis, but is embodied in the candidate herself as practitioner-employee.

A current Flinders doctoral student, Annabelle Murphy, is contributing to creative writing and screen disciplines by focusing on genre (in this case, the feature film and the young adult novel) and the way in which those genres appeal to specific audiences. The process of adaptation provides the functional methodology as well as one of the objects of study. Murphy, who is an experienced screenwriter, has been engaged in studying the theory and practice of what she calls 'reverse adaptation', a process whereby she turns her own feature screenplay into a novel.[8] She examines how this illuminates conventional adaptation by comparison, and also analyses the impact on style and form when a performative genre is transformed into a text for young adults. In addition, she investigates the social drivers of sourcing new products from established work by considering how the various publics who consume contemporary media prolong engagement. These foci might advance understanding of more than one craft and discipline or specialty: for example, screen and novel writing and adaptation and audience studies. By influencing artistic peers, scholars and critics, the project might condition future adaptation choices and production modes and point to new directions in young adult audience psychology. These two distinct doctoral projects demonstrate not only possible models for creative theses and their methodologies, but also the variety of knowledge forms that can result.

Conclusion

This chapter has focused on the two guiding principles of creative writing doctoral education, practice and research, which shape the PhD dissertation, comprising creative work and critical components, whether presented separately or as an integrated whole. This hybridity can sometimes prove problematic, as every candidate must, in a sense, reinvent the conventional dissertation, discovering a form that will help to explore, if not answer, the research questions. On the positive (and ideal) side, experienced supervisors who are also practitioners,[9] supported by flexible yet clear university guidelines, should provide sufficient educational structure and aesthetic and academic training to allow candidates to become independent researchers who understand how to structure a thesis so that it can make original contributions to knowledge. It is worth emphasizing that the symbiotic relationship or interface between the creative dissertation's components can also be one of the vehicles for demonstrating new aesthetic and/or disciplinary knowledge. No matter what form the dissertation takes, however, the well trained doctoral candidate will learn how to make a case (or let the innovative form make a case) that convinces examiners of its contribution.

The chapter has also explored how refreshed understandings of the concepts of originality and creativity, craft and art, can illuminate the way in which practice and research complement each other in the context of higher education. Artistic practice might be the initial motivation for undertaking a doctoral degree, but it can also become one of the methods of knowledge production, as well as the object of study. The reflexive practitioner's 'knowing' results from a heuristic process, which is grounded in their previous apprentice or professional experiences and the subsequent theoretical and craft training acquired in an institution of higher education. Candidates, supervisors and examiners need to consider, therefore, craft and art as generators that can produce a variety of creative and critical artifacts that might demonstrate originality in myriad ways. In fact, as the chapter has argued, craft and art are not easily distinguished, so can be conceived of as part of a continuum. The creative artifact becomes a kind of rhizome, with its own subterranean root system. Innate skill honed by experience, deepened by domain knowledge and sharpened by debate with peers in the academy and a supervisor's feedback, allows practice to actualize the creative potential in projects. Doctoral candidates, mentored by supervisor-practitioners who are also 'field experts', can generate a range of outcomes, among them critical knowledge based on the literary or cultural context and craft knowledge based on the art-form and its methodologies.

Exploration

(1) Creative writing postgraduates and supervisors can interpret the concept of practice-led research in a variety ways and might call it by other names: research-led practice, practice research and so on.

(2) The hybrid creative–critical doctoral thesis can take many forms and produce various types of knowledge.

(3) Research refers to 'any creative systematic activity undertaken to increase the stock of knowledge' and is usually directed by questions for which the researcher wants to find answers.

(4) Creative writing researchers must in some way contribute to this stock of knowledge, but the doctoral journey might include finding the right questions for their practice.

(5) Every culture does not equate originality with creativity. When are the products of a creative process recognized as being original? Is this a useful question?

(6) Cultures can foster creativity within domains that include artistic, scientific and technological communities (among others) of like-minded people who share types of knowledge, values and skills.

(7) Experts competent to judge the products of a domain comprise the gatekeepers or 'the field'. They evaluate when a new contribution has been made.

(8) The terms *epistêmê* and *technê*, or knowledge and craft, do not necessarily exclude one another. Both craft and art are subject to rules and can be or can produce forms of knowledge.

(9) Appropriate theory or theories can help practitioners to understand – 'give an account of' – their practice so that they know it in as many ways possible.

(10) Different cultural and higher-educational contexts will determine what forms creative writing doctoral projects take in Australasia, the UK and the US, as well as what types of knowledge they produce.

Notes

(1) Additional models exist, of course, and interdisciplinary study as well as the integration of new technologies or platforms can produce new types of thesis that exploit other methodologies.

(2) The critical component of creative theses has different names, depending on the institutional or national context: 'exegesis', 'critical dissertation' or 'annotation', 'critical commentary' and 'critical accompaniment'.

(3) The definition continues: 'The student ought to be capable by the end of their candidature of conceiving, designing and carrying to completion a research program without supervision. The PhD candidate should uncover new knowledge either by the discovery of new facts, the formulation of theories or the innovative reinterpretation of known data and established ideas.' This is a standard way of formulating doctoral education in Australian universities.

(4) In many cases, this relationship is not mentioned specifically at all (and/or the guidelines are not available on the web or are difficult to locate).

(5) The second sentence is in bold type in the hard-copy document 'Additional Information for Examiners when a candidate is submitting a Dissertation and Creative Work for the PhD degree' (University of Melbourne).

(6) Judging by university websites and also my file of guidelines from a decade and a half of examining, I have found that there is much replication of phrases, some overlap and some striking differences in the articulation of creative product standards.

(7) Sharon Kernot graduated with a PhD from Flinders University in 2012. Her novel, *Underground Road*, was short-listed for the 2012 Wakefield Press Adelaide Festival of Arts Unpublished Manuscript Award and was published in 2013. The original doctoral thesis was entitled 'Writing poverty – The reflexive practitioner: Social welfare worker and creative artist'.

(8) Annabelle Murphy's feature script has already received state and federal arts funding for development.

(9) In candidatures where practitioners are not available to act as principal or associate supervisors, universities should provide formal or informal creative mentorship advice to the supervisory panel. This is particularly important in the case of candidates who commence study as apprentices rather than professionals.

References

Andreasen, N. (2005) *The Creating Brain: The Neuroscience of Genius*. New York: Dana Press.

Boden, M.A. (2004) *The Creative Mind: Myths and Mechanisms*. London: Routledge.

Bolt, B. (2004) Heidegger, handlability and praxical knowledge. Australian Council of University Art & Design Schools Conference Proceedings. Available at http://acuads. com.au/conference/2004-conference/article/heidegger-handlability-and-praxical-knowledge (accessed January 2015).

Brien, D.L., Burr, S. and Webb, J. (eds) (2010) *Creative and Practice-Led Research: Current Status, Future Plans*. Special issue of *TEXT*, Website Series, No. 8 (October). Available at http://textjournal.com.au/speciss/issue8/content.htm (accessed January 2015).

Brook, S. (2012) Introduction. Part 2: The critiques of practice-led research. In S. Brook and P. Magee (eds) *Beyond Practice-Led Research*, Special issue of *TEXT*, Website Series, 14 (2) (October) (pp. 1–10). Available at http://www.textjournal.com.au/speciss/issue14/content.htm (accessed January 2015).

Bournemouth University (2011) *8-A Code of Practice for Research Degrees*. Available at https://microsites.bournemouth.ac.uk/graduate-school/files/2013/02/code-practice.pdf.

Brien, D. (2004) The problem of where to start: a foundation question for creative writing higher degree candidates and supervisors. In J. Fletcher and A. Mann (eds) *TEXT* Special Issue 3 (April). Available at http://www.textjournal.com.au/speciss/issue3/brien.htm.

Carter, P. (2004) *Material Thinking: The Theory and Practice of Creative Research*. Melbourne: Melbourne University Press.

Cohen, H. (2010) Knowledge and a scholarship of creativity. Interactive Media 5: 2009 Conference Proceedings: Dietetic Life Forms and Dietetic Logic. Available at http://wwwmcc.murdoch.edu.au/nass/issue5/pdf/im5-article-2-cohen.pdf.

Csikszentmihalyi, M. (1990) *Flow: The Psychology of Optimal Experience*. New York: Harper-Perennial Modern Classics (2008).

Csikszentmihalyi, M. (1996) *Creativity: Flow and the Psychology of Discovery and Invention*. New York: HarperCollins.

Csikszentmihalyi, M. (1999) A systems perspective on creativity. Edited extract. In R.Sternberg (ed.) *Handbook of Creativity* (pp. 313–325). Cambridge: Cambridge University Press.

Dacey, J.S. and Lennon, K.H. (with contributions by L.B. Fiore) (1998) *Understanding Creativity: The Interplay of Biological, Psychological and Social Factors*. San Francisco, CA: Jossey-Bass.

Eliot, T.S. (1919) Tradition and the individual talent. In J. Hayward (ed.) *Selected Prose: T.S. Eliot* (pp. 21–30). Harmondsworth: Penguin Books (1965).

ERA (Excellence in Research for Australia) (2012) *National Report*. Canberra: Australian Research Council.

Flinders University (2013a) Research higher degrees: Definitions (section 3.6). Available at http://www.flinders.edu.au/ppmanual/student/research-higher-degrees.cfm (accessed January 2015).

Flinders University (2013b) Creative MA and PhD degrees: Information for postgraduate students and examiners. Available at http://www.flinders.edu.au/ehl/fms/english_files/pdf/Creative%20MA%20and%20PhD%20guide%202013.pdf (accessed January 2015).

Fisher, J. (2012) The publishing paradigm: Commercialism versus creativity. In D. Hecq (ed.) *The Creativity Market: Creative Writing in the 21st Century* (pp. 54–65). Bristol: Multilingual Matters.

Foucault, M. (1972) Intellectuals and power: A conversation between Michel Foucault and Gilles Deleuze. Available at http://www.libcom.org/library/intellectuals-power-a-conversation-between-michel-foucault-and-gilles-deleuze. This transcript first appeared in English in D.F. Bouchard (ed.) *Language, Counter-Memory, Practice: Selected Essays and Interviews by Michel Foucault* (pp. 205–217). Ithaca, NY: Cornell University Press.

Harper, G. and Kroll, J. (eds) (2008) *Creative Writing Studies: Practice, Research and Pedagogy*. Clevedon: Multilingual Matters.

Haseman, B. (2006) A manifesto for performative research. *Culture and Policy* 188, 98–106.

Hecq, D. (2012) Banking on creativity: My brilliant career. In D. Hecq *The Creativity Market: Creative Writing in the 21st Century* (pp. 29–39). Bristol: Multilingual Matters.

Kernot, S. (2012) Writing poverty – The reflexive practitioner: Social welfare worker and creative artist. PhD thesis, Flinders University.

Kernot, S. (2013) *Underground Road*. Adelaide: Wakefield Press.

Krauth, N. (2011) Evolution of the exegesis: The radical trajectory of the creative writing doctorate. *TEXT: Journal of Writing and Writing Courses* 15 (1). Available at http://www.textjournal.com.au/april11/krauth.htm.

Kroll, J. and Harper, G. (2013) *Research Methods in Creative Writing*. London: Palgrave Macmillan.

Macdonald Cornford, F. (trans.) (1963) *The Republic of Plato*. New York: Oxford University Press.

Macquarie Library (1981) *Macquarie Dictionary* (2nd edn). Sydney: Macquarie Library.

Melbourne School of Graduate Research (2011) *PhD Handbook*. Melbourne: University of Melbourne.

National Health and Medical Research Council (2006) *Australian Code for the Responsible Conduct of Research*. Canberra: NHMRC.

NAWE (National Association of Writers in Education) (2008) Creative writing subject benchmark statement and research benchmark statement. Available at http://www. nawe.co.uk (accessed January 2015).

Neumann, R. (2003) *The doctoral experience: Diversity and complexity*. Canberra: Department of Education, Science and Training.

OECD (Organisation for Economic Co-operation and Development) (2002) *Frascati Manual: Proposed Standard Practice for Surveys on Research and Experimental Development* (6th edn). Paris: OECD.

Randall, J.H., Jr (1960) *Aristotle*. New York: Columbia University Press.

Sawyer, K. (2006) *Explaining Creativity: The Science of Human Innovation*. Oxford: Oxford University Press.

Sennett, R. (2008) *The Craftsman*. New Haven, CT: Yale University Press.

Sinclair, M. (2004) *The Pedagogy of 'Good' PhD Supervision: A National Cross-disciplinary Investigation of PhD Supervision*. Canberra: Department of Education, Science and Training.

Smith, H. and Dean, R. (2009) *Practice-Led Research, Research-Led Practice in the Creative Arts*. Edinburgh: Edinburgh University Press.

Stanford Encyclopedia of Philosophy (2013) Michel Foucault. Available at http://plato. stanford.edu/entries/foucault (accessed January 2015).

Stanford Encyclopedia of Philosophy (2014) *Episteme* and *techne*. Available at http://plato. stanford.edu/entries/episteme-techne (accessed January 2015).

Sternberg, R.J. (2003) *Wisdom, Intelligence and Creativity Synthesized*. Cambridge: Cambridge University Press.

Strand, D. (1998) *Research in the Creative Arts*. Canberra: Department of Employment, Education, Training and Youth Affairs.

Commentary 6

Taking Creative Writing Seriously in Schools

Maggie Butt

It has just been announced that although we can continue to teach art and music to children up to the age of 11, from 11 to 18 they have to get serious, and art or music practice can be taught only as a subsidiary subject to art history or music studies, in order to shed light on those more academic critical disciplines.

Okay, that isn't true; but it does reflect the situation we've had with a third creative art for far too long. Creative Writing has been all but invisible as a discrete craft and practice from the ages of 11 to 18 in UK schools, subordinate to the academic study of English Literature and Linguistics – until now.

In the UK, young people aged 17 normally choose four specialized 'A-level' subjects, which they take concurrently throughout the two final years of school. The A-level is the exit qualification from secondary school (age 11–18) or further education college (age 16–18) and operates as preparation and entry qualification for degree courses, which are highly focused in the UK. But up to September 2013, although it was possible to choose from a wide range of subjects, there was no A-level in Creative Writing, except as a small element of an English Literature or English Language A-level. This is in spite of a flowering of Creative Writing courses at undergraduate level, with 141 UK institutions of higher education currently offering a total of 504 degree courses in Creative Writing in some form.

The invisibility of Creative Writing in secondary schools was removed in September 2013, when we started to teach the first A-level in Creative Writing, validated by the AQA examination board.[1] Secondary schools and colleges right across the UK clamored to take it up, recognizing its importance not just for those who want to study Creative Writing at degree level, but also its value in teaching clarity of expression, critical and analytical skills, teamwork, giving and receiving feedback and creative problem-solving to students who will leave school for a wide range of jobs and other degree courses.

At last, aspiring writers will be able to trace a route through school on to higher education and beyond, into professional practice within the creative industries, as it has always been possible for aspiring actors, musicians and artists.

The A-level draws on university-level experience of Creative Writing as a discipline, with a distinct base and a well evolved pedagogical practice of workshopping. The term 'workshopping' can be used in a number of different ways, but here I mean the practice of each student sharing draft creative work with a group of peers on a regular (preferably weekly) basis to receive feedback from 'critical friends'. This practice gives students distance from their own work and develops their own critical faculties in giving feedback. Giving helpful critical feedback is a skill which has to be taught and learned. The new A-level also draws on other university good practice, including the involvement of professional writers, and links to the creative industries whenever possible. The curriculum was devised by a small team with years of experience of Creative Writing in higher education, and of teaching at A-level. It included the Director, Paul Munden, and Chair, myself, of the UK's National Association of Writing in Education (NAWE), the subject association for Creative Writing, which has been responsible for issuing benchmark statements for the subject.

Although the A-level was based on our experience in universities, there will be a number of differences when it is taught in schools and colleges. At university level, Creative Writing is almost always taught by practicing writers. The A-level, on the other hand, will be largely taught by English literature teachers – though many of them may be unpublished writers. It will be a conceptual leap for those teachers. In terms of its underlying principles, processes and assessment practices, the new A-level has more in common with art and design than with traditional English Literature courses and took inspiration from the curriculum and accepted assessment practices of those subjects, where it is understood that students need to develop their craft by studying masters of their art and producing an experimental portfolio of many sketches and ideas before embarking on a final piece.

The new A-level gives students the chance to explore the practical stages of producing creative work in a range of written forms, and allows them to learn how fresh forms of expression are devised in order to express individual visions. It requires them to write regularly in a range of forms and genres, to read widely and critically, to keep a journal, and to share work in progress with others. This will be quite different from teaching *Pride and Prejudice*, but the teachers who have so far enrolled on preparatory courses have embraced the new pedagogy and happily engaged in writing workshops themselves.

English Literature teachers are used to preparing students for assessment by examination but the majority of the assessment of the A-level will be by work developed and refined over the course of each year. At the end of the first year this will be two creative pieces of work in different forms (of a maximum of 3000 words) and a reflective commentary (of a maximum of 1500 words). At the end of the second year this will be a portfolio of creative work (a maximum 4000 words or equivalent) and a full reflective commentary (a maximum of 2000 words), with bibliography and evidence of redrafting.

The assessment practice of Creative Writing is based on the writers experimenting, drafting and redrafting, leading to a final piece. Their creative work can be from a wide range of genres, including fiction, poetry, writing for performance and new media, and a variety of non-fiction. As in university settings, students will submit the creative work alongside an accompanying critical commentary in which they reflect on their own process, detailing the aims, influences, response to feedback and technical decision-making which has led to the final piece. The commentary is like a recipe for the creative work, giving both its ingredients and the method of cooking. Educationally, this encourages deeper and more reflective learning than traditional rote-learning-and-regurgitation forms of assessment.

Unlike university courses, assessment will also include one module each year to be assessed under timed examination conditions. The timed examination is a government-required element of the A-level, so we had to devise an innovative approach to creative writing under timed conditions.

The first of these is a unit called 'Writing on demand', which seeks to emulate the real-life requirements on professional writers to write to order, with short deadlines and a tight focus, in a range of genres. Professional writers are asked to write book blurbs, biographies, reviews, short articles like this one, full academic papers, journalistic pieces and all manner of reports. We try to bring our skill as writers to bear on the requirements of each project. In the new exam, students will be given a brief, with detailed instructions, for example: to write a restaurant review; to write a pitch for a project to put poetry on buses; or to write copy for an exhibition catalogue. It is therefore a test of careful reading, of précis, of ability to grasp what the most 'newsworthy' angles are, as well as a test of writing craft and skill. We will not require students to write poetry or fiction 'to order' in this exam, although if someone chose to write a poem which met the brief, it would be looked on kindly. The first students took this end-of-year exam in the summer of 2014, and the results were very successful.

The second examination, a year later, assesses a unit called 'From reading to writing', which invites students to use published texts as a stimulus for their own creative work, and also to demonstrate their ability to analyze aspects of other writers' craft and apply this to their own writing. This seeks to replicate, on paper, the kind of Creative Writing workshop where extant writing is offered as inspiration for new work. It tests students' ability to read critically as writers, to apply techniques or themes and to reflect on their own process. Students will be given unseen extracts from published work (or whole published poems) in an examination paper and will be required to write creative pieces of their own which respond in some way to the published work, within the three-hour examination. The question paper will include five pieces of published creative work across the range of: prose fiction, prose non-fiction, poetry and script. Each text will be accompanied by a prompt for students' own writing.

In their original piece, students must respond to the instruction given in the writing prompt. This task is designed to allow students to demonstrate the use of published texts as inspiration for their own writing. Their original writing does not have to be in the same form or genre as the stimulus text, but it does have to arise from it in some demonstrable way.

They will also produce a commentary exploring aspects of the author's craft in the stimulus text they have selected, and the ways in which they have used the text to inspire their own creative work. This might include exploration of the author's craft, ideas, technique and use of form and genre, and how this has influenced and informed their own creative piece. The commentary should also give an explanation of their aims, and the techniques they have used to achieve them, and finally allows students to acknowledge that their writing is a first draft and to show how it might be developed further.

We wait to see how successful this will be. Who knows, perhaps Creative Writing examinations will prove so successful that they will be replicated at a higher level in university courses?

Whether or not the examination is adopted at higher levels, there will undoubtedly be ripples of effect from the introduction of the new A-level, although the magnitude of these is of course speculative at this stage.

Hopefully, there are highly positive implications for the increase in creativity generally right across the curriculum, resulting in a generation of students who will take improved imaginative, writing and critical skills into their jobs, whether they become lawyers, botanists or accountants.

Probably, there will be a new intake of students to Creative Writing at university, who will already have two years of study of the subject, and two years of directed creative development before they arrive. This may lead to a need to rewrite first year undergraduate courses, or at least to ensure flexible differentiation within them to allow for students entering with more focused experience than ever before.

Certainly, there will have to be changes to teacher training, addressing the particular pedagogic needs of Creative Writing, both for existing teachers who have specialized in English Literature until now and for the teachers who are starting out.

Possibly, there will be increased opportunities for writers to be invited into schools to share their craft with school students.

Finally, we hope there should be talent which is spotted, nurtured and directed early on, to produce some exceptional writers in the future.

I have known I was a writer since I was seven; I worked as a journalist and a television writer/producer before finally getting my first collection of poems published at the age of 51. Perhaps if the Creative Writing A-level had been available when I was at school, I would have got there much sooner!

Note

(1) The AQA A-level Creative Writing specification is available at http://www.aqa.org. uk/subjects/english/a-level/creative-writing-2750.

Chapter 11

The Poetry of Evaluation: Helping Students Explore How They Value Verse

Michael Theune and Bob Broad

Virtually every great poet has possessed axiological self-awareness. In other words, they are keenly aware of how poetic value is constructed. Of the vast number of subjects that poets have thought about, meditated on and agonized over – love, nature, sex, death – one of the major subjects is poetry itself and how it should be valued. The history of poetry includes vital, energetic, charged statements about the art of poetry. In defenses, manifestoes, essays, prefaces, letters, lectures and *ars poeticas*, great poets have strived to articulate what they value in and about poems. To cite just a few examples by (fairly) recent American poets: 'If I feel physically as if the top of my head were taken off, I know *that* is poetry' (Dickinson, 1958: L342a); 'The poem itself must, at all points, be a high-energy construct and, at all points, an energy-discharge' (Olson, 1966: 16); 'A poem should not mean/But be' (Macleish, 1952: 41); 'Ideally a poem will be both mysterious (incunabula, driftwood of the unconscious) and organic (secular) at the same time' (Guest, 2003: 20); 'A sense of cultural responsibility prompts [Black poets] to affirm the place of poetry in the struggle against social injustice' (Dove & Nelson, 1991: 220).

Such aesthetic statements, and the axiological insights at their core, are not peripheral to poetry but, very often, comprise a vital part of the action of poem-making. By formulating such statements, poets reveal to themselves and others what characteristics they do and do not appreciate in poetry – often such statements reject earlier or commonly accepted values to then formulate, embrace and/or endorse something new, and then the statements can lead poets to new creative territory by encouraging them to work to enact/embody their axiological self-awareness in their creative work.

Take John Keats's great ode, 'To Autumn'. It is mistaken to think that Keats's work toward composing 'To Autumn' began when he penned the poem's first words, 'Season of mists…'. Much influenced and pushed Keats toward this poem – its origins were multiple and complex. However, one major influence on the creation of 'To Autumn' certainly was Keats's axiological searching and self-reflection, as recorded in his letters. Of special relevance are those reflections that, on the one hand, record Keats's praise for the mental state of 'disinterestedness' (letter 159 in Rollins, 1958) and the ways that properly disinterested poets – including the great 'camelion Poet' Shakespeare (letter 118) – could disappear completely into their characters and, on the other hand, offer a concomitant critique of some other stances toward thinking and writing, including, especially, the work of 'Egotist' poets (letter 59) such as William Wordsworth, whose work imposes a 'palpable design' upon its readers (letter 118). According to Keats's biographer Walter Jackson Bate (1963), these related trends in Keats's thinking were succinctly encapsulated in Keats's formulation of the term 'Negative Capability', that is, 'when man is capable of being in uncertainties, Mysteries, doubts, without any irritable reaching after fact & reason' (letter 45). And it is only as a result of such axiological inquiry and investigation that 'To Autumn' – a poem which critic Hartman (1975: 133) claims is 'the most negative capable of all of Keats's great poems' – could have been written. So, in part, Keats articulated his aesthetic values and then wrote a poem that embodied those values.

The intimate relationship between poem-making and axiological self-awareness cannot be stressed enough, for even if all those invested in poetry – poets, scholars, critics, teachers, readers – generally acknowledge this connection, teachers of poetry writing generally do not do a good job of teaching it. Here, we will argue, though, that axiological investigation *should* play a role in poetry writing pedagogy. Additionally, we will recommend that those who teach poetry writing should employ the most current and potentially revelatory form of axiological investigation: dynamic criteria mapping.

The omission of discussion of value from the poetry classroom is not the fault of individual teachers but reflects a much larger trend. In *Contingencies of Value*, Smith (1991: 17) describes what she calls 'the exile of evaluation', noting that 'the entire problematic of value and evaluation has been evaded and explicitly exiled by the literary academy'. Ameliorated somewhat in intervening years by some significant projects and publications in the literary academy, this exile of evaluation has made its way into poetry writing pedagogy. This is not to say that there is no evaluation in poetry workshops – there is a great deal of it. It is to say, rather, that the evaluation that occurs – often formulated by an individual reader on her/his own, with subtlety, speed, silence and in solitude, and then simply shared – largely is unreflective, un-self-aware. Traditionally, workshops invite participants to announce evaluations but not negotiate them.

It is precisely this situation that Bizzaro (1993: xi) reflects on and tries to address in his *Responding to Student Poems,* a book that acknowledges 'our profession's lack of curiosity concerning what happens when teachers read and evaluate student poetry' (Bizzaro, 1993: xi). Bizzaro encourages teachers of poetry writing to become curious about their methods of assessment and to investigate those methods through disciplined self-analysis of one's own methods of revision. Bizzaro (p. 9) specifically advises teachers of poetry writing to carefully analyze the changes made in drafts of their own work in an attempt to discover what literary values are embedded in these revisions.

Such work has multiple benefits. According to Bizzaro (p. 27), as those who must 'act out the role of authoritative reader', teachers 'will perform this task more effectively after they have noted what they value as readers of their own poems, after they have discovered how they employ what they believe to be "standards of excellence" as guidelines for moving from draft to draft of their own writing'. Such work also can free a teacher from the enclosure of her/his own perspective: 'Questioning accepted pedagogy requires that we acknowledge and name the critical lens through which an individual teacher reads and evaluates poems, since only by doing so can teachers render alternative readings' (p. xiv). These benefits for the teacher, then, can be passed along to students; according to Bizzaro (p. 27), '[B]y modeling this procedure in front of their classes, teachers can use their self-examination as a starting point in discussing standards with students who have done little prior reading appropriate to the course'.

Bizzaro's work is uniquely significant. Bizarro contributed something truly new to both poetry writing pedagogy and to the ongoing history of poetic axiological self-awareness: he took a large step forward by approaching his own evaluative processes as an *object of empirical inquiry.* And he did so in an extraordinary way: Bizarro introduced perhaps the single most dramatic shift in literary axiology: from the speculative methods of the humanities (dealing solely with published literary texts) to the empirical methods of the social and physical sciences, adding an analytical, data-driven dimension to what was formerly a largely speculative line of inquiry.

The speculative and empirical need not be understood as antithetical – indeed, any investigation that leads to any degree of axiological self-awareness typically involves some amount of analysis – but rather they exist on a continuum of kinds of axiological engagement. At one end of the spectrum are those working in what Smith (1991: 19) memorably terms '[t]he magisterial mode' – powerful critics and scholars, such as F.R. Leavis and Yvor Winters, who decide how good they think poems (and other texts) are and announce their judgments to the world. Theirs is evaluation without axiology: they devote little or no effort to studying or understanding their processes of poetic judgment, focusing instead on wielding intellectual power through force of will, rhetoric and fame. The next section along this spectrum consists of those poetical/axiological inquiries that – while differing in levels of systematic inquiry – essentially follow the traditional humanities approach: the individual scholar works alone, reading texts and writing her/his thoughts about them. But Bizzaro's close, systematic observations differ greatly from such speculation – albeit seductive, suggestive and even sometimes *potentially* correct. This continuum can be represented visually as shown in Table 1.

Although Bizzaro adds something truly new to axiological inquiry, the self-analysis he recommends is only one kind of analysis and, as he himself notes, it is not even necessarily adequate; Bizzaro (1993: 37) states, '[W]hen it comes to evaluations of matters as private as "preferences" and "tastes" in writing, the self is an excellent place to start. Still, I must also stress that it is a place to begin, not end, our search.' Although Bizzaro does not explicitly develop a different model for the kind of further investigation he espouses, at one point, later in his book, he does seem to suggest a way to move beyond self-analysis: toward the social and collaborative.

In 'Reading the course in poetry writing: Preparing students for the workshop', the seventh chapter of *Responding to Student Poems* (pp. 159–191), Bizzaro – having asked each of his workshop students to assume one of the four theoretical perspectives (listed below) they had examined in order to allow the students to practice critiquing from a specific perspective – records,

Table 1 Types of axiological inquiry

	None	Primarily speculative	Empirical
Characteristics	Lack of self-awareness	Varying degrees of axiological self-awareness and willingness to articulate that awareness	More critical self-awareness as a result of using more data and systematic inquiry
Embodiment	The 'magisterial mode' of critics such as F.R. Leavis and Yvor Winters	Most axiological explorations by poets such as Keats	Bizzaro

transcribes and analyzes their workshop discussion. Through this process Bizzaro finds that he acquires some new, more finely grained information. For example, though each student took on the role of a New Critic, a reader-response critic, a feminist or a deconstructionist, the analysis of group conversation revealed a fluidity in the identities of the conversation's participants, a constant negotiation of roles, which Bizzaro (p. 169) finds 'agreeable', as 'such shifts in the personalities students adopt as readers and writers are necessary if learning is to take place'. According to Bizzaro (p. 169), 'These exchanges between students, sometimes coarse and often more related to the people involved than to the poem, are actually vital indicators that something is happening to the identities of workshop participants'. Bizzaro equates this transformative liveliness with 'underlife', a term used by Robert E. Brooke in *Writing and Sense of Self: Identity Negotiation in Writing Workshops* to mean 'patterns of behavior which show that individuals resist aspects of the assigned role, that there is more to them than this' (Brooke, 1991: 74; quoted in Bizzaro).

Following on Bizzaro's discovery of the underlife of poetry assessors, it is clear that the investigation of assessment in poetry writing pedagogy needs to move to social group, for this is where evaluation happens. As Smith (1991: 14) reminds us, '[E]valuation is a form of *social* behavior'. And, so, such social behavior needs to be studied, with new methodologies, *as social behavior*. And there is a way to do this: through dynamic criteria mapping.

The phrase 'dynamic criteria mapping' was introduced in Bob Broad's 2003 book *What We Really Value: Beyond Rubrics in Teaching and Assessing Writing*. Broad (2003: 13) described dynamic criteria mapping (DCM) as 'a streamlined form of qualitative inquiry that yields a detailed, complex, and useful portrait' of the criteria and dynamics by which people evaluate texts. DCM invites assessors – scholars, editors, teachers, workshop participants – to listen as they examine and evaluate texts together, discussing in detail what they value or do not value in those texts. DCM then analyzes the record of this conversation in order to publish a map, a rich description, of their textual and contextual values. Such a map proves useful to a range of audiences – students, instructors, administrators and the general public – and a range of uses: teaching and learning, program assessment and research (see Broad *et al.*, 2009).

What allows the map to be so rich and therefore so useful is the fact that it derives from around-the-table, face-to-face conversation, which, according to one prominent researcher, allows for more spontaneous interactions and permits not only speech but also social cues to be considered (Opdenakker, 2006). Face-to-face interactions allow for increased spontaneity, volatility, surprise, drama, humanity, civility, fluidity, responsiveness and discomfort in challenging a respected colleague's evaluation while she/he sits across the table from you, listening and preparing her/his reply. Additionally, by listening in on face-to-face conversations, DCM recreates the circumstances under which many assessments in fact get made – by a group of evaluators, such as judges, editors, teachers. In short, through the face-to-face inter-action of DCM, we are permitted access to the 'underlife' of evaluation, and we are witness to what Smith (1991: 15, original emphasis) calls '*the dynamics of a system*'.

DCM developed in the field of rhetoric and composition as a means of studying instructors' evaluations of students' texts (usually analytical, per-suasive and narrative texts). Our (Mike Theune and Bob Broad's) ongoing collaboration imports DCM into the world of poetry, so we call our project 'Poetry DCM'. Communal assessment is not foreign to poetry. It happens often when there are multiple evaluators – for example, in workshops or when there are multiple editors of a journal or multiple judges for a poetry contest. However, as with the bulk of poetry evaluation, these assessments are more 'primarily speculative' than 'empirical'. That is, decisions are made either without inquiry into the values behind those choices, or using representations of what the values are (e.g. the aesthetics *claimed* by an editorial board), which may differ greatly from the criteria by which evalu-ations in fact are made. DCM can be used to investigate and much more accurately articulate the dynamics of group assessments. It also can be used to determine more acutely the evaluative dynamics of any member of that group. In short, DCM fills a gap in methods of axiological investigation, providing a way to perform poetic assessment that is both empirical and communal. We can visually represent the contribution that DCM makes to poetic axiology in the manner indicated in Table 2.

So far as we, Mike and Bob, are aware, poetry DCM has been performed twice. A description of the first was published in *College English* (Broad & Theune, 2010). The second poetry DCM was performed by students. During the fall semester of 2012, we coordinated and collaborated on a teaching project based in poetry DCM. We wanted our undergraduate students to use and experience poetry DCM as a way to better understand poetry and

Table 2 Individual and communal types of axiological inquiry

	Primarily speculative	*Empirical*
Individual	Most axiological explorations by poets	Bizzaro
Communal	Group of editors/judges	DCM

themselves as readers of poetry. Throughout this project, our classroom assignments and activities were substantively the same; however, because Mike secured prior approval from the university's institutional review board to gather data in his classroom, this chapter will focus exclusively on Mike's class, his students and what they wrote.

Mike's class, English 370, was called 'Issues in Contemporary American Poetry'. This literature class enrolled 12 upper-level undergraduate students at Illinois Wesleyan University. Following is a brief summary of what Mike directed his students to do, pulled from the assignment handout for the poetry DCM project:

1. You and a small group of your fellow students will form an editorial board charged with creating a (very small!) anthology of contemporary American poems about which you are passionate.
2. [Each student] will submit ... a packet of five contemporary American poems that you love, along with a Works Cited and a brief (600-word) reflection on your selection....
3. [Mike] will create two small groups of six students each, and for each group [he] will assemble one packet of twelve poems from out of the packets each of its members submitted.
4. ... discuss with your small group the poems in your packet.... The point of these conversations will be to try to select the five contemporary American poems your editorial board is, overall, most passionate about, and so will include in its anthology.
5. ... your small group must record your conversations ... and then transcribe them soon after....
6. ... your small group will analyze your discussion ... you will try to identify, group, and rank ... the criteria that came up in conversation.
7. ... your [editorial board] must submit your five-poem anthology and a five-page (1500-word) introduction to your anthology that
   a. presents (and promotes!) the anthology's poems
   b. discusses briefly the selection process; and
   c. makes clear the criteria that are embodied by the anthology's poems....

Thus Mike required his students to work through a series of steps with a special focus on the values that inform their judgments of poetic texts.

This assignment had multiple purposes. It asked students to begin to engage with the publishing venues for contemporary American poetry in order to find poems they loved. By imitating an actual communal assessment process – that of a group of anthologists deciding what might be included in an anthology – it tried to give a sense of how poetic evaluations actually get made. It offered students the opportunity to be better informed about how they and their peers value poetry, and to get a sense of the many different complexities of poetry assessment. And it did all of this in a relatively short time frame: two weeks of class time. Valuable in itself, the insight gleaned from this exercise also prepared students to be more critical readers and assessors of three anthologies that the class read during the final third of the semester.

Carefully noting recurring patterns and themes – and also anomalies – in the poetic values students highlighted, we studied the introductions to the anthologies composed by both editorial teams in Mike's class. Based on our review of these introductions, we argue that poetry DCM makes students better as both writers and readers of literature. The work of inductively and empirically exploring and articulating one's criteria for judging poems makes one more attuned, sensitive, self-aware and flexible regarding one's framework(s) for judging poetry. While some of the poetic values – such as tone, readers' emotional-experiential connection to content, and vivid images and descriptions – student editors discovered in and among themselves were those we would expect to hear from most evaluators of poetry, other criteria these editorial boards discovered and developed were more nuanced and surprising.

One group of students noticed that they 'often gravitated toward' incongruity of paired images and themes. They discussed their penchant for 'shocking image pairs', explaining that '[t]hese jarring contrasts both created powerful images and gave us the satisfaction of seeing connections between seemingly unrelated things'. This same student editorial board attempted to develop and explain its emphasis on what it called 'complementary formatting', that is, 'when the format of the poem enhanced or at least did not detract from the subject of the poem'. This group also recognized that, for them, 'forms that drew our immediate attention were generally seen as a distraction'. This editorial board took an unconventionally dynamic and context-sensitive approach to the well worn criterion 'form'. In its decisions, form interacts in volatile ways with other poetic elements (subject matter, tone, imagery) and therefore has literary impact that involves a great deal more than form as, say, container.

The other student editorial board in Mike's class achieved equally interesting insights, and added the feature of giving their more distinctive criteria special names. 'Endfectiveness' was the term they came up with to describe 'powerful or effective endings'. Endfectiveness either 'leaves the reader thinking, or is powerful enough to cause them to sit back dumbstruck'. This group was 'captivated by endings that left us hanging and gave us something to think about'. And it especially appreciated the ending of one poem that 'left our group thinking "Wow!" and gave us a sense of hopelessness and comfort at the same time because of the bittersweet image at the end of the poem'.

The final distinctive criterion this editorial board illuminated stands out perhaps more for its courage and honesty than for its originality: they termed it the 'Shakespeare effect' and they noted that it was 'one of the most powerful pieces informing our criticisms'. The 'Shakespeare effect' refers to how knowing a poem's author changes one's assessment of that poem. In fact, this group wrote: '[w]e eventually discovered ... that the author of a poem did not just "matter", but was often vital in shaping our evaluation of the poem before we even began reading'. This discovery seems particularly insightful. Many teachers, readers and editors proclaim that their judgments of poems are unsullied by historical or biographical information about the authors of the texts they are evaluating. And occasionally this is true. This editorial board, however, shone a light on just how powerful the Shakespeare effect was for them.

Although the DCM undertaken by our undergraduate students took place in the context of a literature course, this work certainly can be performed productively in a poetry writing class. We believe that – though this claim has yet to be tested – the enhanced knowledge of self and text that poetry DCM yields also makes one a better poet. The process itself is valuable, especially the part of the process in which students seek out poetry they deeply admire. The work students do to gather their favorite poems can be deeply informative – it can introduce students to various publishing venues (websites, journals, books, anthologies, etc.) and offer them a glimpse of the spectrum of poetry being published.

There are many ways students and instructors can use the information and insights gathered through poetry DCM. For example, the findings could become a revision tool. A poetry writing class might create an idiosyncratic, perhaps playful set of guidelines that the student poet, while drafting a poem, might consult in answering a series of questions: Have I used the form so that it complements the subject and/or action of the poem? Have I included any of the shocking images I value? Is my final stanza endfective? An instructor might use similar questions in the form of a rubric to evaluate student drafts and final portfolios, and to invite students to further discuss and debate the criteria brought to the evaluation. By explicitly articulating their values, students can come to recognize their standards and then work to attain that level of quality they expect in other poems. And being explicit about the values by which they are assessing student work, instructors will reveal that they do not simply use the magisterial mode and grade according to 'what they like'. At its best, poetry DCM helps students see what they love in poetry and so better equips them to emulate it, or it might help students see that there is poetry out in the world that they do not admire, and so they might write in contradistinction to or against it, as Keats did with Wordsworth. Instructors will play the vital role of encouraging this evolving inquiry.

Of course, undertaking DCM in a poetry writing class might mean a bit less poetry writing. This is true, but it is not too much time – just two weeks. And those two weeks are a relatively small investment of poetry writing time for some very large gains in student preparedness, engagement and perceptiveness, and so better workshops. However, there is at least one other way to incorporate the systematic, grounded study of poetic value into the education of undergraduate poets: create a whole class devoted to the study of literary axiology. In such a class, students could engage in DCM to learn more about their own values and/or to learn about the values of others. For example, students might create their own anthologies of contemporary poems they love and, through DCM, further explore and articulate their values. While work would be needed to establish a class devoted to literary axiology, it is through such concerted efforts that literary evaluation finally would emerge fully from its exile.

Whatever the particular method, it is vital that undergraduate poetry writers become better acquainted with their own and others' poetic values – and the best, fullest, most complete way we know of to do this is DCM. By engaging in DCM, students will be at the methodological forefront of the noble tradition of axiological self-awareness and expression and, as a result, they will become better, more alert and engaged readers, and they will become more creative critics of their own and others' work – all of which are a big part of becoming a real poet.

Exploration

(1) Axiology is the study of how things are valued. Many of the greatest poets possess axiological self-awareness. To help students apply or transform their literary values as they read and write poetry, teachers must promote such self-awareness.

(2) Far from rote or predictable, the evaluations at the core of such self-awareness are vital, charged. They boost the energy of the creative writing classroom.

(3) Despite the exile of evaluation, assessment remains at the core of much poetry writing pedagogy. Currently, this assessment is usually tacit. Teachers must make it more explicit.

(4) While typically reserved for editorial boards and admissions committees, poetic evaluation is work of which undergraduate students are fully capable. Through such work, they can begin to articulate criteria with the energy and charge one finds in famous poetic statements.

(5) To become more fully conscious of the dynamics of evaluation, poetry writing classes should undertake dynamic criteria mapping (DCM). DCM transforms individual/speculative assessment into evaluation that is communal/empirical.

(6) The face-to-face interaction and even evaluative conflict produced by DCM are both enlivening and productive: they lead to more finely grained articulations of value and more creative revelations.

(7) DCM can and should be incorporated into poetry writing classes. Additionally, poetry writing faculty might consider offering a class on literary evaluation.

Acknowledgment

We thank the reviewers of the initial manuscript for this chapter. We have incorporated many of their comments, some verbatim. We also thank the students of English 370 for allowing us to use their work.

References

Bate, W.J. (1963) *John Keats*. Cambridge, MA: Harvard University Press.

Bizarro, P. (1993) *Responding to Student Poems: Applications of Critical Theory*. Urbana, IL: National Council of Teachers of English.

Broad, B. (2003) *What We Really Value: Beyond Rubrics in Teaching and Assessing Writing*. Logan, UT: Utah State University Press.

Broad, B. and Theune, M. (2010) How we value contemporary poetry: An empirical inquiry. *College English* 73 (2), 113–137.

Broad, B., Adler-Kassner, L., Alford, B., Detweiler, J., Estrem, H., Harrington, S., McBride, M., Stalions, E. and Weeden, S. (2009) *Organic Writing Assessment: Dynamic Criteria Mapping in Action*. Logan, UT: Utah State University Press.

Brooke, R.E. (1991) *Writing and Sense of Self: Identity Negotiation in Writing Workshops*. Urbana, IL: National Council of Teachers of English.

Dickinson, E. (1958) *The Letters of Emily Dickinson*. T. Johnson (ed.). Cambridge, MA: Belknap Press.

Dove, R. and Nelson, M. (1991) A black rainbow: Modern Afro-American poetry. In R. McDowell (ed.) *Poetry After Modernism* (pp. 217–275). Brownsville, OR: Story Line.

Guest, B. (2003) A reason for poetics. In *Forces of Imagination: Writing on Writing* (pp. 20–23). Berkeley, CA: Kelsey St Press.

Hartman, G. (1975) Poem and ideology: A study of Keats's 'To Autumn'. In *The Fate of Reading and Other Essays* (pp. 124–146). Chicago, IL: University of Chicago Press.

Macleish, A. (1952) Ars poetica. In *Collected Poems 1917–1952* (pp. 40–41). Cambridge, MA: Riverside Press.

Olson, C. (1966) Projective verse. In R. Creeley (ed.) (pp. 15–26) *Selected Writings*. New York: New Directions.

Opdenakker, R. (2006) Advantages and disadvantages of four interview techniques in qualitative research. *Forum Qualitative Sozialforschung/Forum: Qualitative Social Research* 7 (4), article 11. Available at http://www.qualitative-research.net/index.php/fqs/article/view/175/391 (accessed 30 January 2012).

Rollins, H.E. (ed.) (1958) *The Letters of John Keats*. Cambridge, MA: Harvard University Press.

Smith, B.H. (1991) *Contingencies of Value: Alternative Perspectives for Critical Theory*. Cambridge, MA: Harvard University Press.

Chapter 12

The Radical Future of Teaching Creative Writing

Nigel Krauth

The migration of readership from the paper page to the e-page forces teachers of writing to address major changes in publishing and the kinds of outputs writing students produce. Stephanie Vanderslice notes that with web 2.0 'the terrain shifted' for creative writing teachers and admits that, like many teachers, she was tempted 'to hide from this new technology' (Vanderslice, 2013: 138). Graeme Harper observes 'the impact of contemporary digital technologies' on writing and publishing, especially how – using the internet – writers now publish and distribute their own work (cutting out traditional publishers) and talk directly with their audiences. Harper suggests that the 'role universities play in supporting and developing creative writing needs to be considered in light of this 21st century evolution' (Harper, 2012: 22).

While forward-thinking individual academics note the changes and ask questions about them, university creative writing programs have been slow to reflect, or even recognize, this evolution. Discourse at departmental levels has largely avoided questions like: 'With the prospect of paper publishing becoming a thing of the past, what writing processes should we teach?'; 'What will everyone be reading in 10 or 20 years' time, and what will publishers be looking for?'; and 'What do our students need to know now in order to make a living in the future?' Writing for hypermedia has been thought of as someone else's business – belonging to the IT and Communications people, or the New Media Arts people. Creative Writing, and the English departments it is often housed in, need urgently to address this situation.

Eminent librarian and historian Robert Darnton contends that 'whatever the future may be, it will be digital. The present is a time of transition, when printed and digital modes of communication coexist' (Darnton, 2009: xv). Jeff Gomez, a marketing director for Penguin Group (USA), says: 'While print is not yet dead, it is undoubtedly sickening' (Gomez, 2008: 3). One well published American children's author, Roxie Munro, declares: 'I don't

think, sadly, that the average house will have a bookshelf in 30 years [time]'
(National Public Radio, 2012).

Gunther Kress states the situation clearly: 'The *book* has now been
superseded by the *screen* in the role of dominant medium of communication'
(Kress, 2003: 12, his italics). He writes:

> One might say the following with some confidence. Language-as-speech
> will remain the major mode of communication; language-as-writing
> will increasingly be displaced by image in many domains of public
> communication, though writing will remain the preferred mode of the
> political and cultural elites. The combined effects on writing of the
> dominance of the mode of image and of the medium of the screen will
> produce deep changes in the forms and functions of writing. This in
> turn will have profound effects on human, cognitive/affective, cultural
> and bodily engagement with the world, and on the forms and shapes of
> knowledge. *The world told* is a different world to *the world shown*. (Kress,
> 2003: 1, his italics)

During and beyond the period of transition – a time of uneasy co-
existence between print and hypermedia (which may, of course, last a long
while yet) – Darnton predicts that 'book professionals [will continue to]
provide services that will outlast all changes in technology' (Darnton, 2009:
xvi). Darnton includes editors, designers and marketing consultants among
his 'book professionals', but surely creative writing teachers need to be
counted there too.

So what are teachers doing in reacting to the technology changes their
students have to cope with? Adam Koehler, commenting on the proliferation of creative writing studies research in the last four years, observes:

> While all this work admirably approaches some of the urgent pedagogi-
> cal, methodological, and institutional concerns developing in creative
> writing, one set of concerns ... remains largely unaddressed: the ways in
> which creative writing, or creative writing studies, engages with, under-
> stands, responds to, and thrives in an age of digital writing. (Koehler,
> 2013)

And what are these researchers'/teachers' departments doing about the
problem? Joseph Moxley says, in a vaguely hopeful way:

> Eventually innovative English departments will develop their own
> interactive writing environments to support the excellent works of their

students. With students leading the way our disciplinary identity will be substantively revised. It's just going to take a little time. (Moxley, 2010: 237)

Many books have been published in the debate about technology change and the future of the book (e.g. Birkerts, 1994; McGann, 2001; Nunberg, 1996; Striphas, 2011; Thompson, 2005; Vandendorpe, 1999) but major questions for creative writing teachers remain: Where is the teaching of creative writing headed? What will the fiction and non-fiction of the future look like? How significant are the changes we need to make? What new infrastructures must be put in place? Are we dealing with these matters too late? And, are English departments as we know them really capable of handling these problems?

Children grow up reading some of their books as apps now. I have seen infants try to turn the pages of paper books by swiping them. In various US, UK and Australian primary schools, iPads are distributed to pupils from first to fifth grade as the official learning device and their use is integrated into a wide spectrum of the curriculum, including the teaching of writing, literature and technology (see e.g. Burley School, 2014; Department of Education Western Australia, 2014; Square Group, 2013). Leading publishers Pearson, Macmillan, Oxford University Press and others now produce university textbooks for iPad (Apple Inc., 2014). The study of the use of hypermedia in education has its own academic research journal: the *Journal of Educational Multimedia and Hypermedia* (*JEMH*) (published by the Association for the Advancement of Computing in Education – see http://www.aace.org/pubs/jemh/default.htm). However, as Jay David Bolter noted in 2011:

Although many, perhaps most, novelists now use word processors to prepare manuscripts for publication as printed books, our literate culture still believes fiction belongs in the space defined by printing. (Bolter, 2011: 121)

Despite extensive experimentation on the radical fringes, and a handful of notable exceptions in the mainstream (see e.g. Foer, 2006), the adult novel in the first two decades of the 21st century is still a print phenomenon at odds with the new literacy products informing primary and secondary school education. Constrained by the fact that adult mainstream publishing (as opposed to publishing for children) has been slow to embrace the range of hypermedia platforms for creative works, the teaching of creative writing at university level has remained significantly focused on paper publishing outcomes.

Among the iPad apps for teenage fiction readers, there is the 2013 Bologna Children's Book Fair prize-winning version of Michael Morpurgo's *War Horse*. This app novel is published jointly by children's publisher Egmont and Touch Press. The former's blurb says:

> The app features a specially filmed performance of *War Horse* by author Michael Morpurgo, accompanied by musicians John Tams and Barry Coope. It also features interviews with Michael Morpurgo filmed by award-winning arts media company Illuminations in Iddesleigh (Devon), where the novel begins and ends; historians discussing the First World War from the battlefields of the Western Front; the National Army and National World War I museums; and more. In addition to the abridged text used for the performance, the original book's full text is included alongside a full audio reading, an interactive timeline packed with narrated quotes, war videos and artefacts, allowing the reader to delve into the historical background of the story. (Egmont, 2013)

So, it's a work of fiction, of non-fiction, of history and it's exegetical. It's richly illustrated with photography, graphics and digital cleverness. It incorporates various performances, including by the author, and has a number of music soundtracks. It costs $6.99. Even in the co-publisher's short website introduction/trailer/blurb (Touch Press, 2013b) you get a feel for the fact that this is a variety of texts and a variety of reading experiences. In a way, it's like reading in three dimensions – it does for the novel what Cinerama, then 3-D and then Sensurround sound did for film. This is the high end of hypermedia fiction publishing in the future.

Another example of hypermedia fiction – in this case a collaborative web novel by Kate Pullinger, Chris Joseph *et al.* called *Flight Paths* – is not so expensive or elaborate (Pullinger & Joseph, 2012). This DIY hypertext novel has cut out the publisher and isn't too fancy, but it does show the potential of the digital novel form. I find as I read this work, with its strong integration of text, images and soundtrack, that I begin to interpret the visuals as text – to accept that the images are replacing paragraphs of setting and description, so I process them in that way. Similarly, I know the music soundtrack is about atmosphere and emotion, and I interpret it as replacing a textual commentary on the characters' situations and feelings. I change, expand and reinterpret these different modes, or channels, of meaning into a hybrid narrative 'reading'. I'm not watching film or listening to music, I'm reading the combination of text, image and sound as text.

The use of several modes at once – several sites or channels of meaning simultaneously – enriches the reading experience; but also we need to know *how* to read in this way. Our current monomodal literacy (that employed in the reading of traditional text novels, for example) does not cope well with multimodal inputs: we get confused, we feel overloaded, we think we can't focus on so many strands at once. We say the novel cannot be multimodal: that it's just too hard to read – 'exhausting', one critic calls it (Bellafante, 2009). (Of course, the actual structure of the paper book – held in linear order by the spine – is part of the problem here, and I'll come back to it later.) But we read films successfully, and they involve at least two sites or channels of meaning – the visual and the auditory. And television advertisements, like computer screens, encourage us to read images and text together, and they even add a soundtrack to help (not hinder) us doing it.

To learn about multimodal reading we can turn to Gunther Kress and others such as Gregory L. Ulmer (2002) and Jan Rune Holmevik (2012) (the latter both call their version of hypermedia literacy *electracy*). In Kress's analysis of multimodality, the way we read has changed due to our exposure to screen-driven culture. We now interact with diverse incoming channels to produce 'a rich orchestration of meaning' (Kress, 2011: 05.05). Not only is the visual more pervasive in communication but, also, we are much more accepting of the idea that visual and written (or spoken) texts will operate in unison. It started with our recognition that – at the simplest level – gestures and facial expressions accompany speech as part of the message. But with the proliferation of screens to be read, especially TV advertisements and websites, we are now required to master multimodal reading in order to know about our world. Kress talks about finding meaning 'where it is' (Kress, 2011: 05.17), on the page, using 'the whole page as an *integrated* text' (Kress & van Leeuwen, 2006: 177, their italics). The reading 'pathways' (where the eyes go) change from linear to spatially oriented in this new literacy, using codes of spatial and temporal composition for meaning-making (Kress & van Leeuwen, 2006: 177). This changes the logic of how we put narratives together. In other words, we read and understand by synthesizing the variety of input modes that come in to us. By selecting, arranging and interpreting what we find most salient among the variety of incoming channels, we form our reading, our created 'text'. Clearly, these changes in reading require a new kind of writing.

In the book *Multimodality*, Kress starts his argument with a simple comparison between street signs (Kress, 2010: 1–4). The first sign, prominently attached to a wall at a set of London traffic lights, gives directions for drivers to get from there to a supermarket, directions which are complex because of access via one-way streets and an obscure entry point to the carpark. He explains that the information transmitted in the sign – which uses text, image and color to present its message – is nuanced to operate multimodally because the sign would not work either as text alone or as image alone. Text and image together create the whole communication successfully.

But Kress shows another figure – an official sign explaining temporary parking arrangements during the European soccer championships in Salzburg in 2008. It is a printed poster attached to a blackboard-style A-frame, set on the footpath beside a busy road. This sign is typical of publications by official cultures which valorize the written text: 'Bureaucracy assumes that as long as something has been announced in writing it has been communicated and the rest will look after itself' (Kress, 2010: 2). The power of laws and tradition allows the Salzburg Traffic Office to rely on a non-sign, a single-mode communication.

I am tempted to use Kress's comparison of signs as a metaphor for what is happening in universities teaching creative writing today, because so many creative writing courses occur in English departments. English departments, like the Salzburg Traffic Office, think they still have the power to insist on the single-mode written text as the definition of the novel. But like the soccer sign in the Salzburg street, the novel as monograph runs the risk of being less and less noticed by a new generation of readers moving on. Kress suggests that sign-writers, advertising agencies and web editors already know more about the reading and writing that will be done in the future than do English and creative writing departments. How much do teachers of creative writing – and the students we are teaching – know about writing multimodally? We all had difficulty when Barthes said the reader makes the story; now Kress tells us the new reader makes the story out of several modes of input.

Writing and literature have complex histories and we might go back to illuminated manuscripts as a multimodal form before the printing press, and how the first printed books carried on that tradition of multimodal illustration (e.g. Chaucer's *Canterbury Tales* as printed by Caxton) before the burgeoning, bourgeois and commercially driven printing press eradicated the visual from adult literary reading. It seems the paper book (the codex) is to blame for the restrictions inherent in our monomodal reading capacity: all that sewing and gluing that holds everything together unrelentingly at the spine! The book sentenced us, it seems, to lives of reading in a linear fashion, page after numbered page, stuck between covers … until the computer, html and hypermedia came along, until text and the page were liberated from ink, glue, sewing and the chronological.

Children were allowed images far earlier, followed by readers of comics, graphic novels, technical manuals and other popular-culture publications. As Kress and van Leeuwen note:

the layout of the densely printed page is still [in itself] visual, still carries an overall cultural significance, as an image of progress.... [Until the late 19th century] [l]ayout was not encouraged here, because it undermined the power of the densely printed page as, literally, the realization of the most literary and literate semiotic mode.... The genres of the densely printed page ... manifest the cultural capital ('high' cultural forms) controlled by the intellectual and artistic wing of the middle class. (Kress & van Leeuwen, 2006: 178–179)

This raises questions such as 'Will multimodal texts acquire the personal and cultural meaning that printed works of poetry, fiction, non-fiction and drama have?' and 'Shouldn't the construction of multimodal texts remain being taught in graphic arts and in entertainment design?' But also 'Should creative writing programs be more blended with such programs?'

It has been said that the older generation is grieving over the passing of the paper book and that we are still in the first stage of that process – *denial*. I agree with this. What we are also denying is the brilliant future of the book, the possibility that the multiply talented multimodal book can reach the literary heights we currently associate with the old form. But this is already happening. Not only do the recently released iPad versions of *Shakespeare's Sonnets* (see Touch Press, 2013a), *The Wasteland*, *A Clockwork Orange*, *War Horse* and others like them provide exciting opportunities for enriched reading with an expanded set of creative possibilities, they also indicate the potential for multidisciplinary and cross-art-form creative writing teaching. Clearly, too, the paper novel has been strongly influenced: multimodal novels such as Jonathan Safran Foer's *Extremely Loud and Incredibly Close* (2006), Reif Larsen's *The Selected Works of T.S. Spivet* (2009), Jennifer Egan's *A Visit from the Goon Squad* (2010) and *S* (2013) by J.J. Abrams and Doug Dorst provide evidence that the multimodal can be employed in highly literate creative writing.

So, let me turn to teaching creative writing. What has been happening? The rise of Creative Writing as a discipline in British and Australian universities in the 1990s and 2000s coincided with the rise of the computer and the internet. These two events are linked by the concept of interactivity. Hypertext showed readers that the reading process did not have to be passive. Of course, it never had been actually so – reading was always about interacting – reacting with one's intellect, imagination and emotions. But hypertext extended the possibilities beyond the limits of the *monograph* into realms which had previously involved further and separate acts of production – the incorporation of visuals, the adaptation to performance, the addition of commentary and glossing mechanisms. In the paper book world, these extended possibilities were seen as value-added publishing, and were silo-ized into add-on categories. One publisher did the original novel. Another did the audio book. A third did the illustrated edition. A fourth published the author's exegetical essays. Yet others did critiques of the book. And so on.

And we have taught writing in this way. Making the original text is taught in the Creative Writing department and the critical text in the English department. The visuals, if we want to include them, have to be done in the Visual Arts department. And if we want to teach making an audio version, well, there are performance experts downtown in the Drama department.

With hypermedia, however, the illustrated book, the play or film based on the book, the talking book, the index or concordance, the exegetical and critical discussions of the book – as we see with the app book – can be part of the book itself. Clearly, now, the digital book can contain what was previously called research for, adaptation of, and extension to the text. This is the new definition of the book – a multimodal, multidisciplinary, multi-art-form entity. A multigraph, not a monograph. The idea of the text for the new book is encompassing; it involves many more awarenesses and potentially more skills. While this multifaceted text changes the way we read, it must change also the way we write and therefore the way we teach. The writer becomes a cog in a larger production process than before – more like a very empowered scriptwriter. And it's more about collaboration. It's as if teaching creative writing just grew into teaching the creative arts. This provides challenges.

To go back to my statement about the coincident rise of hypertext and creative writing in universities, I think students saw creative writing as itself the logical interactive response to a new kind of reading – in fact, they found writing to be a more logical response than learning cultural or literary theory as context for their reading. In her influential 2006 book *Reading Like a Writer*, Francine Prose makes the claim that students did not react well in the 1980s after

> literary academia split into warring camps of deconstructionists, Marxists, feminists, and so forth, all battling for the right to tell students that they were reading 'texts' in which ideas and politics trumped what the writer had actually written. (Prose, 2006: 8)

The migration of students away from literary studies in the 1990s was a retreat from the imposed contextualization of the text in a theory environment and toward a new contextualizing in the digital environment, where reading was defined by the greater interactive capabilities of html. Creative writing based on *doing,* as opposed to English based on *critiquing,* must have seemed more attractive in those circumstances as students recognized the changes in their own reading habits. The continuing migration of students from English courses to creative writing courses at undergraduate and post-graduate levels in the career-fixated 2010s suggests that students take into account the new literacy and the vast audience for electronic platforms. Joseph Moxley says:

> Technology matters.... If impact is a chief measure of success, then we can expect our students to seek access to the millions of online users as opposed to the one hundred or so people who might read an obscure literary print journal.... (Moxley, 2010: 237)

I tell my students how excited I am about who will write the first young adult novel to go to the top of the charts: it will be done by one of their generation – an iPad app novel about an emerging boy or girl band that has a soundtrack included. I wish I'd had such a possibility in my future when I set out as a young writer. They look at me with maybe a glimmer of the future in their eyes when I say: 'Why don't you write that as a multimodal novel on your iPhone? You've got a keyboard, a camera and a microphone pick-up.'

In the future, the writing, reading and teaching of new books cannot be the same – it will have to be multidisciplinary. Or at least have multi-arts and cross-arts awarenesses built in. The ideal department for a creative writing program will be a Creative Arts department where performance, visual arts, digital/new media arts and music are also taught. English should be housed there too. If the current unrepentant, slow-moving English departments don't catch up, they will have to move in with those dead Arts, History and Philosophy (although these, too, have great scope for flourishing in the digital age). While tightening my bullet-proof vest even further, I'll state that the English PhD is dead unless it becomes multi-arts oriented. Every doctoral submission in English should include a creative product – a work which shows that the lessons from reading have been truly learnt. And this begs the question: Why don't English departments just roll over into Creative Writing departments? Teaching English in the future is obliged to be different because fiction, poetry and performance – their genres, products and dissemination – are already different in the digital era.

The academic infrastructures we need for teaching writing in the future are significantly different from what we have now, and involve more col-laboration between departments currently silo-ized and separated. This means more exposure for creative writing students to courses in other creative arts areas. The scary thing for creative writing staff is that most do not have a cross-art-form background themselves. Creative Arts people in general don't like coming out from their silos because the academic silo is, after all, the garret protected by funding, teaching style and public relations potential. *If one of our Creative Writing students does well, we don't want to share her with the Visual Arts!*

There are universities already better set up for the new sort of creative writing teaching, while others are particularly vulnerable. Independent Creative Writing departments will need to decide their own strategies for the future, including linking with other Creative Arts and New Media departments in their vicinity. Where creative writing programs are part of an overarching and previously powerful English department, there will be problems if the formerly dominant partner, in pondering its viability, seeks to warp creative writing teaching back toward a failing critical-ideological pedagogy, as seems to be happening in the US with what is being called 'craft criticism' (Koehler, 2013; Mayers, 2005: 29–64). According to Mayers:

> [t]he historical and material circumstances of craft criticism are the contemporary historical and material circumstances of English studies.... Craft criticism operates within the same system of exchange, reward, and marginalization as all of the other professional activities of English studies. (Mayers, 2005: 34)

In the UK and Australasia we understand what Mayers calls 'craft criticism' to be the exegesis, or exegetical studies. They developed out of the *writerly* approaches taken for teaching and supervision in creative writing programs, not out of the *readerly* interpretative approaches of English studies. Mayers defines craft criticism as 'part of the broader field of "criticism"' (Mayers, 2005: 35) and because of this we should be wary of craft criticism as a desperate rearguard action by English to impose its critical perspective on Creative Writing. This is exactly the kind of study that put English departments offside with students in the first place.

English departments are paper departments; they have difficulty doing the digital (Kirschenbaum, 2010; McGann, 2001). They also have difficulty doing the multimodal, since printed text alone is their speciality. Some few creative writing programs are already housed in multidisciplinary Creative Arts schools, where the notion of cross-art-form and digitally oriented programs works well. Clearly, multidisciplinary teaching is the way forward in dealing with the more-than-just-text-and-print-based writing of the future. We must teach the multimodal and its implications to creative writing students. This requires change.

Exploration

(1) Since 2000, a number of mainstream paper novels have incorporated visual elements. Students can explore the multimodal in fictions by Umberto Eco (2004), Jennifer Egan (2010), Jonathan Safran Foer (2006), Reif Larsen (2009) and W.G. Sebald (1995, 2001).

(2) Reif Larsen, an MFA graduate of Columbia University and a teacher of creative writing, discusses techniques used in turning his acclaimed *The Selected Works of T.S. Spivet* from paper publication into an app novel in Larsen (2011). This perceptive article provides a writerly viewpoint on the possibilities of multimodal writing.

(3) Histories of creative writing's involvement with the digital can be found in Henry Jenkins (2013), where fanzine writing is studied, and N. Katherine Hayles (2008), where pioneering hypertext fictions and other works associated with the Electronic Literature Organization are discussed.

(4) Few experiments with the digital appear to be occurring in the creative writing classroom. Some articles which focus on digital poetry and memoir in college classrooms are included in Herrington *et al.* (2009). Hazel Smith (2005) also includes classroom exercises for creating mixed media, hypertext and hypermedia pieces.

(5) The dark side of digital creative writing – including appropriation, mash-up and other potentially plagiaristic forms – is explored by Kenneth Goldsmith (2011) and Stefan Sonvilla-Weiss (2010).

References

Abrams J.J. and Dorst, D. (2013) *S*. Edinburgh: Canongate Books.

Apple Inc. (2014) iPad in education. Available at http://www.apple.com/au/education/ipad/ibooks-textbooks (accessed 24 May 2014).

Bellafante, G. (2009) Map quest. *New York Times Sunday Book Review*, 19 June. Available at http://www.nytimes.com/2009/06/21/books/review/Bellafante-t.html?_r=0 (accessed 4 January 2014).

Birkerts, S. (1994) *The Gutenberg Elegies: The Fate of Reading in an Electronic Age*. New York: Faber (2006).

Bolter, J.D. (2011) *Writing Space: Computers, Hypertext, and the Remediation of Print*. New York: Routledge.

Burley School (2014) iPads at Burley (30 January). Available at http://ipadsatburley. blogspot.com.au (accessed 24 May 2014).

Darnton, R. (2009) *The Case for Books: Past, Present, and Future*. New York: Public Affairs.

Department of Education Western Australia (2014) iPads for education: Early childhood iPad initiative. Available at http://det.wa.edu.au/ipadsforeducation/detcms/navigation/ipad-initiative/?page=all (accessed 24 May 2014).

Eco, U. (2004) *The Mysterious Flame of Queen Loana: An Illustrated Novel*. G. Brock (trans.). London: Secker and Warburg (2005).

Egan, J. (2010) *A Visit from the Goon Squad*. New York: Alfred A. Knopf.

Egmont (2013) *War Horse* blurb. Available at http://www.egmont.co.uk/ebooks-and-apps.asp?item=war-horse (accessed 13 November 2013).

Foer, J.S. (2006) *Extremely Loud and Incredibly Close*. London: Penguin.

Goldsmith, K. (2011) *Uncreative Writing: Managing Language in the Digital Age*. New York: Columbia University Press.

Gomez, J. (2008) *Print Is Dead: Books in Our Digital Age*. New York: Palgrave Macmillan.

Harper, G. (2012) Creative writing: The ghost, the university and the future. In D. Hecq (ed.) *The Creativity Market: Creative Writing in the 21st Century* (pp. 12–23). Bristol: Multilingual Matters.

Hayles, N.K. (2008) *Electronic Literature: New Horizons for the Literary*. Notre Dame, IN: University of Notre Dame Press.

Herrington, A., Hodgson, K. and Moran, C. (2009) *Teaching the New Writing: Technology, Change, and Assessment in the 21st-Century Classroom*. New York: Teachers College Press.

Holmevik, J.R. (2012) *Inter/vention: Free Play in the Age of Electracy*. Cambridge, MA: MIT Press.

Jenkins, H. (2013) *Textual Poachers: Television Fans and Participatory Culture* (updated 20th anniversary edn). New York: Routledge.

Kirschenbaum, M.G. (2010) What is digital humanities and what's it doing in English departments? *ADE Bulletin* 150, 55–61. Available at http://mkirschenbaum.files.wordpress.com/2011/03/ade-final.pdf (accessed 5 January 2014).

Koehler, A. (2013) Digitizing craft: Creative writing studies and new media. A proposal. *College English* 75 (4). Available at http://www.ncte.org/library/NCTEFiles/Resources/Journals/CE/0754-mar2013/CE0754Digitizing.pdf (accessed 12 November 2013).

Kress, G. (2003) *Literacy in the New Media Age*. London: Routledge.

Kress, G. (2010) *Multimodality: A Social Semiotic Approach to Contemporary Communication*. London: Routledge.

Kress, G. (2011) Making meaning: The role of semiotics and education. Gunther Kress, Professor of Semiotics and Education, in conversation with doctoral student Sophia Diamantopoulou. Available at http://www.youtube.com/watch?v=8-yO04u8MHc (accessed 18 November 2013).

Kress, G. and van Leeuwen, T. (2006) *Reading Images: The Grammar of Visual Design*. London: Routledge.

Larsen, R. (2009) *The Selected Works of T.S. Spivet*. New York: Penguin.

Larsen, R. (2011) How to make an e-book that could not be made. Penguin.com, 31 March. Available at http://www.us.penguingroup.com/static/pages/features/ts-spivet (accessed 4 January 2014).

Mayers, T. (2005) *(Re)writing Craft: Composition, Creative Writing, and the Future of English Studies*. Pittsburgh PA: University of Pittsburgh Press.

McGann, J. (2001) *Radiant Textuality: Literature After the World Wide Web*. New York: Palgrave.

Moxley, J. (2010) Afterword: Disciplinarity and the future of creative writing studies. In D. Donnelly (ed.) *Does the Writing Workshop Still Work?* (pp. 230–238). Bristol: Multilingual Matters.

National Public Radio (2012) The future of children's books (February 18). Available at http://www.npr.org/2012/02/18/147099486/the-future-of-childrens-books (accessed 10 November 2013).

Nunberg, G. (ed.) (1996) *The Future of the Book.* Berkeley, CA: University of California Press.

Prose, F. (2006) *Reading Like a Writer: A Guide for People Who Love Books and For Those Who Want To Write Them.* New York: Harper Perennial (2007).

Pullinger, K. and Joseph, C. (2012) *Flight Paths: A Networked Novel.* Available at http://flightpaths.net (accessed 10 November 2013).

Sebald, W.G. (1995) *The Rings of Saturn.* M. Hulse (trans.). London: Vintage (2002).

Sebald, W.G. (2001) *Austerlitz.* A. Bell (trans.). London: Penguin,

Smith, H. (2005) *The Writing Experiment: Strategies for Innovative Creative Writing.* Crows Nest, NSW: Allen and Unwin.

Sonvilla-Weiss, S. (ed.) (2010) *Mashup Cultures.* New York: SpringerWein.

Square Group (2013) iPad in education – Roger Ascham Primary School (25 February). Available at https://www.youtube.com/watch?v=pS3U97FALGI (accessed 24 May 2014).

Striphas, T. (2011) *The Late Age of Print.* New York: Columbia University Press.

Thompson, J.B. (2005) *Books in the Digital Age: The Transformation of Academic and Higher Education Publishing in Britain and the United States.* Cambridge: Polity Press.

Touch Press (2013a) *The Sonnets by William Shakespeare.* Available at http://www.touchpress.com/titles/shakespeares-sonnets (accessed 10 November 2013).

Touch Press (2013b) *War Horse* for iPad. Available at http://www.touchpress.com/titles/warhorse (accessed 10 November 2013).

Ulmer, G.L. (2002) *Internet Invention: From Literacy to Electracy.* New York: Longman.

Vandendorpe, C. (1999) *From Papyrus to Hypertext: Toward the Universal Digital Library.* P. Aronoff and H. Scott (trans.). Urbana, IL: University of Illinois Press (2009).

Vanderslice, S. (2013) Teaching toward the future. In D. Donnelly and G. Harper (eds) *Key Issues in Creative Writing* (pp. 137–145). Bristol: Multilingual Matters.

'Born This Way': In Celebration of Lady Gaga

Brooke Biaz

I am not me. Lady Gaga is not her: she is Stefani Joanne Angelina Germanotta. Being pseudonymous has its advantages. For example, you can claim responsibility for a great many things and yet suffer the consequences of none of them. Similarly, you can speak out on ideas and ideals but, if you wish, distance yourself from any involvement in the real world to which these ideas and ideals most often relate. Your cost of living is zero. You have no need of credit cards, a driving license or a passport. In fact, you're actively discouraged from seeking out these things and nobody ever sees your lack of them as at all strange. If you are so inclined, you can claim association with certain people and events, with their fabulous successes and tremendous achievements, even if you never once leave the safety and warmth of your fictitious lounge chair. You are, thus, both named and noted but entirely not responsible for anything.

Born this way, as a fictitious person, seeking clarity becomes immediately significant. Unclear fictitiousness is somewhere between confusing and libelous. Either you are unsure of how to act or you are unsure whether, in resembling a real person in some way or some action, you will find yourself accused of misrepresentation. Clarity, which is in this way the actual substance of the pseudonymous, means thoughts turn naturally to your creation. How did the person who created you understand how to create you or, indeed, comprehend the dimensions of your fictitious life, your past, your present and, perhaps if you are lucky, your future? And so you begin to contemplate the relationship between creative writing and education.

Created by 'Creative Writer X', Alice Towngard struggles to lift herself from the sheer weight of her name and her almost daily load of monstrous duties. In addition to being expected to carry the entire load of being a replacement for X in any number of acts of composition and literary construction, she is also required to bring life and adventure to those exact same duties – uncomplaining, unquestioning (largely), in no way compensated and, in a word, yoked. Not only that, X has made her both creator and created, placing her, seemingly with little regard for her feelings or even a passing notion of self-determination, in a range of short stories, even in a one-act play where she heaved herself onto a musty stage with a bag of dialogue so large she reminded the scattered audience at the 'New Playwrights at Brookside Theater Readings' of a seldom-seen stage version of *Miracle on 34th Street*.

All that Alice wishes, and she wishes it with an intensity that only the completely made-up can sustain for this many years, is that X would learn something about some darn thing to do with creative writing – though she means this, at least most of the time, less censoriously than it sounds. Alice actually believes that it is not that X doesn't know something about something, it is that X doesn't seemingly know the thing or things X needs to know about writing Alice. In not knowing how to write Alice, or how to write with her, or how to creatively explore through writing what she is or isn't or might be or might represent or might become or might enhance in the being or becoming of other fictitious or real persons, X simply uses her like someone might try to use a perfectly good kitchen knife to attempt to carve a block of cedar or someone else might add a favorite condiment to a dish, but have no real idea of the quantity to add or the place in the cooking at which to add it.

That comment might seem dismissive; but we fictitious types dwell between the glory of recognition and the certainty that our future killing off will go completely uninvestigated. In essence, we regularly live and die at the hands of others and no one seems to mind all that much. Admittedly, there are moments – and these are moments of excitement for Alice – where it seems that X has discovered exactly what is needed – a wonderful passage or even, now and then, a fully complete piece of work that stands out in a way that Alice can only think to describe as 'hopeful'. But the next day, the next attempt, even the very next moment and X is unable to grasp even the basics. Hope waivers.

'So how might X "firm up" these basics?', you ask. 'Or even go beyond them?' Well, as is a frequently promoted notion, X writes creatively every day – at least for a few hours, but sometimes right the way through from waking in the morning into the late evening. X reads a whole range of great literary works and lesser literary works, so defined, and non-literary works, popular media, the visual world, the people and events all round; reads, therefore, in the broadest sense of the term and pretty much constantly. X takes, and has taken, creative writing classes, in the community, at university, and remembers writing creatively in classes throughout school. But something isn't 'happening', to use that euphemistic word, and it seems something needs to be done if X is to continue. X certainly wants to continue and, in wanting to continue, X wants to learn something or learn more or learn better. In other words, if both X and X's creation, Alice, are to be happier together and individually, then something is going to be worked out between creative writing and education.

As Gaga and I sit here fictitiously together, let us offer this, pseudonymously, from a shared fictitious world of creative writing and song:

- Educate the creative writer and you educate her or his creations. How could it be otherwise? We learn as you learn.
- Treat education as alive and we creations come to life. Imagine creative writing is not a one-directional exchange. My creator is creating me; I have to be talking back. Creative writing is always conversations.
- To educate is to acquire but it is also to abandon. If you know something to be true it is because you have come to believe other things are not as true. The creative writer has to question other truths in order to fully pursue their own.
- It has been proven that physical exercise keeps the heart in good condition and that thinking keeps the brain in good condition. There is no more simple a statement than this in understanding how creative writing and education can best relate.
- It strikes fictitious characters as readily as it strikes anyone else that education must be education for a reason.
- In the song 'Just dance', on the album *The Fame* (2008), Gaga wrote: 'Just dance. Gonna be okay'. But later, in the song 'Hair', on the album *Born This Way* (2011), she wrote: 'I'm as free as my hair'. Given that if your hair was entirely free you wouldn't have any, these seem to be different points of view. These contrasting viewpoints might offer something for how the undertaking of creative writing is understood. Thanks Gaga!
- If you met one of your creations, would you know them? If not, why not? Creative writing education surely has something to do with creating familiarity, creating associations, creating relationships.
- 'Education of a creative writer', 'education in creative writing', 'education about creative writing' are indivisible. We might consider this in another way as 'person', 'activities', 'results'. Or this way: 'human being', 'human action', 'human understanding'. There are probably other ways, but these are a very good start.
- Because the human activity of creative writing has existed for so long, and in so many cultures, and in so many forms, we can be confident

that human beings value it, and value it for many reasons. That sense of human value must make us ask what it is in creative writing that we value and how any education connected with creative writing can best support that valuing.

- Turn to the process of creating and we can see and hear the evidence of choice, empowerment, determination, individuality and society that connect creative writing and education.

Index

Language, xvi, xvii, xix, 7, 10, 18, 19, 23, 26, 30, 32, 35, 39, 41, 42, 45, 57, 60–61, 70, 72, 76, 80, 83–86, 105, 107–109, 114, 115, 117, 119, 120, 184
Learning paradigm, 46–54
Listening, 43, 103, 129, 131, 135–136, 176

Making, xviii, 62, 116, 117, 157, 158, 171, 190
Massive Online Open Course (MOOC), 14, 138–147
Memory, 20–40, 69, 70, 126, 137, 143
Mentoring, 90, 91, 159, 161, 163
Multimodal texts, 132, 187–191, 193

National Association of Writers in Education (NAWE), 10, 14, 68, 152, 167

Originality, 41, 51, 53, 150–155, 159, 161, 162, 179

Pakistan, 37, 38, 83–86
Perfectionism, 23
Play, 94, 102, 105, 106, 114, 120, 130, 131, 132, 179
Power, 21, 22, 26, 88, 133, 174, 188
Practice, 1, 7, 9, 10, 11, 55, 65, 89, 91, 94, 101, 144, 151, 152–156, 157, 161
Practice-led research, 92, 150, 158, 159, 163
Process, 24, 26, 92, 93, 161, 168, 183, 197, 199
Products, 24, 65, 90, 117, 155, 159, 185, 191
Program assessment, 53–54
Publishing, 177, 179, 183, 185–186, 190

Reading, 47, 57, 60, 61, 66, 70, 74–75, 89, 90, 93, 97, 102, 107, 110, 113, 115, 117, 123, 135, 145, 169, 179, 185–191,

Reflection, 50, 62, 63–64, 73, 74, 81, 90, 98, 124, 131, 172
Research, 15, 23, 65, 71, 80, 90, 92, 99, 120, 150–165, 184
   see also Practice-led research
Response, 21, 39, 42, 50, 58–63, 88, 125–126, 168
Revision, 47, 72, 76, 77, 78, 80, 159, 173, 179
Rhetoric, 9, 174, 176
Risk, xvii, 24, 25, 46, 64, 100, 101–105, 130

Self-awareness, 52, 64, 171–174, 180
Service learning, 12, 63–65
Shanghai University, 13, 71
Situational knowledge, 8
Subjects, 23, 139, 171
Sun Yat-sen University Center for English-language Creative Writing, 72
Syllabus, 49, 50, 55

Teacher authority, 46
Technology, 121, 131, 138, 140, 145–147, 183–185, 191
   see also Massive Online Open Course (MOOC)
Text world theory, 107, 111, 117
The Program Era: Postwar Fiction and the Rise of Creative Writing (2009), 6
Theory, 46, 48–53, 57, 65, 92, 94, 107, 110, 122–123, 130, 157, 160, 162, 190
   see also Text world theory
Truth, 17–27, 198

Visual, 69, 90, 120, 123, 124, 126, 131, 133–135, 137, 141, 186–193, 197

Workshops, 72, 75–76, 80, 89, 101, 102, 127, 134, 139, 144, 168, 173, 175, 176, 180
Writing communities, 52
'Writing on demand', 168